THE GREATEST LAUGHS OF ALL TIME

The Greatest Laughs of All Time

BY GERALD F. LIEBERMAN

1961

DOUBLEDAY & COMPANY, INC.   GARDEN CITY, NEW YORK

Dedication

The dedication of a book always presents a problem.

In the past I have been able to get out of it by dedicating my books to (a) a bank, and (b) a finance company, on the grounds that their courage in loaning me money made them worthy. Since these institutions are no longer so inefficacious in their credit policies I thought of dedicating this book to my landlord, whose attitude toward the rent might best be described as "the triumph of hope over experience." But anything complimentary to landlords would not be stylish. I must therefore face the issue without evasion and dedicate this book to the women in my life: to my mother, Mrs. Frieda Seidman; to my daughters, Laurie Jo and Mona Helene; and to my wife, Sylvia.

All equally dear to me, but for safety's sake listed here alphabetically according to first name.

The Greatest Laughs of All Time,
on the following subjects:

(Having had the effrontery to engineer a work titled The Greatest
Laughs of All Time *it has been deemed necessary that introductory
remarks be supplied by way of justification. Normally the task is
given over to someone whose name on the jacket serves to accredit
the author as an authority. However, when such is the case there
sometimes remains a lingering suspicion that the originator of the
manuscript is shirking personal responsibility. I did not wish to
have either my courage or my intentions questioned. This, along
with the incidental fact that all the distinguished persons to whom
I offered this singular honor chose to decline it, leads me to write
my own introduction.)*

Introduction

When television so sophisticated its audiences that they refused to
titter ecstatically at the lighter fare, video genius perfected a
device called dubbed-in laughter. It stands as one of the great
psychological advancements of the century, for in watching comedy
offerings we were not sure whether to laugh or cry, and we thus
subjected ourselves to all the frustrations of repeated decision-
making. Now all doubt has been removed and we can properly
laugh on cue, and if need be give way to gales of laughter, without
that sneaky feeling of idiocy that we may be displaying the wrong
emotion.

Despite this infallible cue to mirth most of us get the same
feeling watching a television comedy that we get listening to a
fervent graveside eulogy delivered for a philanthropist we know

9

made it by robbing illiterate immigrants and foreclosing on hope-less widows. It's hard to believe what we hear.

Today the medium is faced with a problem of greater conse-quence: diminishing audiences. Still we need not despair; the answer is just over the rainbow. The same board of strategists will again meet, and from this summit of the performing arts will come as sweeping a solution as has come before. It will be called dubbed-in ratings. We can then sit back to watch our favorite television show secure in the knowledge that millions of indi-viduals are engaged in the identical form of masochism. It is as obvious as a L'African Ballet dancer's bosom.

The decline and fall of the American sense of humor purports to be a mystery; if so, it is a mystery filled with clues that identify the murderer long before the plot begins to thicken. When we consider the four elements of civilized social order—morals, economics, politics, art/knowledge—and we check the list of mass media taboos, we find that ninety per cent of the areas of laughter have been legislated against and the remaining fragment has been beaten to death.

Humor has four essential functions: to simplify, to enlighten, to stimulate the thought processes, and to inspire laughter. Any one of these may stand on its own if treated properly. In the short form it is uncommon to find a proper blending of two or three, and the masterful anecdote that contains all four is a rarity. I have tried for as many of the latter as possible.

I do not wish to make a non-existent case for this book. It was conceived as a joke book and treated as a joke book, with the advantages and disadvantages of that form. However, it was put together outside the bind of constricting codes, though entirely within the bounds of enlightened propriety. It is therefore possible I have ignored or overlooked many rules that organized groups of elite professionals have sought to make traditional. If this has happened, and it may have, the credit does not belong to me. I had thousands of years of collected thoughts with which to play, the majority of these obviously not my own.

The objective of this book is to amuse and if possible to delight.

Introduction

Any by-product, such as the revival of the sense of humor, or the realization that things can be funny though adult, is merely an extra which, though partially desired, was not the primary target.

For purposes of updating there is much paraphrasing and transliteration; especially with materials drawn from antiquity. It is possible that some will resent liberties taken with favorite stories. My conscience is clear, for the popular versions are products of identical treatment. To those who persist in their indignation, I say:

> Uren fader thie are in heofnas, sio
> gokagud thin noma, to eymeth, thin rick;
> sic thin willa suc is in heofnas and in ertho.

These are the opening lines of the eighth-century English version of the Lord's Prayer. No baritone alive today could sing it, much less understand it. See what I mean?

GERALD F. LIEBERMAN

THE GREATEST LAUGHS OF ALL TIME

Politics and Politicians

An honest politican is one who when he's bought stays bought.
SIMON CAMERON

The habit of nineteenth-century citizens of ducking long-winded orations by office-seekers on the stump gave rise to the institution known as gallows politics. In certain areas bigwigs found it expeditious to combine campaign oratory with a good hanging in order to turn out the crowd. Shrewd politicians usually arranged their tours according to scaffold schedules, and if especially attractive "necktie sociables" came up in the off season state executives granted delays until a more fortuitous time.

Hangings usually took place early. When they did the crowds never waited to hear the speech. So sheriffs would delay executions while the orators delivered their wares. This led to confusion, for, with all interested parties standing on the same platform, the people found it hard to tell which was the politician and which was the criminal. Ingenuity moved to the fore, and it was decided that the main attraction should stand with the noose properly placed. The people still had their doubts.

A condemned man appealed to the courts against this procedure, thus bringing forth a milestone in judicial enlightenment when a federal magistrate ruled: "It is the sovereign right of every

15

American citizen to git hisself hung before rather than after a political speech."

As a result prisoners were allowed to set their own place on the program. The first time a U.S. marshal advised a horse thief of his rights, and asked his choice, the condemned man thought it over awhile, then said: "Who's speakin'?"

In another case the prisoner shrieked: "In the name of mercy, before!" One victim, having listened to the speech, thanked the speaker for making it easier to die. And a bushwacker, his altruism kindled by a lengthy delivery, interrupted the speaker to say: "Don't you think the people have had enough?"

But the finest example of life in a free society occurred when a condemned man listened to a three hour speech. He then moved to the front of the gallows, and, with the noose tightly secured to his neck, delivered a scathing rebuttal. So eloquently did he argue that the townspeople perpetuated his memory by electing him honorary mayor *in absentia*.

It is hard to say why politicians are called servants, unless it's because a good one is hard to find. Traditionally the great men of our country have sprung from poor environments; that being so, it would appear we have long suffered from a severe lack of poverty.

The materials contained in this chapter show that if the people have not always been fooled by the politicians, politicians likewise have not always been fooled by the people; though it has been some time since either condition prevailed.

A foreign diplomat, upon being assigned to the United States after an absence of ten years, attended a congressional session where he asked one of the guards about a senator he had known. "He's dead, sir," the guard said.

"Poor fellow," the diplomat condoled. "Joined the great majority of his colleagues, eh?"

"I wouldn't exactly say that, sir," the guard corrected. "He was an honest enough man so far as I know."

When Teddy Roosevelt departed for one of his African hunting trips a leading financial bulletin carried this message: "Wall Street Expects Every Lion to Do Its Duty."

Political campaigners usually employ variations on recognized gutter tactics; and the latest is always described as the most disgusting, since political memory is short. A candidate for high office insisted, in many of his speeches, that the man opposing him had been a member of the Ku Klux Klan. The trick almost worked until several newspapers tore the accusation apart. A reporter asked the accuser: "Have you any comment now that your opponent has been proven innocent of the charge that he belonged to the Ku Klux Klan?"

"Well mebbe he didn't belong to the Klan," the office-seeker conceded. "But it's my avowed belief that he'd still look a lot better if he kept a hood over his head."

An instance of rare honesty occurred when a politican who had been among the leading exponents of prohibition made this statement, on his ninety-fifth birthday.

"I was eighty-three years old and suffering from hardening of the arteries when we went for prohibition. If I'd knowed that God Almighty was going to give me another dozen years I'd never 'a voted the country dry."

The radical of one century is the conservative of the next. The radical invents the views. When he has worn them out the conservative adopts them.

MARK TWAIN

When a President's golf score is in the high nineties he's neglecting his golf. When his score is in the low eighties he's neglecting his duties.

A schoolboy, visiting the Senate for the first time, asked his father if the duty of the Senate chaplain was to pray for the senators. "No, my boy," the father explained. "The chaplain looks around, and when he sees the senators he prays for the country."

I might have gone to West Point, but I was too proud to speak to a congressman.

WILL ROGERS

A long-winded politician was addressing Parliament. As he droned on one of the cynical members noticed a colleague leaning forward with an ear trumpet to carefully follow the remarks. The cynic nudged a friend nearby, and said: "Look at that fool over there, refusing to avail himself of his natural advantage."

There are two enemies to every bill proposed in Congress—the fools who favor it and the lunatics who oppose it.

During Stalin's blood purge of political opponents a Russian lay dying in his room. There was a determined knock on the door. "Who is there?" the Russian called.

"The Angel of Death," a deep voice boomed.

"Thank goodness," the Russian sighed. "I was afraid it might be the secret police."

When a politician swears on the Bible that a thing is so, and then immediately goes ahead and proves it, I know he's lying.

SAMUEL BONOM

At a closed door session conducted by one of the numerous congressional investigating committees it was determined that a close friend of the President's had accepted five thousand dollars to award a government contract to an industrial firm. In the course of events the man admitted that he also accepted five thousand dollars from a competitive firm to award *them* the contract.

"You say you received five thousand dollars from company A to favor them?" the chairman asked.

"Yes sir, I did," the man admitted.

"And then you received five thousand dollars from company B to favor *them?*"

"Yes, sir. That's true."

"And to whom did you finally award the contract?"

Here the man raised his head, and with dignified sincerity, answered: "Sir, I awarded that contract according to the dictates of my conscience."

A politician, while speaking to a convention of commercial artists, was asked to name his favorite color. Without hesitation he said: "Plaid."

The United Nations appoints its committees by selecting five men who favor a thing and five men who oppose it—while the world wonders why nothing gets done.

GREGORY NUNN

A retired political appointee who had grabbed the ambassadorship to France as a plum was asked by reporters whether or not he had had any difficulty with his French while in office. "No," he replied. "But the French did."

A schoolboy, asked to sum up the one quality of George Washington that distinguished him from all other great Americans, replied: "He didn't lie."

"Here, hold my horse a minute, will you?"

"Sir! I'm a member of Congress."

"Never mind. You look honest. I'll take a chance."

NINETEENTH-CENTURY AMERICANA

Statement of Harry T. Hartwell, of Mobile, Alabama, after defeat in the race for congressman, First District. (As filed with the Secretary of State.)

"I lost six months and ten days canvassing, lost 1000 hours sleep worrying over the results of the election, lost twenty pounds of flesh, kissed 500 babies, kindled 100 kitchen fires, put up ten stoves, cut eleven cords of wood, carried fifty buckets of water, pulled 400 bundles of fodder, walked 1100 miles, shook 20,000 hands, talked enough to fill one month's issue of the New York World, got baptized four different times, made love to nine grass widows, got dog-bit nine times—and then got defeated."

A Texas oilman offered to throw the biggest gol-darned victory party for Thomas E. Dewey this country or any other country ever saw. "It'll be a two-hundred-and-fifty-thousand-dollar complimentary banquet in honor of Dewey's election to the office of President of the United States," he said.

"Fine," said a friend. "But supposin' he don't win the election."

The Texan replied. "Then we'll have the complimentary banquet in honor of his defeat."

A Las Vegas casino operator listened closely while two roulette players argued the outcome of the 1956 presidential elections. "Eisenhower's gonna get it," one player insisted.

"You're nuts," the other challenged. "Stevenson'll win hands down."

A clergyman who had been visiting Las Vegas to witness purgatory broke in and said: "My friends, you are both wrong. I can tell you who will be the next President. It is the Lord, who is coming with his band of angels and shall rule."

The casino operator sensed a live one, and being confident no dark horse stood a chance, said: "I got fifty grand to your five says he don't carry Missouri."

Public relations has figured large in creating a favorable image of office-seekers. In keeping with the Madison Avenue method of auto-suggestion an interview-at-home arrangement was set with a popular magazine, involving a down-to-earth type of office candidate; a good deal of copy was to center on the man's plain-average hobby. "What is the guy's hobby?" the reporter asked.

"He's a trapshooter," the public relations executive answered. "Oh, and Joe, give the typesetter a message for me."

"What is it?"

"Tell him," the p.r. man said, "there's a century note in it for him if he doesn't make it crapshooter."

Franklin Delano Roosevelt met an old neighbor during the third term campaign. "Who you voting for this year?" Roosevelt asked.

"The Republicans," the man said.

"How come?" Roosevelt asked. "Third term issue bothering you?"

"It's not that at all, Franklin," the neighbor said. "It's just that—well—I voted Republican the first time you ran, I voted Republican the second time you ran, and I'm going to vote Republican again because I never had it so good."

The highest praise that can ever be given a General Assembly of Maryland is it might have been worse. It is also the highest praise that can ever be given to a dead cat.

H. L. MENCKEN

The press relations man of a deceased senator called in the Washington press corps to announce his employer's demise. "What can we say about the late senator?" a newspaperman asked.

"Oh, you might say that he was always faithful to his trust."

"Yes," the reporter agreed. "And shall we name the trust to which he was always faithful?"

A candidate seeking re-election to high office presented a bill for two million dollars to his party's finance committee.

"Two million dollars!" exclaimed the chairman. "Why your campaign will cost less than ten thousand dollars."

"I know that," admitted the candidate. "But in case I lose I want to be able to live comfortably."

The least Victorian Victorians, from the standpoint of vitupera-tion, were Gladstone and Disraeli. Gladstone once encountered the Prime Minister in the halls of Commons and could not resist the temptation to state: "Sir, you will come to your end either upon the gallows or of a venereal disease."

To which Disraeli answered: "That depends, sir, upon whether I embrace your principles or your mistress."

The man with the best job in the country is the Vice President. All he has to do is get up every morning and say, "How's the President?"

WILL ROGERS

A Russian citizen named Igor Meispunimvich had taken three phases of an examination for the coveted post of People's Garbage Disposal Deputy, and having done well was called to Moscow for the ideological inquiry.

The first question put to him by the examiners was: "What is your attitude toward religion?"

"Religion is a capitalist fantasy," Igor replied. "Religious belief is an opiate offered to the proletariat to deaden their sensitivity to imperial subjection."

"And what do you think of churches and synagogues?"

"Churches and synagogues," said Igor, "are symbols of decadent democracy and reaction. They should be burned and the ashes dumped in the ocean by the enlightened working classes."

"That is all," the examiner said. "You will be notified."

Igor went outside where a waiting friend asked: "How did it go, comrade?"

"I feel very optimistic," Igor replied. "With God's help it's possible I passed the examination."

A Greek soldier, newly arrived in ancient Athens, was handed a dispatch to be delivered only into the hands of the assembly leader. "But I have never seen him," the soldier informed his commanding officer. "How will I know him?"

"Enter the forum," his officer said. "The man being cursed at the most will be the leader of the assembly."

President Jackson was under constant pressure to dismiss the White House porter, Jimmy O'Neil, who had incurred the wrath of many powerful individuals, including the President's nephew. That they failed in their pressures is testified to by O'Neil's presence at The Hermitage to the day of Jackson's death. But on one occasion O'Neil was accused of an offense so flagrant that the President deemed it beyond his power to intercede.

"Do you believe this story?" O'Neil asked the chief executive.

"Certainly," Jackson replied. "I have heard it from two senators."

"Faith now," the loyal Irishman argued, and saved his own neck. "If I believed all that twenty senators said about you it's little I'd think you fit to be President."

Get your facts first, then you can distort 'em as much as you please.

MARK TWAIN

During the era of fright a federal employee was summoned to testify in executive session. He claimed the Fifth Amendment in refusing to divulge information on his political background. But when faced with immediate suspension he acquiesced and gave this testimony. "My politics are versatile and objective," he said.

"Because of my background I am a natural Republican. Because of my conscience I am a sympathetic Democrat. And because I wish to avoid jury duty, I am an enrolled Communist."

I never said all Democrats were saloonkeepers; what I said was all saloonkeepers were Democrats.

HORACE GREELEY

Tension mounted as members of the senate committee argued a procedural point. "You are nothing but a crooked, lying, over-inflated bag of wind," one committee member fired.

"And you," said another, "are the most consummate, unmitigated jackass that ever lived."

"Gentlemen, gentlemen," interrupted the chairman. "You forget I am present."

Politics and the federal bench are intertwined. A persistent party member once appeared before President Lincoln and demanded appointment to a judgeship as reward for some campaigning he'd done in Illinois. The President, aware of the man's lack of judicial attributes, told him it was impossible. "There simply are no vacancies at the present time," Mr. Lincoln said.

The man left. Early the next morning he was walking along the Potomac when he saw a drowned man pulled from the river and immediately recognized him as a federal judge. Without a moment of hesitation he presented himself to Mr. Lincoln while the President was eating breakfast, told him what he had seen, and demanded an immediate appointment to the vacancy.

Lincoln shook his head. "I'm sorry, sir, but you came too late," said the President. "I have already appointed the lawyer who saw him fall in."

If you shoot a Republican out of season, the fine will be ten dollars and costs.

MISSISSIPPI PROVERB

"He's the greatest man who ever came out of Plymouth, Vermont."

CLARENCE DARROW, *on the qualifications of Calvin Coolidge*

A western judge sentenced a petty politician to be hanged for stealing half of the city treasury. "Reckon that's a bit steep, judge," a friend suggested.

"Look here," the judge replied angrily. "Any man that gits hisself elected by a pack of damned fools, to an office where he

24

kin git his hands on their money, and only takes half of it, deserves whatever he gits."

When a city servant in New York was found to have banked half a million dollars in four years, Tammany Hall launched an immediate investigation—to see what took him so long.

A District of Columbia newspaper of the twenties carried this advertisement: "For Rent. Large double room with connecting bath. Suitable for two legislators or two gentlemen."

When France delivered the Statue of Liberty to this country, a round of speeches took place. At one such event, while the French ambassador was speaking in his native tongue, a politician leaned over to Horace Porter, who had served as Ambassador to France, and said: "Friend, interpret the libretto for me, lest I dilate with the wrong emotion."

A traveler from Mars had the good fortune to land his spaceship in Las Vegas where he saw lines of players grasping the arm of a slot machine. He carefully moved closer and when he was next to the machine whispered: "Hey, pal, I don't know what office you're running for, but try to smile when you shake hands."

His books did not balance, but his heart always beat warmly for his native land.

EULOGY FOR A TEXAS LEGISLATOR

The press displayed its erudition during the latter part of the nineteenth century when an Ohio governor issued a proclamation composed entirely of passages from the Bible. A Democratic editor pounced on it at once, stating without equivocation that he had heard it before, couldn't remember where, but would swear on an oath that it was downright plagiarism from beginning to end. The Republican press would not let this ridiculous accusation stand unchallenged. They vigorously defended the governor, denounced the charge as libelous, and challenged any man alive to produce a single word of the proclamation that had appeared before in print.

A reporter called his editor and said: "I got the greatest news story."

"I know," the editor said wearily. "Man bites dog."

"No," the reporter corrected. "Bull throws congressman."

The following is an excerpt from a dissertation on the modern statesman, made seventy years ago: "The outcome is about as satisfactory to us who watch and who have to bear the brunt of such statesmanship as that of the clock owner who said, 'When the hands of my clock stand at twelve and it strikes two, then I know it is thirteen minutes to nine.'"

A campaign contributor asked the President of the United States to appoint him Ambassador to France, as reward for faithful financing. "Do you understand French?" the President asked.

"I do," the man replied, "when I speak it myself."

When I was a boy I was told that anyone could become President. I'm beginning to believe it.

CLARENCE DARROW

A candidate for office was riding the whistle stop circuit when he came to a town where the cemetery adjoined the railroad tracks. A funeral was in progress and the reverend was in the process of offering up a final prayer. When he had finished he asked if anyone knowing the deceased would care to say a few words. Several seconds passed and no one came forward. Finally the candidate worked his way through the crowd, found a high spot in front of the mourners, reverently removed his hat, and in a condolent voice said: "Friends, if nobody wishes to take the time to speak of the deceased, I'd like to say a few words about the falling price of cattle."

The nineteenth century saw Lichtenberg describe a public figure this way:

"The attributes of the greatest men were all united in him. Like Alexander his head was tilted to one side; like Caesar he always had something in his hair. He could drink coffee like Leibnitz and once settled in his armchair he forgot eating and drinking like Newton; and like him, had to be awakened. He wore a wig like Dr. Johnson—and like Cervantes, the fly of his trousers was always open."

An unschooled Civil War widow, when asked the meaning of government, said this: "Sure ivery child knows what's the guver'-mint. It's half a dozen gintlemin an' the loike maybe, that meets an' thinks what's best for thimsilves, an' thin says that's best for us—an' that's the guver'mint."

No speech can be so poor that the newspapers will not describe it as able and eloquent, these being the lowest terms to which friendly reporters could reduce even a worthless discourse.

WILLIAM M. EVARTS, *in defense of Andrew Johnson*

A conservative is one who does not think anything should be done for the first time.

A diplomat is a man who thinks twice before he says nothing.

When Congress finally passed a Civil Rights bill in the spring of 1960, the law, such as it was, was the result of long and bitter interparty clashes. It reminded many persons of a dog law which a Kentucky elected official asked a lawyer friend to draw up. "What kind of a dog bill do you wish to have?" the lawyer asked.

The public servant replied: "I want a good, broad, safe, warm-hearted dog law, that will please my constituency and won't interfere with the rights of the dogs."

Reader, suppose you were an idiot. And suppose you were a member of Congress. But I repeat myself.

MARK TWAIN

"What do you think of the political situation?"

"Don't bother me just now," replied a senator. "I've got to get out and talk, this is no time to think."

"I just got out of prison this morning," a traveler told the man on the train. "It's going to be mighty tough, facing old friends."

"I can sympathize with you," commiserated the other. "I'm just getting home from the state legislature."

Political expediency is said to have dictated the appointment of a certain Assistant Secretary of State. An idealistic presidential adviser opposed the move. "The man is thoroughly incompetent. He is untrustworthy, stupid, an unbearable snob, and a congenital liar."

"Good," said the chief executive. "Then we won't have to break him in."

At the height of the McCarthy tactics the efforts of a New York sponsor to blacklist everything caused a certain super-patriotic television executive to bow obsequiously to the dictates of fear. His caution included refusal to employ anyone who did not wear an Eisenhower button; anyone he knew to be a registered Democrat; anyone whose name implied foreign origin, no matter the generation; anyone who at any time attended one of several colleges reputedly liberal; any one who had ever written anything with the word 'fascism' in the text; and anyone who had been reading any newspaper other than those on the safe list. Legend has it that this producer was himself blacklisted when in a momentary lapse he ordered a sandwich from the Radio City lunchroom —on Russian rye.

When a writer found himself unable to get work he approached this producer, whom he regarded as a friend, and asked him to find out the reason. "I'll tell you why," the producer said. He took one of the writer's produced manuscripts from his desk and read a circled portion. "Receive the fugitive and prepare in time an asylum for mankind." Then he slammed the manuscript to the floor. "What kind of crap have you been sneaking in on us?" he demanded.

"But those aren't my words," the blacklistee said. "Tom Paine wrote them."

"Paine, huh?" snapped the producer. "Well he won't be getting any work around here, either."

A midwestern paper takes note of the government practice of distributing the speeches of congressmen at no profit. It adds that they are also read that way.

I am inclined to think that the loss of a sense of humor is one of the punishments of success.

When Adlai Stevenson was defeated as a presidential candidate in 1956, post-mortems favored the idea that he had spoken over the heads of the people. A devoted Stevenson booster objected to this theory and stressed that he had spoken clearly, in simple language, and straight to the point. Franklin K. Dane, the ardent independent cornpatch philosopher from the sidewalks of New York, told her it didn't make a bit of difference—and used the old fashioned method of parable to show what he meant. "I once heard a brilliant give-'em-hell preacher exhorting a congregation in the simplest of terms. He denounced atheism, stomped all over atheism, made a jackass out of atheism, and for good measure kicked the hell out of heathenism, and gave secularism a thorough going over too. When he finished a nice, intelligent little lady came over to him and said: 'You're a mighty convincing talker, young man, but I still believe in God.'"

A letter addressed to "Santa Claus, North Pole" was received in the Washington post office. The Postmaster General was touched by the urgency of the request; it was from a little boy who did not want toys, but food and clothing for his destitute family. The cabinet member addressed a reply to the little boy on official stationery, saying that Santa Claus had referred the matter to him and the fifty dollars enclosed was a gift from the North Pole.

The following year another letter addressed to Santa Claus, and written by the same boy, came to Washington and was forwarded to the Postmaster General. When it was opened the cabinet member read the following: "Dear Santa: You were very kind to me last year and I appreciate it very much. But next time you send me money don't forward it through the government. Those men always keep half of what they receive."

A midwestern newspaper used to print the resignations and death notices of politicians under "Public Improvements."

London's Hyde Park is an open forum for debate on any subject.

A Scottish representative was haranguing the crowd when one of his countrymen stepped forward and asked: "Wot's this here proposal aboot anyhoo?"

"Ye see noo, it's so the guvernment canna carry oot the thigamabob withoot need of a hoodayacallit. Ye see noo, unless the thigamabob is done richt the hale thing will burst up. Have ye no air aboot it?"

"Ah'd air aboot it," the Scotsman replied. "But ah didna ken ony details till the noo."

A southern senator was outfoxed in making a deal with a colleague from the West. "You've been a senator for eighteen years," one of the constituency scolded. "By this time you ought to know a good deal about politics."

"Ah oughta," the senator admitted. "But Ah have a friend who has played poker for over fifty years and is no more certain about a one card draw than he was the day he started."

Politics and Politicians

An orator of Democratic persuasion was delivering a speech in an auditorium deep in the heart of Dixie, when a tussel broke out in one section. "What's wrong out there?" he called.

"Someone's picked my pocket, made off with my wallet and watch and chain," a man shouted.

"Sorry to hear that, mister," the speaker sympathized. "I didn't know there were any Republicans in the audience."

"There's one," the man called. "I'm a Republican."

Alben Barkley was asked at a dinner to explain the meaning of the diplomatic term "a qualified maybe." He said the theory is best illustrated by the story of an Irish sergeant in World War I who decided to inspire the men with a pep talk. He outlined the job ahead and then said determinedly: "Boys, will yez fight or will yez run?"

"We will!" they answered to a man.

"Will what?" the sergeant barked.

"Will not!" they chorused.

"That's the spirit, me hardies," the sergeant beamed. "I knew yez would."

Many people consider the things government does for them to be social progress—but they consider the things government does for others as socialism.

EARL WARREN

If fifty million people say a foolish thing it is still a foolish thing.
ANATOLE FRANCE

A senator's stand on civil rights and medical benefits for the aged was reminiscent of the kind of preaching a bishop once said he overheard a minister deliver to wealthy sinners of an aristocratic congregation.

"Brethren, you must repent, as it were; and be converted, in a measure; or you'll be damned, to an extent."

A foreigner once described Congress as "A strange place, where one man gets up to speak and says nothing, nobody listens, then everybody disagrees."

If the average congressman found himself on an airliner about to crash he would take time to appoint a landing committee.

Candidate: A modest man who shrinks from the publicity of private life to seek the obscurity of public office.

A man approached a politician and angrily shouted: "Remember me? You beat up my father, broke my mother's leg, ran my relatives out of town, ruined my business, burned down my house, and seduced my wife; all because I ran against you."

"Go 'way, boy," the unperturbed politician replied. "I hate sore losers."

A farmer kept continually interrupting a Republican speaker, and when challenged from the platform to explain his actions said it was because he was a Democrat.

"And why, sir, are you a Democrat?" the speaker asked.

"'Cause my father was a Democrat and my grandfather was a Democrat."

"And suppose your father was a jackass and your grandfather was a jackass? What would you be then?"

"Wal," said the farmer. "Then I guess I'd be a Republican."

Two senators with presidential aspirations met in the corridors of a federal building. "I had a strange dream last night," one said. "In my dream I traveled through every state in the country and won every presidential primary held. And as I was on my way to the nominating convention God touched me on the arm and said I was going to be the next President of the United States."

"That *is* strange," the other replied. "Last night I dreamed the people of the United States stormed to the nominating convention and demanded that *I* be unanimously selected as the party's candidate on the first ballot. Then God touched *me* on the arm and said *I* would be the next president of the United States."

A political boss came by and said: "I got news for you fellows. I didn't touch either one of you on the arm last night."

You can fool some of the people all of the time and all of the people some of the time—but most of the time they will make fools of themselves.

Any man with a fine shock of hair, a good set of teeth, and a bewitching smile, can park his brains, if he has any, and run for public office.

FRANKLIN K. DANE

A newspaper once carried an editorial which stated bluntly that half the city council were crooks. Under penalty of arrest the editor issued the following retraction: "Half the city council aren't crooks."

He gave the people what they want, and since the vast majority of the people don't know what in hell they want, he gave 'em what they got.

GREGORY NUNN, *on
the Eisenhower administration*

A group of intellectuals once called on a governor to protest the political habit of neglecting the arts. "Gentlemen, you are misinformed," the governor replied. "I've never authorized a single campaign expenditure that did not include a brass band."

A traveling preacher was debating with a Texas oilman who doubted the miracle of divine chastisement. "Let me tell you of a remarkable occurrence," the preacher said. "In this morning's paper there's an article about a politician who was struck by lightning while he was lying. Miraculous incident, wasn't it?"

"I don't know now," the Texan replied. "It would be more of a miracle if lightning struck a politician when he wasn't lying."

Anybody can be a Republican when the market is up. But when stocks is selling for no more than they're worth, let me tell you, being a Republican is a sacrifice.

WILL ROGERS

A liberal is a man who is right most of the time, but he's right too soon.

GREGORY NUNN

A minister, playing golf with a congressman, was dismayed when the man constantly spouted profanity. "Please, my man," the clergyman protested. "Remember the cloth."

"What cloth?" challenged the congressman. "This is golf, not billiards."

A nineteenth-century item carries this quotation by a member of Congress elected to office from a Dutch community.

"Van I vent to da lechislator I taught I vould find dem all Solomons dere. But I soon found dey vas as pig fools dere as I vas."

A southern gentleman was brought before a congressional investigation committee. The chairman of the committee, noting the man's name was prefixed by the title "Colonel," asked sarcastically: "What does the 'Colonel' stand for?"

"That 'Colonel' is like the 'Honorable' in front of your name," the man shot back. "It don't mean a damned thing."

A politican was asked to mitigate a quarrel between a Catholic priest and a Protestant minister; also present was a rabbi, friendly to both. "I have listened to the arguments of the good father," the politico said, "and I am inclined to say that he is right."

The Protestant then presented his case, and when he finished the politician said: "Having heard additional evidence I believe the good reverend minister is right."

The rabbi appeared confused and quietly asked: "While I do not wish to be presumptuous, how is it possible that both are right?"

"Here now," the politician replied. "It is perfectly evident that the good rabbi is also right."

In 1920 the state of Kansas was swung into line on the suffrage amendment as the result of an open debate, in which a suffragette merely uttered a single sentence. When the opposition argued, "Women could not be relied upon to exercise good judgment in voting, they change their minds too often," a young woman carried the day by shouting, "I would like to ask my honorable opponent if he ever tried to change a woman's mind once it was made up?"

The shortest campaign speech on record was made in Nevada. It consisted of eight words and the speaker was elected by a landslide. "Fellow countrymen," he said. "Follow me to yonder liquor saloon."

Confusion with mythology and governmental procedures led to a candid definition of just what a member of Congress is. "A senator," wrote a student, "is half man and half horse."

Since television about all a man needs to be elected President is the kind of profile that looks good on a postage stamp.

GREGORY NUNN

John Allen of Mississippi used a sense of humor to steal the election from a Confederate general who had served three terms in Congress. The general referred to his war record and stressed the times when he bivouacked under a clump of trees on the very soil where he now sought re-election, so that he might defend it as he had in those trying times.

35

Allen complimented the general's war record, verified it, and then went on to say: "It is also true, my fellow citizens, that I was a vedette picket and stood guard over him while he slept. Now, fellow citizens, all of you who were generals and had privates to stand guard over you while you slept, vote for General Tucker. And all of you who were privates and stood guard over the generals while they slept, vote for Private John Allen!"

Heinrich Heine (1797–1856) described an influential personage who had resorted to expediency, in these terms:

"He has the same experience as the ostrich, which considers itself sufficiently hidden when its head is stuck in the sand and only its backside is visible. This illustrious bird would have done much better if he stuck his backside in the sand and given us a view of his head."

Feuds have always characterized our political machinery. Two southern senators were riding to Washington, in pre-Civil War days. While passing through Virginia they spied a hangman's device on a hill. "Where would you be today if the gallows received its due?" one asked.

The other replied: "I'd be riding alone."

A conservative is a man who wants the rules enforced so no one can make a pile the way he made it.

GREGORY NUNN

Rome had senators too—that's why it declined.

Not all stomping statesmen were unaware of mob fickleness. When Otto von Bismarck was scheduled to visit the Teutonic hinterlands an aide came to him with a public relations device. "For one thousand marks," he said, "I can line the roads with a thousand men who will cheer vigorously as you pass. The cheers will become contagious, and you will enter every province on a wave of triumph."

36

"Save your money," advised Bismarck. "There are always jackasses willing to bray for nothing."

Hidden in the obscurity of time is Phocion, the Greek statesman-general (c. 402–317 B.C.). When he returned from his successful campaign against Philip of Macedon, at Byzantium, mobs crowded the streets of Athens to cheer him. Berated by an aide for failure to show exhilaration at the experience, Phocion said: "They will cheer just as loudly when I am hanged." He never lost his disdain for the mob no matter the honors heaped upon him. He carried his arguments to the people, and once when he addressed the citizens of Athens his speech was interrupted by thunderous cheers. The accolade continued unabated for several minutes and finally Phocion turned to his aides to inquire: "Did I say something *that* stupid?"

His remark following Byzantium was prophetic, for the Athenians forced him to drink hemlock. Later, as though to emphasize his conclusions, the mob repented and raised a statue in his honor.

Phocion was a staunch advocate of democracy. He was compassionate, intelligent, and he refused to speak condescendingly. He was ahead of his time. Had he lived in the television age he would not have died by the mob—he would never have been elected.

A newspaper editorial of the twenties carried this item:
"The Chinese in New York City are putting up huge posters urging America to unite in a boycott against Japan. The posters tell Americans: 'Write to your congressman today and the thing is done.' The Chinese are great thinkers, but they have no sense of humor."

Typographical Errors

"In addition to his wife the good pastor heaves four children."
OBITUARY OF A REVERED THEOLOGIAN.

With the advent of the printing press came a curious editorial by-product known as typographical errata. As the art of typesetting became more widespread the virus responsible for the typographical error went right along, achieving heights of mischief never before imagined. Things got so out of hand that Pope Sixtus V felt moved to issue an editorial bull threatening with excommunication any printer responsible for typographical errors in a pending new edition of the Bible. The *Bible of Sixtus* V has since become a valuable collectors' item, setting as it does a record for typographical errata. The fate of the printers remains unrecorded.

Baron de Grimm, in his *Memoirs*, makes note of a highly sensitive French author who died in a fit of anger as the consequence of a favorite work having been printed with upwards of three hundred errors, half of which were inserted by the proofreader.

A British clergyman almost suffered banishment as 'a man who lost the faith' when his book, *Lives of the Saints*, appeared as *Lies of the Saints*. And in the same period a company of stationers was tried in star chamber proceedings and fined heavily for neglecting to correct a version of the Bible that read: "Thou shalt commit adultery."

So severe was the punishment inflicted upon publishers holding biblical patent in England that one printer gave up his company to study medicine, giving as explanation: "A printer's errors are exposed to the eye; but a physician's are buried with the patient."

It was about this time that a London paper published an unsurpassed correction: "For '*her* grace, the Duke of Bedford,' read, '*his* grace, the Duchess of Bedford.'"

The most brilliant minds have attempted to explain the phenomenon—but a sixteenth century monk offers the most likely reason. His book, *Anatomy of the Mass*, was one hundred seventy-two pages in length and had an accompanying fifteen page list of errata. The pious author explained that the purpose of the book was to forestall the artifices of Satan. He supposed that the devil, to ruin the fruits of his work, employed malicious frauds in obliging printers to commit blunders never before equaled in number for so small a book. To combat the machinations of Satan he was obliged to re-edit the work in condensed form, thus cutting the size of Satan's field of operations.

The devil remains as good an explanation as any.

If newspaper and book publishers suffer nightmares as a result of this form of error think of the pain authors feel, particularly when a book called *Drunkenness is Folly* appears as *Drunkenness is Jolly*.

Typos per se come to us as errors of commission as well as omission; yet, for all the havoc caused, the typographical error remains the most pungent and funniest kind of written humor, often thoroughly devastating in editorial insinuation impossible to achieve any other way.

Witness the evidence. . . .

A travel brochure aimed at encouraging the tourist trade to visit Toulouse, France, highlighted its attractions this way:

"Toulouse is a large city with one hundred thousand inhabitants built entirely of brick."

An over zealous clergyman once advertised that he would conduct Sunday school classes twice a week.

The obituary of a politician with a notorious lust for life was intended to read: "The subject, in the throes of his final illness, could hardly bear the demise of his life."
Instead it was printed: "The subject, in the throes of his final illness, could hardly wear the chemise of his wife."

A history of the reign of Queen Victoria details the incident of a mad horse that ran amuck and caused considerable damage to Her Majesty's royal east end.

The United States Supreme Court has lately been responsible for much in the way of controversy, but never more so than when it caused the headline: LEWIS LOSES UNION SUIT.

HOTEL BURNS. TWO HUNDRED HALF GLAD GUESTS ESCAPE.
This story also contained the following report. "Mrs. B. was one of the less fortunate. Caught in her bathtub when the alarm was sounded, she slipped on a bar of soap and broke her etaoin etaoin."

Linguistic barriers have produced their share of mistakes. Shakespeare's, "Out brief candle," was translated into French as, "Get out you short candle."

Alexander Pope would never recognize the edition carrying his *Shoot folly as it flies*—POPE, as, "*Shoot Polly as she Lies*—POP."

An all-time classic came into being when the deeds of a famous military man were lauded thusly: "The general will remain unequaled in history for his accomplishment on the bottlefield."

Juvenile delinquency may have its roots as a protest against this mistake. Meant to read: "Girls of fifteen and sixteen are fond of beaus," the report appeared, "Girls of fifteen and sixteen are fond of beans."

Household safety certainly received careful consideration when the manufacturer of an electrical opening device flooded supermarkets with a pamphlet headed: "Jagged cans cut more housewives in the pantry than anywhere else."

A court trial was responsible for this information.
"Midway through her testimony the beautiful Mrs. W. stripped to the waist to show the court how her wealthy husband amused her."

A report on the sermon of a fiery preacher noted the fact that among other things the clergyman 'called upon all singers to repent.'

When the handsome faces of a smiling society couple appeared in the centerfold of a New York tabloid, it was noted they "recently exchanged marriage cows."

Though devoted to family life a certain magazine may well have encouraged birth control with a story banner that announced: "Good News for Would-be Mothers. Infant Morality Declines."

A well-known fashion expert, after addressing the ladies' auxiliary of a national organization, was herself criticized by a reporter for her lackluster clothing. The reporter wrote: "The lady lecturer on dress wore nothing that was remarkable."

A proofreader allowed the insertion of a period to go undisturbed, and the published report read: "The lady lecturer on dress wore nothing. That was remarkable."

Was it wishful thinking when a headline reported the failure of justice this way? MOBSTERS EVADE NOOSE: JURY HUNG.

A typographical error once started a unique fad. During the era when devouring live goldfish was part of a college curricula the following errata was bannered in a midwestern paper: FALLS FROM THIRD FLOOR WINDOW. BREAKS EGG.

It started a rash of fraternity activity, each pitted against the other, to see from what height one could fall without breaking an egg. A southern sophomore set the unofficial record by toppling six stories into a net, cracking the egg in flight, and hitting a greased frying pan with a bulls-eye as he descended.

Item: "Mrs. F., leader of the local temperance movement, continues to be under the doctor's car."

The trend of the times was illustrated by this startling report in a New York newspaper: PRESCRIPTION DEPARTMENT ADDED TO LOCAL DRUG STORE.

An especially vicious crime was recorded when a Pennsylvania sheet told its readers: THUGS EAT THEN ROB PROPRIETOR.

A renowned newspaper publisher, after backing the views of a certain politician with regard to proposed amendments, had a change of heart. The day before the polls opened his newspaper carried this black bordered correction:

"Regarding our editorials of the past few weeks, for 'No' read 'Yes' and for 'Yes' read 'No.'"

"Amicus Plato, Amicus Socrates, sed majer veritas."

The phrase, used by an itinerant lecturer, was reported in a local newspaper as: "I may cuss Plato, I may cuss Socrates, said Major Verit Ass."

A news magazine, covering the national scene, printed the following correction: "In last week's editorial on the Republican tax proposals the words 'pigs' and 'cows' should have been 'pros' and 'cons.'"

The photograph of a debutante, taken at her coming-out party, showed her clinging affectionately to her portly, overly buxom aunt. The society page caption described the young lady as "extremely lovely on the whole."

In print, however, it was reported that "Miss F.E.A. looked extremely lovely on the whale."

A suburban community was shocked to read that, "Mr. W. was badly burned when he came in contact with a live wife."

Nobody could help but admire the honesty of the staid institutional mercantile establishment that advertised: "Why go elsewhere to be cheated when you can come here?"

The sermon of an itinerant preacher was printed under the title head: "The Ford is my Shepherd. I shall not walk."

The city of Albany was once described this way:

"Albany is a town of eight thousand houses and twenty-five thousand inhabitants with most of their gable-ends to the street."

Bar and Bench

Whene'er a bitter foe attack thee,
Sheathe thy sword, thy wrath restrain:
Or else will magistrates and lawyers
Divide thy wealth, thy purse retain.

ARCHEVOLTI, *Sixteenth Century*

The legal profession, like the medical profession, has a canon of ethics, and, as in the latter instance, it is generally ignored. This is understandable; lawyers, after all, must spend much of their time dealing with other lawyers, as well as with magistrates who at one time themselves practiced law. No other calling requires its practitioners to concentrate their efforts among a class thoroughly immersed in its own shenanigans. (Imagine the chaos if plumbers were limited to repairing the accouterments of other plumbers.) The result of this natural accident has been a clan constantly exposing itself through self-criticism. The perfect anecdote, one of the best bits of nineteenth century humor, concerns itself with the legal profession. A midwestern judge, while strolling through a graveyard in Philadelphia, came upon a headstone that read: HERE LIES A LAWYER AND AN HONEST MAN.

"Ah," he remarked, "I see back East they bury 'em two in a grave."

On the subject of justice itself, Diogenes Laertius wrote in the third century: "Laws are like cobwebs. If a trifling or powerless thing falls into them they hold it fast; while if it is something weightier, it breaks through them and is off." Charles Dickens was more outspoken with: "Law is a ass, a idiot." And William Shakespeare, when laying the grounds for a utopia, in *King Henry* VI, suggests as the initial step: "—let's kill all the lawyers." To which Montaigne might have added: "For a desperate disease a desperate cure."

It is unfair to believe everything we hear about lawyers—some of it might not be true. In a way we must pity them; no other group has had to stand up to the most brilliant minds of the ages, and so consistently come out second best. Law and lawyer baiting goes back to the Bible ("Woe unto you, lawyers! For ye lade men with burdens grievous to bear."—Luke 11:46) and comes right down to the present ("There is no such thing as justice, in or out of court."—Clarence Darrow). Even Philo warned that a judge must bear in mind that when he tries a case he is himself on trial; which probably explains the popularity of closed-door sessions, especially with some pseudo-judiciary groups.

Because law deals with humanity under duress it is an inexhaustible reservoir of good stories, creating an illusion wherein attorneys and magistrates appear to be the epitome of wit. This is easy to understand, especially when the attribute of wisdom is so closely associated with advocacy, particularly judicial advocacy. In many instances wit and wisdom have blended in the persons of legal practitioners, and these unusual men have stood forth brightly as examples to be copied and admired. But close inspection of classic courtroom situation and commentary shows that the legalites are not responsible, rather that the wit and wisdom spring from the people harassed by them. Witnesses, clients, defendants, and jurors emerge as the ray of light in the austerity of pomp and circumstance found in the Halls of Justice. The professionals merely serve as *modus operandi* or corpus delicti.

It was an outstanding case in one of the small mining towns. Joe was brought in on an assault charge. The State presented the weapons he used. A huge telegraph pole, a dagger, a pair of shears, a saw, a gun, and a Civil War saber. Counsel for the defense produced the weapons used by the alleged victim to defend himself. A scythe, a hoe, an ax, a shovel and a pair of tongs. After deliberating, the twelve men filed in slowly and the foreman read the verdict: "We the jury would give five dollars to have seen that fight."

Backwoods justice is often exacting and to the letter of the law. The magistrates are conscientious and strict observers of legal protocol. It was in such an area that a judge one day told a witness to raise his right arm.

"Can't, your honor, got a shot in it," the man said.

"Then hold up your left arm."

"Can't. Got a shot in that one too."

"THEN HOLD UP YOUR LEG," the judge roared. "No man can be sworn in this court unless he holds up something."

I was never ruined but twice, once when I lost a lawsuit and once when I gained one.

VOLTAIRE

If I was to give you an orange I'd simply say, "I give you this orange." But when the transaction is entrusted to a lawyer he puts down, "I hereby give and convey to you all and singular, my estate and interests, rights, title, claim and advantages of and in said orange, together with all its rind, juice, pulp, and pits and all rights and advantages with full power to bite, cut, and otherwise eat the same, or give the same away with and without the rind, skin, juice, pulp, or pits, anything herein before or herein after or in any other deed, or deeds, instruments of whatever nature or kind whatsoever to the contrary in anywise not withstanding."

Then another smart lawyer comes along and takes the orange away from you.

The witness fainted on the stand and the judge, seeking to revive her, noticed the only liquid in the court was a bottle of brandy. "I'd offer her a drink," he whispered to the bailiff, "but I know she's the head of the temperance league."

"Oh, no," corrected the groggy woman. "I'm president of the Anti-Vice League."

"Well," said the judge, "I knew there was something I shouldn't offer you."

In some states they no longer hang murderers. They kill them by elocution.

WILL ROGERS

In negligence cases the injured party is always torn between two professional opinions: his doctor's, who says he no longer needs crutches, and his lawyer's, who says he does.

The loser was finding defeat difficult to accept. "I'm far from through," he threatened. "I'll law you to the Appeals Court."

"I'll be there," replied the victor.

"And if need be I'll law you to the Supreme Court."

"I'll be there," the winner complacently repeated.

"And if necessary," the angry one shouted, "I'll law you to hell."

"In that case," said the other, "my lawyer will be there."

Contingency fee: An arrangement in which if you lose your lawyer gets nothing—and if you win you get nothing.

Let him whose coat a court has taken,
Sing his song and go his way.

THE TALMUD

A law school graduate considered setting up office in the deep South and sought advice of an elder, prominent attorney. "In politics I am a Republican," said the novice, "and by nature an honest man."

The great southerner replied: "If you are an honest lawyer you will have no competition here—and as you are a Republican the game laws will protect you."

Courtroom ego reached new heights when a learned judge, after sentencing a man found guilty of a capital crime, concluded his remarks with: "Young man, you will soon have to appear before another, and *perhaps* a better judge than I."

An extremely verbose attorney droned on and on in a manner both nerveracking and boring. Finally, after five hours, he ceased his pleading and awaited the court's verdict. The jury filed back into the room and the foreman read: "Despite the arguments of his attorney we the jury find the defendant not guilty."

Under the laws of this country a man is innocent until he is proved guilty—then he is usually insane.

American judicial procedure's great difficulty seems to be how to proceed.

A Pennsylvania magistrate was also a cashier of the hometown bank. A stranger presented a check for payment one day, but the judge refused to tender cash, feeling as he did that the evidence of identification was not satisfactory.

"Why, judge," the man protested, "I've known you to sentence men to be hanged on lesser evidence than this."

"Very likely," his honor admitted. "But when it comes to cold cash I gotta be mighty careful."

Judge: "Have you ever been up before me?"
Accused: "I don't know, your honor. What time do you get up?"

Jury: Twelve men chosen to decide who has the better lawyer.

Bar and Bench

An attorney, on being called to account by a bar association for having acted unprofessionally in that he took less than the prescribed fee, argued that he had taken everything the man had. Whereupon he was most honorably acquitted.

Following the presentation of evidence against a Kentucky moonshiner the federal judge charged the jury, then asked, "Are there any questions the jurymen would like to ask before considering the evidence?"

"A couple of us jurymen, your honor," said the foreman, "would like to know if the defendant boiled the malt one or two hours, and how he keeps the yeast out."

"Have you ever appeared as a witness before?"

"Yes, your honor," replied the advertising man.

"In what suit?"

"In my gray flannel."

It was Clarence Darrow who lost his temper in court one day and started to leave. "Are you trying to show contempt for this court?" demanded the judge.

"No," shouted Darrow. "I'm trying to conceal it."

The legal council of the League of Nations met one day and issued the ultimatum that if Japan did not get out of Manchuria on a given date the council would hold another meeting.

A successful lawyer once toured the country as a lecturer. His subject was: "The Trial of Jesus from a Lawyer's Standpoint." On which one critic wrote: "I can imagine only one lecture which might prove more interesting to an audience. That would be, 'The Trial of a Lawyer from Jesus' Standpoint.'"

Law is a strange thing. It makes a man swear to tell the truth, and every time he shows signs of doing so some lawyer objects.

A late arrival at the funeral service for a millionaire political financier seated himself beside a lawyer and asked, "How far has the service gone?"

Nodding toward the clergyman in the pulpit the attorney whispered, "Just opened for the defense."

"Silence in the court," the judge hammered. "Half a dozen men have been convicted without the court being able to hear a word of the testimony."

If nature had as many laws as the State, God Himself could not reign over it.

LUDWIG BOERNE

The famous judge was being interviewed for a national picture magazine article. "Could you tell me, sir," asked the reporter, "how you manage, year in and year out, to try more than twice as many cases as any other judge in the country?"

"Certainly," said the austere gentleman. "I listen to the complainant, and I render my decision."

"You mean you do not hear the arguments of the defendant?"

"Well, I used to," said the judge. "But I found it confused me."

A man left the bulk of his fortune to his lawyers. If everybody did this a lot time would be saved.

LONDON OPINION

A judge once ruled against a man who wanted certain gifts returned when the lady of his affections married someone else. "Request denied," was the decision. "I am certain the amount spent was more than covered by the fun. I courted that girl myself once."

The law is a system that protects everybody who can afford to hire a good lawyer.

To a recently arrived immigrant the processes of law and order were baffling. He had the misfortune to be arrested for peddling without a license. Now he stood before the bar of justice with three young ladies arrested for soliciting. When the first young lady gave her profession as "actress" the judge sentenced her to thirty days in the workhouse. When the second said she was "a model" she drew a sixty-day sentence. "And what do you do for a living?" the judge fired at the third girl.

"To tell you the truth, your honor," she answered, "I'm a prostitute."

Taken back by this burst of frankness the judge said, "Honesty has become such a rare commodity in these parts that for telling the truth I'm suspending sentence. You are free to go." Then he turned to the peddler, his face hardened. "And what do *you* do for a living?"

"To tell you the truth, judge," he replied, "I'm a prostitute also."

The backwoods judge had a queer habit. Before rendering a verdict he would look in a book which resembled a legal tome but was in reality a Sears Roebuck catalogue. One day he pronounced: "For being drunk and disorderly I fine you $1.98 and two days on the road."

As the prisoner filed from the courtroom he said to the sheriff, "He sure was tough on me."

"You were lucky," the sheriff answered. "If he'd opened that book to the plumbing section instead of the pants section you might a got life."

The most famous reply to a lawyer's direct question occurred in a slander suit. Asked to repeat the exact conversation between defendant and complainant, the witness replied, "I cain't remember rightly, 'cept each was callin' de other what dey both is."

"Have you a lawyer?"
"No. I'm going to tell the truth."

It is the duty of our courts to try anything presented to it, from which a dispute detrimental to public interest might occur were the matter not decided by authority. In this country one of the most graphic examples concerns the discovery of a human toe in a package of chewing tobacco. After finding against the manufacturer in a negligence proceeding, the Mississippi jurist stated: "We can imagine no reason why, with ordinary care, human toes could not be left out of chewing tobacco. If toes are found in chewing tobacco it seems to us that somebody has been careless."

The populace of antiquity was unaware, as are peoples today, that the rendering of court decisions quite often had little to do with justice.

When a praetor assigned as counsel to a Sicilian, a Roman, who though patrician was also stupid, the Sicilian entered this plea: "I pray you, great praetor, assign this gentlemen as counsel to my opponent; then you needn't give me any counsel."

Appropriately, the oldest joke in the world deals with justice. The text was discovered in one of the noble ruins stumbled upon now and then in the jungle recesses of the world. This particular find was made in India where it is given a possible longevity of six thousand years. It concerns a conflict in which one lawyer argued both sides. His advocacy for each cause was so brilliant that the court of the day rendered the only logical verdict. They hanged the lawyer.

History and Diplomacy

"We learn nothing from history except that we learn nothing from history."

The trouble with history is its dependence upon diplomats. Heinrich Heine's description is appropriate to the general breed. "Ordinarily," said Heine, "he is insane. But he has lucid moments when he is only stupid." It has been said that fifty-one nations rushed to embrace the United Nations, and, if the UN fails it will be because all had one thing in common: the foregone conclusion that fifty of the member nations were not to be trusted!

Historical comparisons are worse than odious; they are incorrect. Recently, when the South African prime minister was fired upon and wounded as a result of apartheid policies, a constituent at the United Nations compared the shooting with that of Abraham Lincoln. The very nature of the remark typifies the attitudes of diplomats, for it should be noted that the only similarity was the nature of the wound and the most important difference was the accuracy of the assassin.

That it is difficult to live with one's national history is shown by the Frenchman who renounced his citizenship to become a British subject. "What have you gained by it?" a countryman demanded.

"Well," said the man, "for one zing, I win ze battle of Waterloo."

Today we stand on the brink of nowhere. At stake is the penultimate of social achievement, the free society. Somewhere in the montage of liberty, subjugation, and nuclear fission, are the peoples, wondering how this situation came about. Their bewilderment can be capsuled by a Christopher Columbus story. On the evening of October 11 in the year of the great voyage Columbus stood on the bridge of his ship, puzzled. Luis de Torres, the interpreter, came to him. "It is a shame, my captain," said De Torres, "that we flounder this way, not knowing where anything is."

"That is not my problem, De Torres," Columbus said. "I know where everything is. The part that concerns me is, where are we?"

History tells us that the next day Columbus discovered America. Knowing history, I wonder if he really did—or if a persistent rumor might have foundation in fact and he couldn't help himself, having run aground. In which case America discovered him.

A foreign diplomat assigned to the United Nations could not speak English. During the luncheon interlude he placed himself behind a stranger at a food counter and heard the man order apple pie and coffee. He too ordered apple pie and coffee. For the next two weeks he continued to ask for apple pie and coffee. He finally decided on a change of diet and listened attentively while another man ordered a ham sandwich. "Ham sandwich," he said to the counterman.

"White or rye?" the counterman asked.

"Ham sandwich," the diplomat repeated.

"White or rye?" the counterman asked again.

"Ham sandwich," the diplomat replied.

The counterman grew very angry. "Look, Mac," he roared, shaking his fist under the diplomat's nose. "I haven't got all day. Do you want it on white or rye?"

"Apple pie and coffee," answered the diplomat.

A gentleman from Washington returned from a European trip in the early part of the current century. Since his butler was of Irish origin he thought he would advise him of things in the old country. "I made a rush trip through Ireland, Patrick, and the people seemed extraordinarily happy and content," he told the employee.

"It's rarely they are so," replied the butler. "You must have been there while the fighting was going on."

I know I am among civilized men because they are fighting so savagely.

VOLTAIRE

The legend of that fighting Irishman, Patrick O'Flynn, probably started at the battle of Trafalgar. Through the hell of fire and smoke, the crashing of cannon, and the cries of men in anguish, Lord Nelson signaled a halt. Silence permeated the atmosphere and his lordship asked: "Is Patrick O'Flynn on deck?"

"He is, m'lord," a junior officer reported.

"Then," said his lordship, "let the battle go on."

During the thirties a Parisian was considerably irked by a fascist who insisted on praising the glories of Il Duce. "Il Duce ordered us to subdue the savage Ethiopians," said the Fascist diplomat. "And we did, in spite of half a hundred nations of the world determined on our destruction. We are unbeatable. We have the power to conquer and destroy—we cannot be stopped." He paused for effect, then said to the gentleman from Paris: "If Il Duce commanded his army to march immediately into France what could possibly stop us?"

"Ah," the man replied. "Monsieur apparently has forgotten the French Customs Service."

A United States senator was irked by the refusal of the Secretary of the Navy to appoint a young man to Annapolis who had been recommended by the politico. "But the boy has no teeth," the Secretary declared.

"What do you expect him to do in the event of war?" asked the senator. "Bite the enemy?"

Assassinations have figured in the destiny of the world. Some logicians believe the passing of assassination as a stylish tool of criticism has resulted in the decline of effective government. Politicians are able to sit back content in the knowledge that they might be voted out of office but never carried out. The only solution appears to be more elections or more assassinations.

In Russia, during the reign of one of the tyrannical Czars, a plot was hatched calling for the assassination of a key nobleman. A band of anarchists set themselves behind a clump of bushes to await his passing, a practice which had been carefully noted as taking place at the same time every day. But as time passed it became obvious that the notorious Baron Paskutstve would not follow his schedule today. Hours went by, and finally one of the killers whispered to an accomplice: "It is difficult for me to understand. The Baron passes here every day at the same time. I hope nothing has happened to him."

Abraham Lincoln's difficulties with his generals are history. When McClellan's waiting campaign finally got on his nerves Lincoln sent the following note: "My dear McClellan: If you do not want to use the Army I should like to borrow it for a while."

Metternich approaches close to being a great statesman. He lies very well.

NAPOLEON

A British seaman was taking his examination for a higher grade. "Now, Summerville," said the inspector, "you are quartermaster on duty at night. Your ship is tied up at the wharf in a dangerous area. You see a figure crawling and stumbling towards your ship in the dark. What do you do?"

"Why," replied Summerville, "I 'elps the skipper aboard, sir."

"Who was the first man?" a teacher asked a young child in her first grade class.

"George Washington," answered the boy.

"I'm afraid you are wrong. It was Adam."

"Well," said the lad, "if yer talkin' about furriners I guess he was."

Count von Bismarck wished to show the patriotism of his rank-and-file to a visiting dignitary. In the course of a special ceremony he approached an enlisted man and said: "I have authorization to bestow upon you, in lieu of the Iron Cross, the amount of one hundred thalers, Which do you choose?"

"What is the Cross worth?" asked the hero.

"Approximately three thalers."

"Well then, Your Highness," said the soldier, "I'll take the Cross and ninety-seven thalers."

In England they've been changing the guards for three hundred years. I guess they're not old enough to change themselves.

Lafayette, at the time of the American Revolution, was introduced to two young candidates for officer rank in the American Army. He asked one: "Are you married?" When the candidate said he was, Lafayette replied: "Happy man!"

The marquis then put the same question to the other young fellow. "I am a bachelor," was the reply.

Lafayette said, "Lucky dog!"

America had often been discovered before Columbus—but it had always been hushed up.

OSCAR WILDE

Lincoln was once told that twelve mules and a brigadier general had been captured by the enemy in a Confederate advance. "Too bad," said the President. "Those mules cost two hundred dollars apiece."

America's political history, capsule version:
The passing of the buffalo.
The passing of the Indian.
The passing of the buck.

Patriotism is the last refuge of a scoundrel.

SAMUEL JOHNSON

In the middle of the nineteenth century one of the British diehards remarked to an American: "If things do not improve in your country it might be necessary for us to send an army to chastise you."
The American replied: "What, again?"

Every man loves his native land—whether he was born there or not.

IRISH PROVERB, *attributed to*
THOMAS FITCH

When news reached England of the destruction of the stamp papers in the colonies, Benjamin Franklin was serving in London as representative of the province of Pennsylvania. The British ministry sent for him and after a lengthy discussion a proposal was offered whereby, if the Americans would agree to pay damages for the destroyed paper and other items connected thereto, Parliament would agree to repeal the act.

Franklin gave the following reply: "I am put in mind of the Frenchman, who, having heated a poker until it was red hot, ran furiously into the street and addressed himself to the first Englishman he met. "Aha monsieur! Voulez-vous give the pleasure, zee satisfaction if you pleez, to let me run zee pokair only one foot eento your rear?" The Englishman hesitated, whereupon the Frenchman amended his request, "Veree well zen, perhaps six eenches?"

"I say, are you mad?" returned the Englishman. "If you don't go about your business I shall be obliged to knock you down."

"Well zen," said the chastened Frenchman, "weel you, good sir, only zen be so obliging as to pay me for zee trouble and expense of heating zee pokair?"

(With that Franklin left—and the colonies did not pay.)

In statesmanship get the formalities right, never mind about the moralities.

MARK TWAIN

A man from outer space landed in the hills of this country, where he set up housekeeping, listened to the radio, and watched television. With his space ship out of commission he soon tired of the spot and decided to take an ocean voyage. He appeared at a travel agency one day and requested accommodations for a trip abroad. "Where to?" asked the agent.

"Oh yes, where to?" returned the spaceman. "May I look at your globe?"

He turned the globe several times, studied it carefully, and after a few minutes he turned back to the clerk. "Pardon me," he said. "Do you have anything else to offer?"

A man whose religion allowed him deferment in the war, on the grounds of conscientious objection, was hailed into court for hitting a neighbor with a brick. "You say you are a lover of peace," the judge reprimanded. "Yet you go ahead and hit Smith with a brick."

"Yes, your honor," he admitted. "And he was indeed very peaceful after I hit him."

Curious how Napoleon's greatest detractors have all come to horrible ends. Londonderry cut his throat. Ludwig XVIII rotted on his throne, and Professor Saalfeld of Goettingen is still professor at Goettingen.

HEINRICH HEINE

When the State of Israel came into existence severe fighting broke out in the Negev. King Farouk decided to visit an Egyptian outpost. He found the troops reluctant to stand their ground. In a voice full of pathos Farouk called up memories of the glorious Egyptian past, and then said: "Soldiers, I'm asking for volunteers. I want four men to retreat a little slower."

My constitution grows worse—even worse than the constitution of Prussia.

HEINRICH HEINE

"Remember, my son," a World War I mother cautioned her boy, "do not get hurt. Stay near the general."

Every government has spies in every other country, and every other country knows about them. It is merely a form of international courtesy, like exchange professors. . . . In fact, they give a rather nice cosmopolitan air to the streets.

ROBERT BENCHLEY

Adolf Hitler was very much disturbed when a clairvoyant let it be known that she could predict the exact day of the Führer's death. Since her predictions were always based on astrology, and since Hitler himself was a believer in the stars, he sent for the woman. After much divination the woman finally said that the omens indicated no specific date for the passing of the Nazi leader, other than that it would definitely take place on a Jewish holiday.

"Which holiday?" Hitler demanded.

"I cannot be sure," said the astrologist.

"You've got to be sure," Hitler ordered, going off into one of his spastic shrieks. "I demand that you be sure."

"What difference does it make?" shrugged the woman. "Any day on which you die will be a Jewish holiday."

An enemy of dictatorship fought hard and at great sacrifice for democratic principles. But gradually the secret police learned his true identity and the man barely managed to escape before he was killed. As he made his way from country to country little was heard of him, except for an occasional announcement that he had been captured or slain. Finally, after years of fighting and hiding, he made his way into Lisbon and appeared at the American Embassy. There he was treated in the fine style accorded all fighters for democracy, until he asked: "Can you give me a visa to get into your wonderful country?"

The American consul sighed. "I'm sorry," he said, "but our immigration laws make it impossible. You will have to come back in ten years."

Slowly the man walked to the door. Then he turned and hopefully asked, "Morning or afternoon?"

About a century ago a famous politician from Philadelphia paid a visit to Boston and was being shown around the city. He was critical of the physical layout of the place and did not hesitate to ask his host why Boston was not laid out like Philadelphia.

"Well," said the Bostonian, "if Boston ever gets to be as dead as Philadelphia, we'll lay it out."

At the height of the apartheid insanity in South Africa all mail going out of the country was carefully censored. One of the anti-apartheid soldiers was incensed when he received word from home to the effect that his last few letters had been totally illegible because the censor had obliterated whole sentences and words. In his next letter he remonstrated against this and in conclusion wrote: "Look under the stamp."

As usual the letter was opened by the censor. The man in charge decided to handle this one himself, and spent a great deal of time carefully detaching the stamp from the envelope. But the

61

soldier had used an extra strong adhesive and the job was extremely painstaking. Finally the stamp was steamed from the envelope and the censor read: "Was it hard to get off?"

The time will never come in this country when the people won't know exactly what sugar-coated means.

ABRAHAM LINCOLN

War is what results when one country takes steps to defend itself from another country that is taking steps to defend itself.

"I just learned why the Scotch bagpipes make a Scotsman brave in war."
"Why?"
"He'd rather die than have to hear them."

Fame is fleeting, even for historical figures. Wellington, immediately after his greatest victory, was stopped by a polite gentleman who inquired, "Mr. Brown, I believe?"
"My good man," said Wellington. "If you believe *that* you'll believe anything."

The least pain in our little finger gives us more concern than the destruction of millions of our fellow beings.

WILLIAM HAZLITT

Two American soldiers, in England during World War II, were having difficulty with the British public pay phone system. One of them entered a booth which had the customary dialing buttons A and B. He pressed one button at precisely the moment a Nazi V-bomb exploded near by, leveling the entire community. As the soldier came stumbling out of the wreckage of the booth he said to his buddy: "Honest, Joe, all I did was press button A."

Prior to the Civil War, Wendell Phillips, the abolitionist, (best remembered today for his remark: "You can always get the truth from an American statesman after he has turned seventy, or given up all hope for the Presidency") was lecturing in the Middle West when he ran into a group of clergymen returning from a convention. "Are you Mr. Phillips?" one of them asked.

"I am," Phillips replied.

"You trying to save the slaves?"

"I am an abolitionist, sir, if that's what you mean."

"Why preach up here? Why don't you go down South?"

"Are you a preacher?" Phillips inquired.

"Yes, sir, I am."

"And are you trying to save souls from hell?"

"Yes, sir, that's my business."

"Well?" asked Phillips. "Why don't you go down there?"

Following the Crimean War, a driver in London drove two officers to their barracks and received a less than liberal fare from the gentlemen. He launched into a blasphemous denunciation of the Czar. "My good man," said one of the officers, "why do you speak so badly of the Russian Emperor."

"Because, sir," the driver replied, "it appears that 'e 'as killed off all the gentlemen in the British Army."

In the heart of Dixie the driver of a sight-seeing bus highlighted southern battlefields to his passengers. In glowing terms he spoke of the many victories piled up by the Army of the Confederacy, until one man from the North asked, "Didn't the Northern armies win any battles in the Civil War?"

"No, mister, they didn't," the driver answered. "And they ain't going to so long as I'm driving this bus."

A Union soldier was being tried before an army court-martial, the charge being cowardice and desertion under fire. "Now, John," said the prosecuting attorney, "you say the sight of your first Secesh scared you, that the man fired three shots in rapid succession, and didn't hit you with any of them? How far were you from him when he fired?"

"The first shot or the last one, sir?"

"Why? What's the difference?"

"Not too much, sir," the soldier replied, "I'd say about half to three quarters of a mile."

Two Russian judges met after the overthrow of the Czar. "A terribly trying day today," said one. "I was forced to sentence a comrade to five years in Siberia only because he stole a case of food."

"I had a more difficult time of it this morning," said the other. "I was forced to let a non-Party member go free only because he was innocent."

A senator who opposed federal aid to education on the grounds that his constituency was educated more'n they could ever use, found himself stranded when the railroad line in his state was flooded. He waded along until he came to a hotel where he asked for a room. As he signed the register he remarked to the clerk: "Just like the deluge."

"What was that, stranger?" asked the clerk.

"I said, my good man, that this is just like the deluge. I'm certain you read about the deluge. You know—Noah, the Ark, Mount Ararat."

"Sorry, no," said the clerk. "We ain't had no papers here for more'n two days."

Gallantry was never overlooked in the olden days. When your great-great-great-grandmother was waiting to be burned at the stake, the executioner wrapped a blanket around her to keep her warm until they got the fire started.

The difference between a moral man and a man of honor is that the latter regrets a discreditable act even when it has worked.

H. L. MENCKEN

One super-patriot recently remarked. "The United Nations is a good idea, but it's too bad we gotta have so many foreigners in it."

The Red Army captured a Nazi outside of Stalingrad and sentenced the man to death. The day of the execution came and it was miserably cold and damp. The firing squad marched the German SS man some distance into the woods until the prisoner protested. "What brutes you Communists are," he said, "forcing me to march through muck like this."

"Think of us," said the Red officer. "We gotta march back."

When Napoleon escaped from Elba in 1815 the Paris newspapers reported events as follows:

"The Corsican monster has landed in the Gulf of Juan."

"The cannibal is marching towards Grasse."

"The usurper has entered Grenoble."

"Bonaparte has entered Lyons."

"Napoleon is marching towards Fontainebleau."

"His Imperial Majesty is expected tomorrow in Paris."

A group of doughboys, going over in 1917, were receiving battle information. "Sergeant," said the officer. "Supposing you suddenly rounded a turn in the road and came upon a large detachment of Boche. What would you do?"

"Why, sir," said the sergeant. "I'd spread the news through all of France."

A hillbilly recruit told his buddy he was going to take out the full amount of government insurance permitted soldiers, ten thousand dollars. "Don't be silly," said his friend. "Why pay all them premiums when you'll only get shot anyway, and could have had so much more fun for the money."

"I know what I'm doing. That's mah insurance, boy."

"Whaddaya mean?"

"Listen," said the hillbilly, "you all don't suppose that Uncle Sam is gwine 'a let a ten thousand dollar man into the front lines, do you?"

It is a reflection on our times of superior happiness that a student committed suicide, leaving behind a note reading: "I'm tired of being so damned happy."

An ambassador, on a mission to Sparta from Perinthus, overdid himself by speaking at great length. "What answer shall I give to the Perinthians?" the diplomat asked.

"You may say," replied the King, "that you talked a great deal —while I said nothing."

We are only cave men who have lost their caves.

CHRISTOPHER MORLEY

When General Buller, during the Boer war, sent word from South Africa that he had retired without losing a man, a flag, or a cannon, Whistler added: "Or a minute."

When World War I broke out, the War Ministry in London dispatched a coded message to one of the British outposts in the inaccessible areas of Africa. The message read: "War declared. Arrest all enemy aliens in your district."

The War Ministry received this prompt reply: "Have arrested ten Germans, six Belgians, four Frenchman, two Italians, three Austrians, and an American. Please advise immediately who we're at war with."

Two draftees were in the PX at Camp Dix when their sergeant entered and asked: "Did you guys see the colonel?" They said they hadn't. About fifteen minutes later the sarge came in again, and said: "You sure you didn't see that son-of-a-b——colonel?" Again the recruits said they hadn't. Shortly thereafter an officer walked up and reprimanded them for not saluting. "Who the hell do you think you are?" one asked.

"I'm the colonel," the man said briskly.

"Boy, are you gonna get it," said the other. "The sarge has been looking for you."

The Big Three dinner at Teheran, in 1943, saw Marshal Stalin explaining to President Roosevelt and Prime Minister Churchill the classic attitude of the Russian people. "The honors paid to me are not mine, but belong to the people of Russia," said the Marshal. "It is easy to be a great leader, or a proud hero, when one has to do with such people as the Russians. The Russian citizenry will not tolerate any other qualities from those in the armed forces. Why, even people of mild courage, and even determined cowards, become heroes in Russia." Here the Marshal paused, and added: "Those who do not—are killed."

An American correspondent who had spent a great deal of time in Nazi Germany returned after the war. The first day in Berlin he walked into a shop and asked for a photo of Hitler. "We do not have photographs of Hitler," said the clerk. The man walked around the block, then entered the store again and asked: "Do you have photos of Hitler?" Again the reply was in the negative. Once more the correspondent circled the block, came back to the shop, and asked the clerk if he had photos of Hitler.

"Sir," shrieked the clerk. "I have repeatedly told you that we do not have photographs of Adolf Hitler. Those days are over. Why must you keep asking again and again?"

"Because," said the newspaperman, "I like to hear it."

Two Irishmen were assigned to the trenches for the first time, while serving with a British outfit. Their captain promised the company a reward of five shillings for every German they killed.

Patrick fell asleep while Michael had the duty. Before long Patrick felt the insistent hand of Michael rousing him. "They're coming, they're coming!" shouted Mike.

"Who's coming?" asked Pat.

"The Germans," Mike answered. "And we're alone out here, the others have gone back for food."

"How many Germans are there?"

"I'd say at least twenty thousand."

Michael leaped to his feet. "Begorrah, man," he yelled, grabbing his rifle. "Our fortune is made!"

On the obstacle course a sergeant noticed one of his men lying on the ground. "What's the matter with you?" the sarge asked gruffly.

"It's my leg, sergeant," moaned the recruit. "I broke it on the last hurdle."

"Well now, don't waste time," ordered the sergeant. "Instead of just lying there do push-ups until the ambulance gets here."

At the United Nations an American and a Russian debated the relative merits of their political societies. "But you have no freedom in Russia," argued the American.

"We have as much freedom as you have in America," the other insisted.

"Very well then, let me give you an example," the American said. "If I wanted to I could take a plane to Washington, go to the White House, walk into the President's office and tell him right to his face that I think he's an idiotic fool. Then I could walk right out and nothing would happen to me."

"So what?" countered the Communist. "We have the same thing in Russia. If I wanted to I could take a plane, fly to Moscow, go right to the Kremlin, walk into the Premier's office, tell him your president is an idiotic fool also. Then I could walk out and nothing would happen to me either."

A diplomat is a person who is appointed to avert situations that would never occur if there were no diplomats.

It was Napoleon's genius to be able to ignite the common man to fevered patriotism. To exemplify the French spirit he is said to have told this story:

Once, while visiting the provinces, he came upon an old soldier who had one arm and still wore his uniform, on which was displayed the Legion of Honor. "Where did you lose your arm?" the Emperor asked.

"At Austerlitz, sire," the soldier replied.

"And for that you were decorated?"

"Yes, sire. It is a small token to pay for the Legion of Honor."

"It seems to me," Napoleon said, "that you are the kind of man who regrets he did not lose both arms for his country."

"What then might be my reward?" asked the old soldier.

"Oh, in that case I would have awarded you a double Legion of Honor."

With that the old soldier drew his sword and immediately cut off his other arm.

For years the story circulated and was accepted without question, until one day someone asked: "How?"

Complacency has failed to still the knowledge that in our time civilization plunged to the depths of degradation. There is, however, a particle of consolation in the awareness that the noble innocents reached out from damnation to grasp a dignity which refused to be suppressed, not even when smothered in the bowels of hell.

In 1943 there remained alive and confined behind a ghetto wall in Poland forty thousand men, women, and children—remnants of what had been half a million subjected to the sophisticated social order of the Third Reich. Weary of the graces of this Teutonic cultural creation, they had dispatched couriers to investigate tales concerning the fate of the others. Word came to Warsaw, and the worst was confirmed. The crematoria operated twenty-four hours a day.

A band of ghetto-dwellers achieved an ingenious escape and sought to join the partisans in the hills. But they were machine-gunned by their friends, the partisans, for the crime of being living testimony to a godly heritage, and, in the most bitter irony of social disorder, had to fight their way back to the safety of the wall.

From their illegal radio came news that Allied Headquarters had decided to cancel a parachuted munitions rendezvous. The cost was too high, the results dubious; they were expendable. Denuded of hope, they decided to fight anyway.

Where there is life there is wishful thinking, and some were reluctant to join the resistance. "Of what use are bare hands and obsolete weapons against superguns and superaircraft manned by supermen?" they argued. "Whereas any moment the British will surely pour through the gates to free us." The others could fight, if they so desired; the dissenters would wait.

A rabbi rose to address this group. "There are two ways we will ever leave the ghetto alive," he said. "One way involves the practical, the other way involves the miraculous. One would take place if the heavens were to open and God was to send an avenging angel to strike down our oppressors and free us from torment. The other would take place if the British were to send a flight of paratroopers to liberate us. The angel," he said, "is the practical. The British the miraculous."

(In April 1943 fighting broke out in the Warsaw ghetto. By the end of May the resistance fighters were dead. But not before they had determined that six thousand German casualties would no longer practice the subtle barbarisms of the Third Reich.)

If you want to understand the social and political history of modern nations, study hell.

THOMAS MERTON

Status and Snobbery

I knew a woman once whose name was Mrs. Mabel Jallup. She had taste. One day she saw a vase at an auction. She bought it. She brought it home and put it on her table. It was Ming, and it made the Grand Rapids furniture look cheap. She was very sad, so she sold the Grand Rapids furniture and bought period. But the period furniture made her mail-order house look cheap. So she sold the house and took an exclusive apartment in town. But this apartment was so exclusive it made Mr. Jallup look cheap. Naturally she got a divorce, and married a Mr. Preston Potter. But she was stymied. Mr. Preston Potter made her look cheap. . . .

from Curiouser and Curiouser DOROTHY RICE SIMS

In *The Anatomy of Snobbery* (Anchor Review #1, Doubleday, 1955) Arthur Koestler tells of a young lady, employed by a left-wing publishing firm in pre-Hitler Germany, whose promiscuous favors were bestowed only upon authors whose books sold above twenty thousand copies. She became the mistress of a man whose work as a Communist correspondent gave him an audience not of twenty thousand but of two million. Eventually the man disappeared, the apparent victim of a totalitarian purge, and she with him; thus, the consequence of quantity over quality.

71

Koestler's story brings to mind an incident somewhat lower on the cultural pole, that happened ten years ago.

A young lady appeared one day at a hangout for unemployed night-club comics. She asked if there were any impersonators present. There were several. "Can either of you do Cary Grant?" she asked. In a sidewalk audition each did his version of Cary Grant. She selected the best, handed him a card with an address penciled on the back, and told him to be there at ten that evening.

Anticipating his first employment in months, the comic arrived fifteen minutes early for band rehearsal, to learn there was no band. Neither was there an audience, other than the young lady dressed in a sheer negligee. Protest obviously futile, the young man permitted himself to be compromised. The lights were out, and at the height of the adventure the object of the audition was made clear. "Speak to me like Cary Grant," she ordered.

The Cary Grant obsession gratified, the young lady returned to the hangout periodically, and held talent auditions for a gamut of celebrity impersonations: Gary Cooper, James Cagney, John Barrymore, etc. News of this haunted Venus reached into the better hangouts, and soon there appeared a real life figure of her imaginary exercises to pluck her away from the artificial embrace of the unemployed.

The story should have ended there, with the heroine nestled in bliss. But it didn't. Six months later she returned to the less pretentious hangout, disillusioned by the fullfillment of her objective and seeking vicarious pleasure without the letdown of reality.

It is the way of all status-seekers.

Augustus Caesar was touring the provinces when he noticed a man in the crowd who bore a striking resemblance to himself. Calling the fellow to him, he asked: "Tell me, did your mother ever find herself in my family employ?"

"No, sire," the man replied. "But my father did."

Status and Snobbery

A certain university is said to be so absorbed with protocol that students not formally introduced refrain from sociability. An upperclassman came upon a freshman who had fallen into the athletic house pool while touring alone. As the drowning student went down for the last time the senior muttered: "Oh, the shame of it all that I was not introduced to that young freshman. Perhaps I could have saved him."

That which we call a snob, by any other name would still be snobbish.

WILLIAM MAKEPEACE THACKERAY

At a cocktail party the irrepressible Gregory Nunn was accosted by a dowager who alluded to her ancestral background—a heritage she claimed could be traced back to Noah. "Noah?" shrugged Nunn. "A mere mushroom."

"How so?" challenged the lady.

"Well, recently, while cleaning the attic in my Larchmont estate I came across a pleasant surprise," Nunn confided. "Several scrolls of parchment and copper filled with the family pedigree. And in the middle of the fourth scroll was a marginal note which read 'Along about this time the world was created.'"

John D. Rockefeller was asked how he managed to control his children, in view of the great family wealth. He replied: "Whenever a situation arose that might not be good for them I asked, 'Who do you think you are—the John Jacob Astors?'"

Portentous aristocracy was described by Margot Asquith as: "Rectitude, platitude, high-hatitude."

Prior to the Civil War two southern gentlemen determined to put their prejudices aside and listen attentively to a negro gentleman whose argument against slavery was said to be especially erudite. They listened and were completely carried away. As they

73

were leaving the hall one said, "John, that was absolutely magnificent."

"What of it?" John replied. "He's only half a niggra."

"Half a niggra? Half a niggra?" said the other with astonishment. "My God! What would he have done if he was a whole niggra?"

A dowager was teaching her itinerary to a new footman. She started a round of visits but found that she had forgotten her calling cards and dispatched the man with orders to bring the cards which she had left on the mantel. When the lackey returned she told him to keep them in his pocket and leave one, or sometimes two, as instructed, wherever they called.

At a particularly ostentatious town house the man was instructed to leave three.

"Cahn't do it, mum," said the footman.

"Why is that?"

"You see, mum," he replied. "I've only two left. The ace of hearts and the nine of diamonds."

A gentleman visiting a certain New England city, and desirous of attending Sunday services, called upon the minister of an exclusive church. Upon hearing the man's southwestern twang, and noting his conventional dress, the clergyman tried tactfully to evade the issue by suggesting that he consider the matter carefully and make it the subject of prayers for guidance; in his own hotel room.

The following day the minister met the man again. "Ah done mah prayin'," the traveler said. "Jest like you said. And last night Ah got mah answer from the Lord."

"And what was it?" asked the clergyman, somewhat taken back. "What did the Lord say?"

"Well, suh, it was like this. He asked me what church Ah intended to join, and Ah told Him it was your'n. And he says 'Ho, ho, that there church.' He says, 'You cain't get in there. Ah knows you cain't, 'cause Ah been trying' to get in that church for twenty years mahself—and Ah cain't do it.'"

Status and Snobbery

Several members of an exclusive country club were discussing the funeral of a departed colleague. "It was fine, quite fine," said one. "I understand it cost forty-eight hundred dollars."

"Holy cow!" another interrupted. "Five bills more and he could 'a been buried in a Cadillac."

During the Christmas vacation a co-ed entertained several sorority sisters at her home. The first day, while they were being shown the house, the girl kept remarking on the origin of every object in sight. "This was imported from Japan," she said of a vase. "This was imported from England," she said of a silver service. "This was imported from India," she remarked of a dinner gong. Until it was firmly established that not a single object in the house was of domestic origin.

Eventually the girl left the room to seek out her maid. "You know, I think Linda Sue is obsessed with foreign things," one of the girls whispered. "I hope her mother isn't as snobbish as all that or the whole vacation will be ruined."

Linda Sue's mother entered. As she did she sneezed, pressing a dainty handkerchief to her nose.

"Oh," said one of the girls. "I see you have a cold."

"Yes," replied the lady. "I imported it from Switzerland."

"That soprano isn't as young as she appears on her publicity photos," an opera-goer remarked to his wife. "Have a look at her through these opera glasses."

"I can't," she replied. "I forgot to put on my diamond rings."

Snobbery is not the affliction of any one class. A New York City relief investigator called on a new applicant and found four families living in one room. Chalk lines were drawn to quarter off each area to one family.

"How do you manage here?" the investigator asked.

"Not bad," said the applicant. "We're the only ones who don't take in boarders."

An Austrian diplomat remarked to one of Queen Victoria's ministers that the British speak French quite poorly. "True," admitted the diplomat. "But, you see, we have not had the advantage of having the French twice in our capital."

I am his Highness' dog at Kew;
Pray tell me, sir, whose dog are you?

ALEXANDER POPE

Elbert Hubbard patronized the Palmer House whenever he had reason to be in Chicago on one occasion he glanced at the register and noticed the last entry: "Richard Harding Davis and man."

Immediately beneath Davis's signature he wrote: "Elbert Hubbard and satchel."

A lady, traveling in a set determined to outdo one another in their search for antiques, one day called upon the leader and excitedly remarked: "I came across something marvelous. An archaeologist friend sent me the very cup from which Socrates drank the hemlock."

"Are you sure it's authentic?" gasped the pace-setter.

"Authentic?" repeated the woman. "Why when they dug it up it was marked 350 B.C."

At a hospital in England, sometime during the last war, two Tommies were standing about when a neat looking major came upon them. They immediately snapped to attention, but as he passed the officer cast an annoyed look in the direction of one soldier.

"I say, Bill," the other remarked. "You must be on his blacklist."

"No," replied Bill. "That hain't hit. 'E resents being 'it by the same shell as me at Dieppe."

Zangwill said this of GBS: "The way Shaw believes in himself is very refreshing in these atheistic days when so many believe in no God at all."

Status and Snobbery

A lady of early American lineage was being quite fussy in the selection of a horse for her stables. Each time the proprietor of the academy produced a specimen for her consideration she found some reason for rejecting the animal. Finally she selected one, and, to confirm her opinion, asked: "Is this a pedigreed?"

"Pedigreed," flouted the trainer. "Lady, if this horse could talk he wouldn't speak to either of us."

In 1901 the reign of Victoria, Queen of England and Empress of India, was drawn to a close by her final illness. "I wonder if she will be happy in heaven?" a member of the royal household speculated.

"I don't know," said the Prince of Wales. "She will have to walk *behind* the angels—and she won't like that."

When science discovers the center of the universe a lot of people will be disappointed to find they are not it.

BERNARD BAILY

It's the high class people you have to give passes to.

FLO ZIEGFELD

A man from the wrong side of the tracks spent his day off patrolling a restricted cemetery. The sumptuous mausoleums fascinated him, and he found the immaculate landscapes awe-inspiring.

"Belle," he called to his wife upon arriving home, "I spent the whole day in the cemetery. And you should see how the rich people live there."

Having failed to obtain the services of Frank Lloyd Wright for the purpose of remodeling his recently purchased estate, a manufacturer called in a lesser known architect and was delighted when an immense lagoon was suggested as added décor; complete with a thousand swans. Soon the work was done and hordes of graceful swans filled the water.

Several months later the architect phoned to ask how the swans were getting on. "They're dead," the industrialist sighed.

"Dead?" was the incredulous shout. "What did you feed them?"

"My God!" gasped the landowner. "Do you have to feed *swans?*"

"The end of the world is coming in less than a month!" a gloomy preacher predicted to a New England dame.

"That does not concern me," she replied. "I live in Boston."

In the midst of preparations for an outdoor barbecue, considered *the* social event of the season, the matriarch of a blue-chip family summoned her butler. "James," she said, "I find that our lawn party is set for the same day as the eclipse. I'm afraid I'll have to get it put off."

"Oh, you couldn't do that," James advised. "Not a *total* eclipse you couldn't."

"Read a book," a status-seeker advised his wife. "Any book. Then when you are at a party you don't have to just sit around and talk over last year's jewelry. It's important that a person be a conversationalist."

"But what if I'm asked to converse on something I know nothing about?"

"If somebody asks you a question on something you know nothing about steer it to something you know."

She read a book, and at the next party awaited the opportune moment for revealing her erudition. At last one of the women turned to solicit her opinion of the Congo situation and the United Nations. "To tell you the truth I haven't one," she admitted. "I'm too upset over Marie Antoinette."

A case wherein the money objective was sublimated by the cultural drive involves a former manufacturer who retired to Scarsdale. He wanted his home to be an art center and towards that objective had walls of his study lined with alabaster and mahogany bookcases. Then he consulted an expert as to the types of books to be placed in this setting. "Deluxe gold gilt, embossed with your family crest, will look appropriate and richly modest in that setting," he was told.

A mass of cultural texts was made to order. When they were in place the gentleman discovered a small vacancy on one shelf. He called the advisor. "What kind of books do you want?" the book expert asked.

"Something by an outstanding author," the culture-seeker replied. "In nine inches by twelve inches."

Editor-publisher Bernard Baily reported this conversation with a visiting society columnist. "My husband spends money on the most ridiculous things. He bought an Irish setter and an Italian automobile—and he knows very well I do not intend to mingle with either the Irish or the Italians."

Abraham Lincoln, when asked the proper spelling of his wife's family name, replied: "God is satisfied with one *d* but the Todds need two."

The man who worships mere wealth is a snob.

ANTHONY TROLLOPE, *Life of Thackeray*

During World War I a top-ranking British army officer resented the presence of a civilian on an African expedition. To his cramped mind the mission required specialized military knowledge and breeding. Overruled by superiors, the officer sighed with resignation and handed the man a book on Syria, saying: "Take this. Study it carefully and have a report ready whenever it is most opportune for you. Perhaps you might be able to digest it in six months."

"Perhaps I might," the man said. "It took me only three months to write it."

At their first social dinner since attaining financial stature a middle-aged couple did everything according to protocol. However, try as they would, neither could figure out the exact purpose of the fingerbowls set before them. Against the better judgment of his wife, the man leaned towards a dinner table companion and asked: "Could you tell me what these are for?"

"Certainly," said the man. "Their primary function is to allow one to clean one's fingers if they become sticky during the repast."

"See, stupid," the women whispered. "You ask a silly question, you get a silly answer."

A baron of the Schleswig-Holstein district in Prussia decided to organize a dangerous expedition to the Near East and beyond. His company was completed when he felt it advisable to have a chief lieutenant along as an added measure of safety and expediency. Unable to find anyone suitably qualified in his immediate circle, the baron decided to advertise the post. The requirements listed were linguistic mastery of ancient and modern Arabic tongues, unquestionable courage and efficiency with the sword, expert horsemanship, physical superiority, and marked Prussian characteristics. For several days nobody appeared. The baron was discouraged when, on the fifth day, his man announced that a shabby appearing individual of not overwhelming stature had come in response to the advertisement. "He does not sound very much like what I want, but show him in," said the baron.

The butler had been more than kind in his description. But the baron knew first appearances could be deceiving. "You are no doubt a seasoned traveler?" he declared.

"Hah!" the man laughed. "I despise boats. They make me seasick till I want to die. Trains are worse. All in all I hate traveling."

The baron went on. "I assume, however, that you are a linguist. That you have mastered all the idioms of Araby—Persian, Turkestan, Hindustani and the like."

"Me? You mean me?" The applicant looked incredulous. "I talk nothing but Yiddish."

"No doubt, though, you are quite adept with the sword?"

"Sword? Me? What would I do with a sword?"

"And your horsemanship? Tell me of that."

"What horse? I wouldn't go near a horse. I can't stand them."

"Then tell me," said the baron, "why you are here?"

"Well, I saw your ad," the man answered, "and I just came to tell you that on me you shouldn't depend."

The sanctum of the literati is not immune to the hypocrisy manifest in snobbery; though it should know better. Thomas Carlyle, 1795–1881, the British man of letters, is an example.

"Speech is silver; silence is golden;" stands as his most quoted observation. Yet this worshiper of quietude expounded elaborately, and profanely, on the quality of his contemporaries. To Carlyle the beloved Lamb was "a despicable abortion." Lamb stuttered, and Carlyle did not hestitate to call him a pitiful, rickety, gasping tomfool, saying, "His speech is more like a convulsion fit."

Tennyson was a ruler on a dung heap to Carlyle, and he derided viciously Shelley, Macaulay, Spencer, and Milnes, with epithets such as: "Fricassee of dead dog"; "The most unending ass in Christendom"; "Adulatory lick-spittle"; and, "A little ape."

It is natural that the pleader of speech as silver and silence as golden should receive an appropriate answer. It came when John Merley reviewed his collected works.

"The canon is definitely made up and the whole of the golden gospel of silence effectively compressed in thirty-five volumes."

The ability of international diplomacy to fail superbly was proved by the Treaty of Versailles. Clemenceau was once ridiculed for the part he played in drawing up the treaty, which he did in collaboration with Woodrow Wilson and Lloyd George.

"It was the best I could do under the circumstances," Clemenceau defended, "seated as I was between Jesus Christ and God."

Psychiatry

Why, O Ariston, old and bald-headed
Did'st to the sun to bake give thy noddle?
          DIOGENES LAERTIUS, *Third Century A.D.*

Psychiatry has emerged as a new science, the aim of which is to chart our symptoms at the expense of our amusements. It is a form of horizontal confession subscribed to by those who would like to know why they do things that have always been done. It is a diversion for the rich, a palliative for the poor, and a boon to the furniture industry. To the sex connotation of the common couch it has added the luster of a college diploma.

The greats of by-gone eras had their peculiarities which they indulged freely without asking why. Petavius could do nothing unless he twirled a chair five minutes every two hours; Jonathan Swift liked to run up and down stairways; Spinosa would set spiders to fight each other—a sophisticated forerunner of pulling wings off flies. And one chronicler speaks of the habit indulged by ancient titans, that of singing airs while accompanying themselves on a flute. The latter adds substance to the legend of two-headed genius.

Perhaps the most eccentric habit was that of Percy Bysshe Shelley. Shelley was educated at Eton and Oxford; as high a recommendation for normalcy as one could have. Yet he liked to make paper boats. The sight of water was an irresistible compulsion. When coming upon a lake, or a pond, he would lose himself in a rapture of torn books, letters, posters, and what have you, and watch the results of his action take form in a great armada. Once, having gotten his kicks in Kensington Garden, he found himself on the north bank of the Serpentine River, all scrapped out. A one-hundred-year-old edition of the *New Century* describes his torment.

"Not a single scrap of paper could be found, save only a bank note of fifty pounds. He hesitated long, but yielded at last. He twisted it into a boat with the extreme refinement of his skill, and committed it with the utmost dexterity to fortune, watching its progress with a still more intense anxiety than usual."

Today Shelley would have been told by a psychiatrist that his was a syndrome of psychosis; bed-wetting, accompanied by a complex id balance catering to the obsessional libido, praecox, bicox, and shmicox.

All of which would have cost him a pretty pound. For, as Keith Preston warns: "The alienist is not a joke, he finds you cracked and leaves you broke."

The Russian diplomat was sent to a Kremlin analyst who diagnosed his ailment. "Comrade, you are suffering from confusion of purpose brought on by loss of confidence," the neurologist said. "The antidote is auto-suggestion. You must spend fifteen minutes of each day studying yourself in a mirror and telling yourself over and over again, 'I am a diplomat. I am important. I am indispensable. I mean something.'"

"It's useless, comrade," the man replied. "I don't believe a word I say."

An important politician called to visit a friend at an insane asylum and while there tried to phone his office. But his connection was constantly delayed, and in exasperation he said to the operator: "Young lady, do you know *who* I am?"

"No," she replied. "But I know *where* you are."

A Hollywood actor suffered from overactive sexual characteristics to a point where his career was threatened. He took six months off, underwent analysis and hypnotic treatment, and reported back at the studio saying he was cured. "Maybe you ought not to hang around today," the cautious producer told him. "We're filming that Lady Godiva sequence."

"Great!" the actor said. "It's been months since I last saw a horse."

An employer noticed that one of his clerks had not been looking well for months. He had black circles under his eyes, his cheeks were sunken, the color was gone from his face, and his general attitude was one of fatigue. "Don't you sleep well, Ashley?" he kindly asked.

"No, sir, I do not," Ashley replied. "My roommate and I both suffer from alternating insomnia."

"Alternating insomnia? What's that?"

Ashley explained: "Whichever gets to sleep first keeps the other awake."

At the doctor's office she needed only one general question and was off on a two-hour dissertation of her troubles. "You know something," she finally said. "You're wonderful. When I came in here I had a terrible headache, but it's disappeared."

"You are wrong, madam," replied the psychiatrist. "I have it now."

The mother of a boy in the fifth grade was urgently summoned to the principal's office. "I called you here on a matter of grave concern," the headmaster solemnly declared. "Today your son came to school wearing a dress, feminine underthings, and heavy lipstick——"

"I'm so ashamed," interrupted the parent. "I told him a thousand times he's not to wear his father's things."

After several sessions in which the analyst sought to have the woman retrogress, a point was reached where it became necessary to discuss the death of her husband.

"How did he die?" the psychiatrist asked.

"Must I?" the woman asked hesitantly.

"You must. It is absolutely necessary that you speak of it. You cannot go on keeping it to yourself."

"It's just that I—— Well, I'm ashamed," she said. "My husband was a college football star and he never got over his football days. He used to get drunk, come home, and kick me between the bedposts. One day I was off a little to the left. When he sobered up and saw he had failed to convert he died of a broken heart."

The woman said, "I cater to his every whim and get nowhere. He's something of an epicure, and I go out of my way to make unusual dishes for him, but he's so unresponsive."

"Tell me about some of those meals," the psychiatrist said.

"Well," she sighed. "Last week is a good example. I bought a twelve-pound rabbit. Monday I gave him rabbit steak, Tuesday rabbit's feet, Wednesday barbecued spare rabbit ribs, Thursday rabbit hamburger, and Friday—Friday I outdid myself to prepare the most delicious goulash a la rabbit."

"That's interesting," the analyst remarked. "What did he say on Friday?"

"He didn't say anything," she sobbed. "He just sat there and stared at me with his big pink eyes."

"I'll admit my education is spotty. I had all kinds of chances, but I even played hookey from correspondence school."

"How could you play hookey from correspondence school?"

"I sent in empty envelopes."

"Psychotherapy shows that this young lady developed all sorts of phobias because of her husband's unnatural preoccupation with the game of baseball," the alienist testified.

"That's a damned lie," the husband shouted, leaping to his feet. "My interest in baseball is no greater than that of the average man of normal intelligence. It's got its time and place and that is all."

"You sound sincere, young man," the judge said, "but I must fine you ten dollars for contempt of court for jumping up that way."

The man agreed to pay the money, but when he stepped over to the clerk's window he could not find his billfold. "What a day," he sighed to the judge. "First my business burns down, I just about lose my wife, the Orioles lose to the Yanks, and I lose my wallet. Fantastic, isn't it—and they were leading by four runs going into the ninth."

During proceedings to have an eccentric millionaire declared insane, the attorney for his relatives offered a quick test to show the man to be an imbecile. With the court's permission he questioned the beleaguered old man. "Who was our first President?" he asked defiantly.

"Er—uh—let me see—I think it was Washington."

"Uh huh. And who was our second President?"

"Why, now, let me think awhile. Uh—hmm—I'd say it was John Adams, I think."

"Uh huh."

There was a pregnant pause. The lawyer's assistant leaned forward and whispered, "Go on, go on, you're doing well."

"Can't," the lawyer whispered. "I'm not sure who was third President myself."

After several visits to the psychotherapy clinic a vagrant was reprimanded by the senior doctor. "Stop deluding yourself," he scolded. "You're healthy in body and mind. Why don't you go to work?"

"What for?" asked the vagrant. "To support a bum like me?"

Psychiatry

Although the young lady had never seen the psychiatrist before, the moment she entered his office he threw his arms around her, kissed her first on one cheek then on the other, and said: "Well, that takes care of my problem. What's yours?"

An affluent female called to visit a relative confined in an exclusive asylum. On the way out she was chatting with the institution's supervisor when she let out a cry of terror. "My God," she shrieked, "look at that vicious woman coming down the corridor. Is she dangerous?"

"At times, yes," the supervisor said cautiously.

"Why do you allow her so much freedom?"

"I have no control over that."

"But as an inmate shouldn't she be under your supervision?"

"No," the doctor said. "She is neither under my supervision nor an inmate. She is my wife."

On a cross-country train an executive watched in amazement as a dog and its master played two games of checkers. Unable to constrain himself he walked over and said, "Your dog, sir, is the greatest I've ever seen."

"I don't think he's so hot," the man replied. "I beat him three out of four."

"Doc, you've got to do something. Every time I go to the grocery I hear the sardines talking."

"What do they say?"

"We're packed in like commuters."

"I've got such troubles," cried the mother. "My daughter is going around with someone who sings like Sinatra, fights like John Wayne, and wriggles like Elvis Presley."

"That's trouble?" questioned her neighbor. "I'd be very proud if my daughter had a guy like that."

"Guy, nothing," the mother said. "It's a girl."

"This is a simple test to determine ordinary response," the psychiatrist told his patient. "What would happen if I cut off your left ear?"

"I couldn't hear."

"And what would happen if I then cut off your right ear?"

"I couldn't see."

"Why?"

"My hat would fall over my eyes."

A housewife was undergoing hypnotic treatment as the result of an ordeal suffered on the desert when her car ran out of gas. The analyst felt that if she would relive the moment she passed up the last filling station he could create an illusion in which she would drive in and thus rid herself of the experience. "Now, Betty," he said softly, "you are on Route 99. Can you see Route 99?"

"Yes."

"It's a clear day and Dead Man Gulch is just up ahead. Do you see the gulch?"

"Yes, I see it."

"Now you drive past the gulch and as you turn Skeleton Ridge you see a service station with a sign that says LAST CHANCE TO GAS UP. You look at your fuel gauge and it shows only a quarter tank. You are an intelligent woman. You know that if the gauge is at all off you will be stuck in the middle of the desert. So turn in and buy gasoline, Betty."

"I can't. I can't."

"You've got to or else you'll be stuck in the middle of the hot desert. You must pull in and buy gasoline."

"I can't."

"Why?"

"They don't give green stamps."

The eccentric five-year-old son of an affluent family was spoiled; and, with the purchase of a motor-driven hobbyhorse his odd behavior became bizarre. He refused to leave the saddle, taking his meals there and sleeping in an upright position. Family doctors were unable to budge him. In desperation a psychologist was called.

The specialist put a fatherly hand on the boy's shoulder, whispered gently into his ear, and the boy leaped from the horse.

After the fee was paid and the family was alone the boy's mother said, "You refused to obey the doctors, me, your father, or your tutors. What did the man say that made you obey?"

The boy refused to divulge the information unless he was promised a new motorboat. A check was drawn, placed in his hand, and again the mother asked: "Now, what did he say?"

"Well, mother," the child confided. "He said, 'Get the hell off that lousy horse or I'll break every bone in your body.'"

When a patient confided to his psychiatrist that he was in love with an elephant, the neurologist spoke candidly: "Animal love is fairly common. Among some ancient civilizations people were forbidden to keep pets until they had produced a full quota of offspring. However, this sort of attachment is only genuine where the object of human affection is small, cuddlesome, dependent upon protection. It is not possible to be in love with a mammoth. Now what do you think?"

"You convinced me, doc," the patient said. "Where can I get rid of a large engagement ring?"

A stranger called on a famous surgeon and told him that he had received a beautiful set of cuff links for Christmas but did not own a single shirt with french cuffs.

"Why come to a surgeon?" the doctor asked.

"I'd like to get my wrists pierced," the man replied.

As his eyes grew accustomed to the dark, a movie-goer noticed that the occupant of the adjoining seat was a gorilla. Hastening to find the manager, he demanded: "How come you sold a ticket to a gorilla?"

"Well," the manager replied, "he said he read the book and now he wants to see the picture."

A doctor, experimenting with love potions, discovered that sexual impotence could be easily solved by convincing the male partner he had the virility of a horse. A woman called on the doctor and prevailed upon him to allow her husband to undergo treatment.

A few weeks later the doctor met the woman on the street. "Do you see the kind of change you wanted?" he asked.

"No," said the woman. "But now he runs the mile in 1:39."

"My most embarrassing moment came when I fell off my kiddie car and everybody laughed," an army general told his analyst.

"That can happen to anybody in his youth."

"I know," the general answered. "But this was yesterday."

Two psychiatrists passed each other on the street, and one said: "Nice to see you."

A few steps away the other scratched his head and said: "What did he mean by that?"

"Where's the defendant?" the judge asked.

A man stood up in the jury box and said he was the defendant.

"What are you doing in the jury box?"

"I was told to come here."

"Come now, sir, you know you can't be the defendant and a jury member at the same time."

"No? I thought I was sort of lucky."

A bopster couple sat in an espresso café, when a waiter in the kitchen dropped a trayful of dishes. "Listen, darling," cooed one. "They're playing our song."

A child, having given educational authorities reason to suspect he was mentally retarded, was sent to a psychologist for examination. "How many tails has a cat?" the psychologist asked.

"One."

"And how many legs has a cat?"

"Four."

"And how many ears has a cat?"

The boy looked questioningly at the psychologist, then said: "Hey, doc, ain't you never seen a cat?"

"Life is like a suspension bridge."

"How is that?"

"How should I know?"

"Are you bothered by dreams of romps with half-naked men?" a psychiatrist asked a career woman.

"No," she sighed. "I rather like it."

At a PTA meeting a pupil's mother met his teacher for the first time. The teacher complained of the boy's conduct, and the mother listened attentively. "Next time he's bad use a little psychology," advised the mother. "Hit the boy next to him. That will frighten Arthur."

An eighteenth-century story tells of a woodsman who called at the home of a pioneer family. "Reckon you folks had ought-a come out to the bog with me," the woodsman said. "Yer son, Ephraim, is stuck there."

"How deep's he in?" asked the father.

"Up t'his ankles."

"Then let's crack the jug a bit," the father said. "There's plenty o' time."

"No, there ain't," the woodsman replied. "He's in head first."

"Severe depression brought on by worry," diagnosed the analyst. "You've got to stop worrying. Your case is not unlike another I recently had. The man worried himself into a case of nervous dyspepsia, over an unpaid dentist bill. I told him to stop worrying; he has, and now he's cured."

"I know," said the patient. "I'm his dentist."

The new patient at the asylum was extremely difficult to handle. He kept insisting he was an ancient Egyptian pharoah and would not cease his ravings until a throne room was prepared and he was given back his royal scepter. Having no other choice, the supervisor went to a good deal of trouble to cater to the man's whim. He had the walls of his room repainted and decorated with hieroglyphics. He had ancient accouterments added and brought in a scepter borrowed from a local museum.

For a while it worked, but a month later the noise started again. "Get me outta this tomb," the man shouted. "I left Egypt long ago."

When the supervisor was sent for the man insisted he was Napoleon and demanded a ferryboat ride away from Elba. "Now look here," the supervisor said angrily. "You demanded the Egyptian atmosphere and we went to a great deal of expense to produce it. Why don't you show some consideration and——"

"What are you arguing with me for," the man interrupted. "*I'm* supposed to be crazy."

An orderly in a hospital for the mentally disturbed reported that one of the inmates had escaped. "Got away, huh?" the chief neurologist asked. "Did you guard all the exits?"

"I did," said the orderly. "He must have left by one of the entrances."

To a chronic sufferer from imagined illnesses a psychologist gave this advice: "Immediately upon arising you are to say 'Every day, and in every way, I am feeling better and better.' Repeat this fifteen minutes daily and you'll be fine."

After some months the man called again. "How is everything?" the doctor asked.

"Well," shrugged the hypochondriac. "Every day, and in every way, I am feeling better and better. But at night I'm still lousy."

A female premium maniac asked a friend to visit her new home in the suburbs. "We furnished the entire playroom with disinfectant box tops," she said proudly.

"Only one room?" the friend asked. "What about the others?"

"Can't put a thing in them," the woman replied. "They're full of disinfectant."

A husband convinced his wife to seek psychiatric help for her problem—an unchecked enthusiasm for the horses. At the neurologist's office she protested vigorously. "I'm only doing this because my husband insists," she said. "He has this wild suspicion that I am a horse-player. The only thing I know about horses is they are used to pull wagons. I wouldn't know how to place a bet, where to place a bet, when to place a bet."

"Your husband seems pretty certain the opposite is true," the psychiatrist said. "He told me you neglected your own mother's funeral for horses, and wouldn't even know which cemetery she's at."

"THAT'S A DAMNED LIE!!" the woman roared. "It's the fifth cemetery on the left when you pass the jockey stable at Santa Anita."

Joseph Stalin was very proud of Russian enlightenment under the Communist regime, and when the Minister of Internal Affairs told him a modern institute for the mentally disturbed was being opened in Kiev the late premier insisted on attending the dedication ceremonies. As he walked from floor to floor prior to making his speech, the inmates cheered loudly! "Hurrah for Stalin! Hurrah for Stalin!"

In the ward set aside for the violent cases everyone cheered except one man. Stalin walked up to him and angrily demanded: "Why are you not cheering?"

"I'm not crazy," the man replied. "I'm the head keeper here."

His first day on duty at a sanitarium a neurologist was flattered when a patient said, "We like you better than any other doctor we ever had."

"Why?" asked the doctor, smiling.

"Because," replied the inmate, "you're more like one of us."

"I want my father committed at once. Every time I tell him to go to Boston he winds up in New York."

"I won't do it."

"Why?"

"Any man who is told to go to Boston and goes to New York instead can't be crazy."

From Paris a patient sent his analyst the following wire: "Having a wonderful time. Why?"

A scientist with a persecution complex sought out a neurologist and complained that the world was plotting to suppress his invention.

"What is this invention?" the doctor asked.

"It's a bar of soap six feet by nine feet."

"But how do you lift it to lather yourself?"

"You don't," the scientist explained. "You just sit on it and slide up and down."

The insane author called for a typewriter, and for six months the sound of clacking keys could be heard in his room. At last he emerged, handed a voluminous manuscript to the doctor, and announced that the work was complete. The psychiatrist eagerly grasped the bulky carton in which the papers lay and started to read. "General Smith leaped on his faithful horse and yelled giddap, giddap, giddap, giddap, giddap, giddap, giddap, giddap. . . ." He paused and dug through the other pages. "Why there's nothing here but five thousand pages of 'giddaps'!" he exclaimed.

"Yeah," said the writer. "Stubborn horse."

"I am very much put out. Anyone who has the advantages of a New England upbringing, the finest family, the best education, and comes from a deeply religious heritage, should never act the way you act."

"Aw, doc, I have to do something crazy once in a while to keep from going nuts."

"Where'd you get that terrific tan?"

"I just got back from Florida. Stayed at the Carol."

"But the Carol is in Georgia."

"It is? No wonder it took me so long to walk to the beach."

A brave Russian volunteered to be the first man fired at the moon in a rocket ship; and now he stood before representatives of the world press and Premier Khrushchev. Khrushchev made a laudatory speech about Russian courage and then asked the flier to explain why he had fought so hard for this privilege.

"I come from a proud family of Russian aviation pioneers," the man said. "My mother was the first woman to jump one thousand feet from an airplane without a parachute. My father was the first Russian to jump five thousand feet from an airplane without a parachute. And my brothers were the first to jump ten thousand feet from an airplane without a parachute." He paused. "So you see, gentlemen, I have nothing to live for. I have no family."

Education and Knowledge

A set o' dull, conceited hashes
Confuse their brains in college classes;
They gang in stirks, and come out asses. . . .

ROBERT BURNS

Pedantry carries a history of moral assertion no other field can boast, little of which is evident today. Gone is the attitude that knowledge is the preparation for experience; it is replaced by the pose that knowledge is a substitute for experience. The mark of the scholar is now only an embellishment to the status conscience, the key to a phenomenon known as boss's-sonism, a process whereby a young man newly academized starts at the top and works his way up. "*Hamlet*," said Tom Masson, "is the tragedy of tackling a family problem too soon after college."

The halls of learning encase memories of teachers whose convictions were unshakeable. From the dust of classical antiquity it is time to revive one. Peregrinus had his roots in Athens, but he was a nomadic professor, traveling widely to experience everything that he might return a better man. No sophisticated snob was Peregrinus, but one of firm convictions who did not hesitate to pass on the boiling cynicism of life. When a complacent Greece would not heed his teaching Peregrinus strode to Olympia where he fired a pyre, turned a look of disdain upon the populace, and gave himself to the flames. As an example of turning positive thinking into positive action it is unequaled.

At its height the Academy of Athens stressed individual responsibility in the universal sense. Commencement exercises included the now unfashionable oath: "I will not abandon the man next to me, whoever he may be." It was here that the first government-financed educational system was established. As for university towns, ancient Athens has never been equaled. Not only was it situated near the libraries of antiquity, but it thrived in the heart of the marketplace, where students could observe the swearing, cheating, and altogether unscrupulous tactics of the merchants. It also gave students easy access to the courtesans; the latter in turn established low student rates as their contribution to a well-rounded education.

As for primitive society, it regarded education as the transmission of skills and the training of character. The apprentice-to-master way of life was encouraged. It was a hard existence, with learning primarily aimed at the preparation for war and the responsibility of marriage; the two were not yet synonymous. Only males attended school, and graduation consisted of tests of strength and playful scourging. The highlight of commencement came when the senior class lined up for their diplomas and were circumcised by the dean.

There were no school songs, and students who yelled the loudest were graduated *cum laude*.

Twenty years after graduating from college the eldest son of a man who had deprived himself to put the boy through school came to realize that his father had learned a great deal. Only one thing puzzled him and that was the father's refusal to deprive himself further so that the youngest son might go to college. "Father," the eldest said, "you were perfectly right in not sending my brother to the university. Mind if I ask what made you so wise?"

97

"Good judgment, son," the old man said. "I got good judgment. Good judgment comes from experience; and experience, well, that comes from bad judgment."

Many persons are both wise and handsome—but they would probably be still wiser were they less handsome.

THE TALMUD

The rash of honorary doctorates being awarded to industrialists —seldom upon receipt of wisdom by the businessman, but often upon receipt of cash by the institution—is an ancient practice.

Samuel Johnson (1709–84) noted that the University of St. Andrews, in Scotland, had a low treasury but a high number of honorary titles to award. He remarked: "Let it persevere in its present plan and it may become rich by degrees."

When a committee sought to learn the reason for sharp increases in the cost of farm produce, the leader of an agricultural co-operative gave this testimony:

"It's this way. When a farmer's got to know the botanical name of what he grows, and the zoological name of the insect that eats it, and the chemical name for what kills the insect—someone's got to pay for it."

The scholastic mind soared to the heights of simplification when a college student turned in this summation: "The Protestant Reformation was when the Protestants broke away from the Catholic Church and decided to forgive their own sins."

A farsighted high school teacher passed a student who, when asked in what battle General Wolfe said, "I die happy," answered: "His last battle."

A teacher in Arkansas called a father to school and asked: "Do you know your son swears terribly?"

"Yes, ma'am, he sure do," the father agreed. "He knows the words, but he don't put no feeling in 'em."

A Sunday school pastor asked a little girl: "What are the sins of omission?"

After some thought, she answered: "They're the sins we ought to have committed, but haven't."

At Oxford two students argued the correct pronunciation of the word "either." One stood firmly by "ee-ther" and the other was just as dogmatic for "eye-ther." An Irish professor happened by, and one of the students asked: "Pardon me, sir, but could you tell us if the correct pronunciation of e-i-t-h-e-r is 'ee-ther' or 'eye-ther'?"

The professor said: "It's nairther. It's air-ther."

Scholarly children are a great source of parental pride. The mother of a junior high school student was proudly displaying a trophy the boy had brought home. "It's for biology," she told her neighbor. "The teacher asked the whole class how many legs an alligator has, and my Alfred said 'five.'"

"But an alligator only has four legs."

"I know," the mother admitted. "But he was the closest."

A college newspaper of the twenties asserted that it would no longer publish any degrading absent-minded professor jokes, except for this last one: "He slammed his wife and kissed the door."

"What did you do in school?" a mother asked her little boy when he returned from his first academic day.

"Nothing," the boy replied. "Some woman wanted to know how to spell 'cat,' and I told her."

A little girl, when asked what she had learned in school the first day, replied: "Nothing, I've got to go back tomorrow."

Some professors live on in the memories of school and student body for reasons other than academic qualities. A fabled New England educator was put in charge of student discipline when schoolboy pranks got out of hand. The college president ordered any culprits caught to be immediately expelled. One night the professor was summoned from his quarters to apprehend some nocturnal frolickers. As a matter of duty he pursued the revelers and, because of his long, gangly form, found he was gaining on them rapidly. "Gentlemen, gentlemen," he called, "if you don't run faster I shall be obliged to overtake you."

The new dean was being shown about a university that had de-emphasized athletics. When he was introduced to the football coach, the dean, knowing the situation, asked sympathetically: "How's our team? It's sportsmanship that counts. Are they good losers?"

"Good?" the coach said. "Heck, they're perfect."

During the period of female emergence two college girls sat in a restaurant. "Anybody looking?" asked one.

"No," whispered the other.

"Good," said the first. "Then we don't have to smoke."

An outstanding mathematics student was walking from the campus when a professor was struck by a hit-run autoist. The student barely was able to catch a glimpse of the departing vehicle, but when he was questioned in the dean's office he offered the license number of the car and insisted he was positive of the matter. "But how can you be so sure?" a detective asked.

"Well, it's true that I barely saw the license plate at a distant angle," explained the genius. "But I recall that if it were multiplied by itself the cube root of the product would be equal to the sum of the digits reversed."

Education and Knowledge

"I was sorry to hear that your brother passed on," one old class-mate consoled another at a reunion. "Had he finished his education?"

"No," said the other. "He died a bachelor."

A boy returned home from school, on New York's lower east side, two hours before the regular lunch hour. The teacher's note explained that he was sent home because his body gave off an odor, and suggested the mother do something about it.

The mother sent the boy back to school with this reply: "Dear teacher. Henry ain't no rose. Don't smell him, learn him."

A college student applied for a job during the summer vacation. "I see you're a math major," the interviewer remarked. "I suppose you can tell me how many sides there are in a circle?"

"Certainly," the student replied. "Two."

"Really? What are they?"

"An inside and an outside."

When a group of Ivy Leaguers were suspended from school for attending a burlesque show, the father of one of them protested to the college professor that the show had educational value. "And what did it teach?" the professor asked.

"Anatomy," the father replied.

A college education seldom hurts a man if he is willing to learn a little something after he graduates.

Confidence is the feeling you had before you knew better.

You can lead a boy to college but you cannot make him think.
ELBERT HUBBARD

A synonym is a word you use when you can't spell the other one.

Illiteracy so concerned Lord Brougham that he saw fit to say in Parliament that he hoped the day would come when every Englishman would be able to read Bacon.

A practical opponent replied: "I hope to see the day when every Englishman will be able to eat bacon."

A high school student asked his father to assist him in writing a composition on how a war starts. "Well, now, let us suppose we got into a quarrel with Canada," father began.

"Ridiculous," mother interrupted. "Why should we quarrel with Canada?"

"That's entirely beside the point, darling," the husband said. "I was merely trying to use an illustration——"

"Don't darling me, you half-wit. If you had an ounce of brains you wouldn't go around showing your stupidity with such——"

"Watch your language. Who do you think you're talking to? Why if I want to teach my son a certain——"

"Your son!! And I have no rights to him I suppose. I had nothing to do with his being here. I just sat by and watched while you found him in a garbage can."

"Let's not get into personalities, or I'll have a few things to say about the way you spend——"

"Please folks, please," the boy interjected. "Forget it. I know perfectly how a war starts."

According to a high school examination paper the world's greatest living inventor is an individual of Irish ancestry named "Pat Pending."

I got no use for a man who can only spell a word one way.

JOE LAURIE, JR.

College professors are men who get what's left over after the football coach is paid off.

The Greeks may have had a word for stoic and cynic, but according to contemporary examination papers their usages were in error. In the modern version a stoic is a bird and a cynic a place to wash dishes.

On a true or false examination several candidates for law school marked "True" the statement: "When a criminal seeks to establish his presence away from the scene of the crime, this is called having an Ali Baba."

A university is an institution that has two thousand seats in the classrooms and sixty thousand in the stadium.

There is nothing so stupid as an educated man, if you get off the thing he was educated in.

WILL ROGERS

A man picked up the phone and asked for the telegraph office. His connection was completed and he told the clerk: "I want to send a telegram to Pottawatomie, Indiana."

"Please spell it," the clerk said.

"Listen, lady," the man said. "If I could spell it I wouldn't send a telegram—I'd write a letter."

A college history paper tells us, "Martin Luther died a horrible death. He was excommunicated by a bull."

That colleges do occasionally get their point across is testified to by the senior who described the government of England as a "limited mockery."

It ain't the things you don't know what get you into trouble, it's the things you know for sure that ain't so.

The father of a student was paying his first visit to the campus, when he mistakenly entered a nearby mental institution thinking it was the college. When the gatekeeper corrected the error, the father laughingly said: "Guess there isn't much difference between them anyway."

"Yes there is," the gatekeeper said. "In this place you have to show some improvement before you can get out."

Mark Twain complained of foreign names. "They spell right," he said. "But they don't pronounce right." Perhaps the leading exponent of simplification of the English language was Teddy Roosevelt. The dispensers of intellect condemned his order altering the spelling methods of the Government Printing Office, and on the day he departed the White House his political epitaph appeared as a one-word newspaper headline: "THRU!!"

I would rather have my ignorance than another man's knowledge, because I have so much of it.

MARK TWAIN

You may have noticed that the less I know about a subject the more confidence I have; and the more light I throw on it.

MARK TWAIN

In youth and beauty wisdom is rare.

HOMER

Facts do not cease to exist just because they are ignored.

ALDOUS HUXLEY

I would rather have experience than education. There is no such thing as formal experience. You take it where you get it. The difference between an experienced person and an educated person is: An experienced person recognizes his mistakes then he makes them again.

FRANKLIN K. DANE

The college backfield ace had failed to score in the first half of a big game and the coach thought he knew the reason. "LARKIN," he shouted angrily, "yer outta condition. Whatcha been doin'? Studyin' again?"

We can look forward to advances in structural pattern if one of our future designers properly defined "buttress." He answered: "A buttress is a butler's wife."

"How many wars did we fight with Spain?" the professor asked the gridiron flash.

"Seven."

"Seven, hey? Can you enumerate them?"

"Certainly," the athlete replied. "One, two, three, four, five, six, seven."

Socrates maintained that an education obtained with money was worse than no education at all. In a discussion of war technique with a military school graduate, the young man said his teacher instructed him to put the best men in the front and rear ranks and the poorer men in the center.

"Accepted," agreed Socrates. "And did he tell you how to distinguish the good from the bad men?"

When the flustered militarist replied in the negative, Socrates said: "Then you had better go and get your money back."

You can educate a fool, but you cannot make him think.

THE TALMUD

An educational system isn't worth a great deal if it teaches young people how to make a living and doesn't teach them how to live.

The type of education a college person gets sometimes depends on the type of institution he attends—educational or coeducational.

"A polygon," says one examination paper, "is a dead parrot."

Colleges don't make fools; they only develop them.

HORACE LORIMER

A high school teacher asked a student: "Bertram, who wrote *Hamlet?*"

"Not me," Bertram replied.

As a consequence of the ensuing uproar the student's father was asked to appear in school. When he arrived the teacher told him of the disruption caused by his son. "When I asked him who wrote *Hamlet,*" the teacher said, "he became very facetious and said, 'Not me——' "

"Look, teacher," the father interjected, "I know Bertram is no angel, but isn't it possible he told the truth? Maybe he didn't write it."

Thoroughly exasperated, the teacher walked away; while the father, unable to understand, went home and reported the incident to his wife.

"Idiot!" she scolded. "An idiot you were when I married you and an idiot you still are. Couldn't you use diplomacy and commonsense? You should have apologized for your son, then you should have explained that while he wrote it this time he would never write it again."

A college student, home for his summer vacation, was asked by his mother: "Did you pass everything?"

"No," the academician replied. "Some of those foreign jobs are too souped up."

Winston Churchill takes his place alongside Mark Twain and Teddy Roosevelt when it comes to resisting the more clumsy laws of grammar. It is said that during World War II he was piqued by a rule requiring him to submit copies of his speeches to other authorities before delivering them on radio. On one occasion a subordinate official had the effrontery to exceed his position by questioning the Prime Minister's practice of ending a sentence with a preposition. Churchill sent for the underling and forcefully declaimed: "This is the kind of arrant pedantry up with which I won't put."

At a business convention an industrialist from the Southwest found himself assigned to a table where all the others proudly displayed recent class pins. Lacking this key to acceptance the industrialist found himself frozen out of the conversation, until, after discoursing on all the major campuses in the country, the young men switched their conversation to Yale. At the appropriate moment the industrialist joined in with detailed information. There was an immediate change, and one of the college men said: "You know quite a bit about Yale. Are you an alumnus of old Eli?"

"No," the man said, "but I have twenty-six Yale graduates working for me."

A noted educator once said there were only two kinds of colleges in this country. Those that fired the football coach before the start of the season, and those that wish they had.

Formal education, even when properly assimilated, can be a drawback. A traveler, while waiting to make a train connection in a southern town, walked through the vintage sector politely viewing its dilapidated structure. The sheriff approached as he was examining some Civil War posters, and said: "Ah hopes you goin' straight through this yere town without stoppin' off none, stranger."

"Why?" the man asked angrily.

"'Cause Ah noticed you readin' them there stickers," the sheriff said suspiciously, "and any man what kin read is mebbe a college graduate or a Republican—and neether one is welcome here."

The next best thing to knowing something is knowing where to find it.

A man profits more by the sight of an idiot than by the orations of the learned.

ARABIAN PROVERB

The value of education was surely overrated by the convict who, upon being strapped into the electric chair, told his executioners: "This electrocution sure is gwan to teach me a lesson."

A symptom of the education mania that is imbedding itself into the subconscious of those who hire and fire is the business of seeking college graduates to do jobs that normally would go to persons less fortified with academic ineptitude. As a matter of prestige, an employer is willing to hire an engineer to do a clerk's job, and to pay a much higher wage, merely to be able to say he has so many engineers working for him, rather than so many clerks.

Birch Kadar, the legendary lumberman of America's Northwest, had a complex about his lack of formal education, and it is said that he was the first American to specify a college degree as prerequisite to working his lumber camps. "I just don't get it," a tough job applicant said. "Now, Birch, here's this big tree to be chopped down, and here is this high-priced college boy on the other side hefting a good ax, and I am on my side hefting a good ax too. He chips away his half, and I chip away my half. The tree falls. Now tell me, what's the difference?"

Birch said: "About thirty dollars a day."

Knowlege is power—if you know it about the right people.

Joel Chandler Harris was in his office one night when a reporter who had been in his employ many years called out: "Joel, do you spell 'graphic' with one 'f' or two?"

"Well," Harris answered, "if you're going to use any at all, Bill, I guess you might as well go all the way."

The day after a campus class reunion one of the students was asked by a professor: "Was that an alumnus I saw you with last night?"

"No," said the student. "That was just an ordinary drunk."

"The time one spends thinking before speaking is most important," a pedant instructed his class. "Let's all get into the habit of counting to fifty before saying anything important, and one hundred if it is very important."

The following day, while the professor was working an intricate formula on the blackboard, he heard low murmuring behind him. As he turned the class shouted in unison:

"Ninety-seven, ninety-eight, ninety-nine, one hundred. THE SCHOOL'S ON FIRE, SIR!!"

When Napoleon ruled that the spirit of "Liberty, Equality, Fraternity" meant just that, without any legal exceptions, a family of pious Hebrews sent their son off to the university—a privilege never before granted them. At the conclusion of his freshman year the youth returned to his village and sought out the rabbi. He told the pious man that at first his body had been liberated, but after one year at the university his mind, too, had been liberated; and he was now an avowed atheist, neither accepting nor believing any theology.

"I see," the rabbi nodded after listening to him. "You say you are an atheist. Have you read the Bible?"

"I studied parts of it, but lately I've had no time for that as I've been busy with my university studies," the boy replied.

"And the *Talmud*—have you studied the *Talmud*?"

"Come now, rabbi," the boy interjected. "You don't honestly expect me to waste time on that."

"What of the great Hebrew philosophers? Do you know the work of Maimonides, and Moses Mendelssohn or Ibn Gabirol?"

"I have never read a line written by those men."

"I see," the rabbi said. "Of the Bible you admittedly know nothing and of the philosophers you know less. Yet you say you are an atheist. Young man, why do you not call yourself what you really are? You are not an atheist—you are an ordinary ignoramus."

"You call yourself a kind father," the college boy remarked. "Five times I wrote to you for money to buy a car and five times you ignored it. What sort of kindness is that?"

"Unremitting kindness," the father replied.

Ego once forced a bright student to expound on Einstein's theory of relativity at inordinate length. At last he finished and waited expectantly for the commentary of his professor.

"Young man, I have listened carefully to your entire pronunciamento and I have come to the conclusion that you are greater than Einstein," the professor declared. "According to reports there are only twelve men in the entire world who understand Einstein. Nobody understands you."

Drinking, Intoxication, and Sundry Liquids

How, they ask, can such a diluent (water) be resorted to by any one above the savage or half-crazed eccentric, when those potent brethren, ale and porter, the brilliant and numerous family of the wines, and the immortal trio, gin, rum, and brandy are in existence? Men, Englishmen, too, have been heard of, who do not know the taste of porter. This cannot be credited; though it may be readily believed that many are quite ignorant of the taste of water.

WESTMINSTER REVIEW, 1846

Midway through the second quarter of the nineteenth century genteel Europeans had the purgatory scared out of them by a movement which made Napoleon's schemes of bloody conquest seem insignificant. From a place called Freidwaldau, in Austrian Silesia, came word that the peasants were using water for human drinking. "Wha'?" an incredulous Briton asked, dismayed. "The stuff ye give 'orses?" It was the start of a thing called hydropathy, or the water cure. Basically it meant the application of water to the mouth and the practice of occasionally dabbing it on the body. The word is obsolete.

It happened when the son of a small farmer named Priessnitz, in the hilly district of Gräfenberg, which was near Freidwaldau, in Austrian Silesia, made the amazing discovery that water puts out fires. If water puts out fires, he reasoned logically, why shouldn't water put out the flame of illness? Nobody had thought of this since Hippocrates, nor did anybody stop to think that fire could be put out with whisky too, at least with cheap whisky.

The results could not be disputed. There was bona fide evidence that water cured the gout, further evidence that a man who thought he was born with a shriveled leg took a bath and found he wasn't crippled at all. Even pimples began to disappear. Naturally Priessnitz's biggest detractors were the medical societies. "DEPRAVED CHARLATAN!" they cried. "QUACK!" They followed up this violent opposition with: "Doddering sheepshead"—"Empiric"—"Foofoo!" And their denunciations of water were unprintable.

News of the miracle worker of Austrian Silesia spread until it engulfed all of continental Europe, bringing schools of "I like Priessnitz" fanatics into existence, and with them the terrible water cure. There were water riots in London, as, for the second time in less than a quarter century, Britain stood alone. Amid this pint-sized version of the finest hour an MP took the floor of Parliament to demand: "What manner of individual is responsible for bringing the throat divine to the level of a common gutter? Let it be known that no rational man, no *Englishman*, is the instigator of this foul notion."

However, by the mid 1840s a group of Priessnitz's adherents managed to establish a bath in the township of Malvern, and to fortify the beachhead with a squad of technical experts. Shortly afterwards a book appeared titled *A Month at Malvern*—by one of the survivors. Others, including prominent medical and political personages, came forward to admit they had dabbled with the less extreme phase of the matter, such as foot and elbow baths.

In 1846 W. H. Ainsworth, Esq., editor of the *New Monthly Magazine*, published *Confessions of a Water Patient* by Sir E. Bulwer-Lytton, in which the distinguished knight revealed that he not only had subscribed to the numerous baths but had given himself over entirely to the treatment, including admission of the fluid into the oral cavity.

Noting this unrelenting swell the *Westminster Review*, in September of the same year, declared: "It (water) may be explained, to a considerable degree, in a popular manner, and we propose to state briefly what it is." It did so, and thus the common man became thoroughly informed.

The die was cast and Britain took the bull by the horns to spread knowledge of the efficacy of water to such faraway places as Scotland and Ireland.

The unflagging quality of Scotch and Irish whisky is sober proof that the knowledge of water was accepted with neither hysteria nor tumult in these provinces, and will forever stand to the undiluted glory of these intelligent people.

Two drunks wandered into a religious service, quite by accident, and listened to a fiery sermon in which the preacher pounded at the proposition that on the last great day some would be sheep and some would be goats. "On that last, great, come and get it day," shouted the preacher, "who will be the goat?"

There was a great silence in the auditorium till one of the drunks rose to his feet and cried: "Sooner than have this wonderful show stop, I'll be the goat!"

Gasoline and alcohol don't mix—but try drinking them straight.

A wet individual was walking through the streets of Kansas City one day when a stovepipe-style fire engine, still in use, came clanging along. Fire and smoke poured out of its funnel, and no sooner had it passed the drunken one when he started after it in more or less hot pursuit, his jacket flapping wildly and his hat bouncing from side to side. For nearly a mile he held his own in the chase, but gradually the engine pulled away. Realizing further chase was futile the man drew himself to an unsteady halt, gazed after the disappearing machine, and shaking his fist called out: "The hell with you and yer damned chestnuts."

What do the vintners buy one half so precious as the stuff they sell?

OMAR KHAYYAM

An itinerant Irish laborer had the misfortune, while working on a project in the city of Philadelphia, to lose his grip and fall four stories to the pavement below. He awoke to find a doctor holding forth a glass of water. "Begorrah," he exclaimed. "How far must a mahn fall in this city before he gets whisky?"

Two gentlemen, somewhat wet, were discussing the mores of civilized man. "Shay," said one. "Itsh funny how shome guy can shtart a rumor that Friday ish unlucky."
"Yeah," agreed the other. "He mushta been a fish."

A visitor to Paris, having spent some thirty days in the city, was invited to dine at a famous restaurant. "They have the most marvelous burgundy and bordeaux wines there," said his friend.
"Please don't speak to me of burgundy and bordeaux," the visitor replied. "What I am looking for is a reliable French bootlegger who can sneak me a drink of ice water."

SCOTCH DRINK

When neebors anger at a plea
An' just as wud as wud can be,
How easy can the barley brie
    Cement the quarrel.
It's aye the cheapest lawyer's fee
    To taste the barrel.

ROBERT BURNS

An aged Scot was threatened with blindness. "Now see here, McGoggle," his doctor warned. "You've got to recognize the facts. Either you stop the whisky or you will give up your eyesight, and I'm warning you, you must make a choice."

"Well, doctor," McGoggle said, after a moment. "It's an auld man I be noo, an' was thinkin' as ha'e I proobably seen aboot everything wurth seein'."

During prohibition days in New York City a cab driver was summoned to an elaborate Park Avenue speakeasy. The doorman escorted four men to the cab, helped them carefully inside, then gave the driver his instructions. "The man seated by the door directly in back of you goes to the Hotel Taft. The one alongside him goes to the Astor. The gentleman on the front seat is to be taken to the Dorchester. And the other one goes to the Hotel Lincoln."

The driver acknowledged his instructions and drove away.

A few minutes later he returned and beckoned the doorman to him. "Hey, Mac," he said. "Would you please sort them guys out again? I hit a bump on Lexington Avenue."

Drinking makes such fools of people, and people are such fools to begin with, that it's compounding a felony.

ROBERT BENCHLEY

"Where are you going?" the cop yelled at a drunkard driving in the wrong direction on a one way street.

"Can't shay, offisher," he burped. "But I musht be late, caush everybody elsh ish coming back."

A man ordered a drink. When it came he withdrew a mouse from his coat pocket and after he belted the drink down allowed the creature to finish the few drops that remained. No sooner was this done than the mouse burst into an aria from *La Traviata*, singing in a brilliant tenor.

A customer standing nearby was intrigued by this and asked

115

the man how much he wanted for the mouse. "Heck," said the owner. "Buy me a bottle of scotch and you can have him."

The deal was made and the new owner departed. "You must be crazy," the bartender admonished. "Why did you give away a fortune like that for one lousy bottle of scotch?"

"Eh-h," the man said disgustedly. "That mouse can only sing in Italian."

A college professor was invited to the Dean's house for cocktails. Later realizing that he had exceeded his normal capacity the prof was determined that no one should be aware of his indiscretion. As the party neared its conclusion the wife of the Dean decided to show the latest addition to her family, and presently a nurse appeared carrying a bassinet containing twins. The prof looked into the bassinet and, trying to sound as normal as possible, said: "My, what a beautiful baby."

"Gimmie a fifth of milk," the new father said to the grocer. "Milk don't come in fifths."

"Oh, I forgot," said the man. "You're right. Gimmie a magnum."

I feel a great sympathy with that woman in Ireland who had something of a field day. She began by knocking down two unwelcome agents of her landlord, then, was seen later in the day dancing a jig on the stomach of the prostrate Presbyterian minister. One of her friends passed admiring remarks on her prowess and invited her in to have a good stiff glass of whisky. The friend said: "Shall I pour some water in yer whisky?"

And the woman replied: "For God's sake, haven't I had trouble enough already today?"

GENERAL HORACE PORTER

"Do you know anything about the robbery of the liquor store?" the judge demanded of the troublesome suspect.

"Well, judge, I'm surprised at ya," the man answered. "Do you suppose I'd be sober if I did?"

Be moderate in everything—including moderation.

A little girl reported: "Father came in late last night and rammed into the garage doors, knocking one right off. It's a good thing he didn't have the car."

The proprietor was furious at the Scotchman. "How dare you, sir," he reproached. "You come into my restaurant, order a glass of water, drink it, and then calmly walk out."

"And what is it ye be expecting me to do, mon," the Scot replied. "Stagger out?"

A do-it-yourself book on gardening contains this advice: "A carbonated headache tablet, placed in a vase of water, will make wilted flowers brace right up."

On which Gregory Nunn wrote, in a critique of the work: "A mere curl. Put the same flowers in a pot of 180 proof and they will burst into song."

A British gentleman was apprised of the fact that his hearing was failing due to excessive drinking. His doctor insisted he give up drinking, as the bottle was causing his deafness. Sometime later the doctor met the man on the street, and spoke to him in a quite loud tone of voice. The man told him it was not necessary to speak so loudly. "I have followed your advice, given up whisky, and as a consequence I am able to hear perfectly."

At another meeting some time later the doctor noticed that the man was again deaf. He leaned over and shouted into his ex-patient's ear. "It seems to me you've forsaken your vow and taken to drinking whisky again."

"You are right," admitted the man. "Drink is once again my habit, and I shall tell you why. So long as I did not drink I could hear, but all that I did hear was not so good as all that I could drink."

A clergyman once encountered a parishioner who was addicted to the bottle. "My dear Frazer," said the man of the cloth, "didn't I tell you that whisky is your enemy?"

"Ay, Father," replied the man. "That you did, and didn't ye also tell us that we should love our enemies?"

"Yes," the clergyman countered. "But I never said you should swallow them."

"Who is the best lawyer in town?"
"Ferris Brown when he is sober."
"And who is the second best lawyer in town?"
"Ferris Brown when he is drunk."

Water taken in moderation cannot hurt anybody.

MARK TWAIN

Women will be as pleasing to men as whisky when they learn to improve as much with age.

FRANKLIN K. DANE

"Ever notice a cactus plant," said Dr. Stitchem to Mr. Tripple, in an effort to get him to give up drinking. "If you pour water around its roots it thrives, turns greener, and grows bigger. Take the same cactus, pour vile liquor on it, and what happens? It shrivels, it shrinks, it dies. Doesn't that teach you anything?"

"Yes," said Tripple. "If you want a cactus growing in your stomach drink water."

Mr. Coffee tore out of his house in an exceptional rush. "Where are you going?" called his neighbor, Mrs. Buttin.

"I'm on my way to George Kinkel's house. He just phoned and asked if I could lend him a corkscrew. I'm taking it over myself."

"Why don't you send it?"

"My dear Mrs. Buttin," said Coffee exasperatedly. "What you have just asked is clear indication of why women are totally unqualified to lead armies and make quick and important decisions in industry, affecting billions in currency. When the psychological moment arrives they do not know what to do with it."

Two old-timers, living on pensions, would meet each day and walk to every saloon in town. One day one of them said: "I read in the papers that if all saloons in the nation were set end to end they would reach from New York City to Los Angeles."
"Wow!" gasped the other. "What a walk!!"

A savage beast had escaped from the zoo, and the sheriff hurriedly organized a posse to search the woods. "Before we start out, fellas," the lawman called, "let's tank up a bit! The drinks are on me."
Inside the saloon all indulged except one meek little man, who only took sarsaparilla.
"Hey, Shortie," the sheriff called. "Whatsa idea of only drinking sass? The boys are all on whisky. Why ain't you?"
"Don't want any," said Shortie. "Whisky gives a man too much courage."

Two guzzlers were rapping one of their fellow office men because he couldn't hold his liquor. "You know the type," one said. "Two hanmattans and he can't chind the ferry."
"Should have invited him anyway," said the other. "He'd have all day sober to Sunday up."

The modern debutante no longer comes out—she's carried out.
GREGORY NUNN

Count Pigerov, of the court of Czar Alexander, once called his orderly to him and said: "Koffnar, the Czar is scheduled to address a group of high dignitaries in the palace reception room today, and we could use your help to make the address a great success."

"Whatever you desire it will be my privilege to obey," said the obsequious orderly.

"Good," the Count said. "The plan is precisely this. You are to seat yourself in the middle of the room. Now, when you see the Czar drink some water from a glass that is set before him you are to start to applaud. Now, when you see the Czar wipe his brow you are to commence laughing. Do you comprehend?"

"Absolutely," said Koffnar. "But, may I kindly ask you to change the signals. It would be much easier for me to laugh when I see the Czar drink water."

"Shay, bartender, can you imagine anyone going to shleep with their shoesh on?"

"Who does that?"

"My horsesh."

The gentleman had plans, but the lady didn't seem to show any effects after a dozen martinis. "Don't you ever feel your liquor?" he asked.

"Of course not," she said. "Why should I get my fingers wet?"

On a rainy night in seventeenth-century England a church dignitary had been driven to his home by a coachman, and felt courtesy required him to give the man something to keep out the cold. However, he found nothing on hand but some liquor and a stand with tiny glasses. So he filled one of them and handed it to the man, saying: "I trust you will think none the worse of this because it was concocted by the holy monks."

"God bless the 'oly monks," the man said, draining the glass. "It's themselves, sire, that can make good liquor. But the man what blew this glass was very short of breath."

The worst thing about some men is that when they are not drunk they are sober.

WILLIAM BUTLER YEATS

Drinking, Intoxication, and Sundry Liquids

In 1927 a speakeasy proprietor whose premises were raided sued the local precinct captain for breach of promise.

"They redecorated my favorite bar."
"How?"
"They put new drunks around it."

An august New England minister was shocked one night towards the close of the nineteenth century when he met one of his wealthy parishioners coming home in a condition severe enough to warrant chastisement. After lecturing the man on the degraded state he was in, the clergyman further remonstrated, "What would you say if you encountered such as myself reeling down the gutter in a state of hopeless intoxication?"
Leaning against the minister the parishioner whispered: "I give the Lord's word, sir, I wouldn't tell a soul."

Two gentlemen from the old sod met on Fifth Avenue and decided to wet their memories. "Have you ever tried using horse-radish in yer whisky?" asked Murphy. "It gives the stuff a grand sparkle."
So on the next round they gingerly sprinkled their glasses with horseradish; whereupon Murphy, after draining his glass, began to weep.
"What are you crying for?" asked his friend.
"Aye, Clancy, I'm crying because my old father was hanged. And it was he who taught me to use horseradish in my whisky."
Clancy belted down his drink and began to cry without inhibition. "And what are you crying for?" asked Murphy.
"I'm crying," said Clancy, "because you weren't hanged with your father."

"Why do you beg?"
"The truth is I beg to get money for booze."
"Why do you drink?"
"To give me the courage to beg."

Ginsburg came home in a state of intoxication to find that Mrs. Ginsburg had suffered a stroke and now lay mortally ill. He staggered into her chamber, and her eyes lit when she saw him. "Penrod," she said, making an effort to speak clearly. "I'm glad they found you. There is one last wish—one last favor, if you will —that I want you to grant me."

"Name it, and if it's in my power to do it I will."

"Pen, dearest, I know you haven't spoken to my mother for fifteen years. But now I am dying, and it is my last wish that when I am laid to my final rest the two of you will be together."

"No," shouted Ginsburg. "You're only trying to take advantage of me because I'm drunk."

"Please. I've been a good wife, a good mother—I tried to be everything a woman can be to her husband. Grant me this last favor. At least——" Here she gasped for breath. Gaining control once more, she continued: "At least promise me that you will drive to the cemetery with her."

"Oh, all right." Then his face tightened as he pictured his mother-in-law. "But I'm telling you right now," he shouted, "it's going to ruin my whole day."

A classic of the damp genre concerns the man who walked into a western saloon, banged on the bar, and said: "Rack 'em up fast. I need it. It's gonna be a terrible fight."

The bartender served the man his drink. He polished it off and turned to the other guests. "Anybody here a doctor?" he asked. When someone admitted he was, the man said, "Stick around, doc, you're gonna be needed. It's gonna be a bloody fight." Then he turned to the bartender and ordered another drink. "And make it a triple. I'm gonna need it, believe me. This fight is gonna be one of the worst."

He finished the triple and asked if there was an undertaker in the house. A man rose and said he was an undertaker. "Don't go 'way, mister," the man called. "There's gonna be a job for you soon. It's gonna be a helluva terrible fight."

He turned to the bartender again. "Set 'em up. Four triples in a row. I need 'em bad. What an awful fight it's gonna be."

As the man gulped the last of the triples the bartender seemed anxious. "Who you going to fight with, mister?" he asked.

"You," said the man. "I ain't got money to pay for the drinks."

A drunk absent-mindedly strolled into a cemetery one night, tripped on a stone, and fell into an open coffin. The next morning he came to, looked around, sat upright, took in the situation, and remarked: "Either I'm the first one riz or I'm damned late."

Chauncey Depew told the story of a temperance lecturer who was caught by a disciple as he was downing a hot whisky punch. "I thought you were a total abstainer," said the shocked fellow.

"I am," said the lecturer. "But I'm not a bigoted one."

Another Depew story concerns the Church of England man who entered a dining car and asked: "Is there any member of the Protestant Episcopal Church here?"

A man came forward and said: "Yes, I am."

The other asked: "Have you got a corkscrew, sir?"

And it was immediately forthcoming.

A teacher called upon a student to correct this sentence, "The toast was drank in silence."

The student replied: "The toast was ate in silence."

Drink is the curse of marriage. It makes you shoot at your wife —and it makes you miss.

A man entered a bar, ordered six singles lined up in a row, then proceeded to drink them rapidly. He then ordered six more and repeated the libation. A stranger, who had just stopped by to use the phone, noticed this and came walking over. "Pardon me, I do not mean to sound personal, but do you make a practice of that very often?" he asked.

"Twice a day, sometimes three," said the man.

"Good Lord. How much do you spend on whisky daily, sir?"

"Between twenty and thirty dollars, I'd say."

"TWENTY AND THIRTY DOLLARS!" The stranger was astonished. "And how long have you been doing that?"

"Oh, I'd say about twenty-five years."

"TWENTY-FIVE YEARS?" The figure was staggering. "My good man, do you see that building across the street?" The man nodded to indicate that he did. "Do you realize," said the stranger, "that if you had taken all the money you spent on whisky and set it aside you could own that building."

"Do you drink, mister?" the man asked.

"No, sir, I do not," said the stranger.

"Do you own that building across the street?"

"Why, no, I don't."

"Well," said the man, "I do."

When you find you can't stand the terrible crashing of snowflakes as they hit the ground, you've had enough.

GERALD BARZAN

A sportsman on a toot strayed into the New York Aquarium where he suddenly found himself facing the tank containing the largest man-eating shark in captivity. "The man who caught that fish," screamed the sportsman, "ish a gawdamn liar!"

Michael and Patrick were on their way to a wake for one of Michael's friends, when they decided on a nip or two. Along about the tenth drink they were pretty well swanked and as a result Michael could not recall the address of the appointment. "Where is your friend's house?" asked Patrick.

"I cannot rightly recall the number, but I'm certain it is on this street," replied Michael.

They walked along until Michael squinted at a house he thought might be it. They opened the door and staggered into a pitch black hallway; then they opened another door and found themselves in a living room which was equally dark except for a set of candles glimmering faintly atop the piano. They walked to the front of the piano, knelt, and prayed. Patrick, after a moment, looked up long enough to study the keyboard of the instrument. "Sure, Michael," he whispered, "I didn't know yer friend, but he had a foine set of teeth."

"Father drinks anything," the boy told his teacher. "Right now he's under the influence of lacquer."

The old British colonel was telling his grandchildren of the horrors of war in Injiah. "Ammunition, food, and whisky had run out and we were parched with thirst——"
"Wasn't there any water?"
"Certainly," said the old soldier. "But it was no time to be thinking of cleanliness."

To scare the old man into becoming a teetotaler, Mrs. Hoolihan had the priest tell him a horrible story. It seems a certain old lady, fond of alcoholic beverages, was so saturated with spirits one day that her breath caught fire and she was instantly cremated on the spot. The good Father could tell by the expression on Hoolihan's face that it had made an impression, so he said: "Mick, let that be a warnin' to ya."
"Begorrah, and sure it will, sir," answered the solemn Mick. "I'll never blow out a candle again so long as I live."

Favorite Hollywood drink: Marriage on the rocks.

> He who drinks a glass a day
> Shall live to die another way.

STANLICUS

The Greatest Laughs of All Time

If the aunt of the vicar
Has never touched liquor
Look out when she finds the champagne.

RUDYARD KIPLING

Men and Women; the Battle of the Sexes

Breathes there a man with hide so tough
Who says two sexes aren't enough?

SAMUEL HOFFENSTEIN

BY ACT OF PARLIAMENT (1670):

(Be it resolved) that all women, of whatever age, rank, profession, or degree; whether virgin maids or widows; that shall, from after the passing of this act, impose upon and betray into matrimony any of his Majesty's male subjects, by scents, paints, cosmetics, washes, artificial teeth, false hair, Spanish wool, iron stays, hoops, high-heeled shoes, or bolstered hips, shall incur the penalty of the laws now in force against witchcraft, sorcery, and such like misdemeanors, and that the marriage, upon conviction, shall stand null and void.

Man having emerged from the dark ages, the above decree, as passed by the British Parliament, evidenced his eagerness to get at basic truths. But once privileged to observe woman without artificial teeth, false hair, scents, cosmetics, Spanish wool, and iron stays, man had reason to question the commonsense of too much enlightenment—and the decree passed into limbo. Not, however,

127

before it helped give rise to the feminist movement, results of which are apparent today.

Isadora Duncan stands out as the prime example of liberated womanhood. Not content to fascinate her audiences with artful dance patterns performed in gossamer, the great Isadora was known to punctuate her art by exposing her firmed-up breasts for all to see, thus preceding by thirty years the contemporary school of beat poets, whose poetry leaves much to the imagination but who habitually combine public readings with displays of the anatomy.

Isadora deplored the boorishness that overwhelmed her when she was presented with an opportunity to enact a seduction scene with Rodin. She blamed it on society's immaturity, coupled with the idiotic mores attendant upon being a virgin. Having deprived the world of what surely would have been an incomparable image, she determined never again to be guilty of such thoughtless restraint. In keeping with this divine dedication she broached an idea to George Bernard Shaw. "Let us have an affair outside the Victorian fantasy of marriage," was her suggestion. The object: a superb infant possessed of her body and Shaw's brains. But Shaw rejected the idea. "What of a mishap?" he asked. "An offspring with your brains and my body?"

It was Isadora's argument that women should be allowed to seduce men with the impunity given men who seduce women. This, she contended, was the only way in which the female would achieve true equality.

While both sexes are agreeable to the plan, Isadora never resolved the main problem! Who would have the baby?

Man's admiration for woman never flags. He will give her half his fortune. He will give her his whole heart. He appears willing to give her everything he possesses—except his seat on a streetcar.

HORACE PORTER

During certain court procedures a gentleman did his best to remain within the bounds of his congenital upbringing. Despite this a hostile attorney asked: "You are aware of the testimony given by the young lady who appeared before you, yet your statements are contrary to hers. Am I to infer that you wish to throw doubt upon her veracity?"

"No. Not at all." The man waved deprecatingly. "I merely wish to make it clear what a liar I am if she's speaking the truth."

When Cardinal Mazarin was at the height of his power as the result of his influence over Anne of Austria, one of his royal eavesdroppers brought news of a terrible row between two ladies of the court.

Each had accused the other of sins which ran the gamut of degradation and which no lady's character could survive without total disgrace. "Have they called each other ugly?" the cardinal asked, after hearing the story.

"No, Monseigneur," the informant replied.

"Well, then," the cardinal rejoined, "it should not be difficult to reconcile them."

A young gentleman, barely in his twenties, requested his jeweler to engrave a recently purchased engagement ring with the statement: "Tom, to his dearly beloved Helen."

"Is the young lady a relative?" the jeweler asked.

"Certainly not. She is the young lady whom I intend to marry."

"Well, then," cautioned the jeweler, "if I were you I would not inscribe 'Tom, to his dearly beloved Helen' on the ring. Should Helen change her mind you could not use the ring again."

"What would you suggest?"

The jeweler said: "I suggest the words 'Tom—to his first and only love.' Then you can use the ring a dozen times."

"If I refuse to marry you will you really commit suicide?"

"That has been my customary procedure."

JOHN BARRYMORE

The last man on earth has always fascinated the unwed female. "If he was the last man on earth," a girl pouted, "and I was the last woman, I wouldn't marry him."

"You're absolutely right," her friend advised. "What's the use of marrying when there's nobody to envy you."

A spinster lady was eager to wed a gentleman who showed interest. But she knew he feared the prospect of marrying a woman with any physical defect, and she was hard of hearing. By pre-arrangement she had a little boy hide in the woods with instructions that at a given signal he give off very faint bird calls. She in turn would pretend to hear them, and her intended would never suspect the handicap.

All went as planned. Her beau walked blissfully along with her, and at the signal the little boy placed his fingers across his lips. But at precisely that moment a train rounded the bend and gave off an ear-wrecking shriek that pierced to the heavens. The spinster smiled. "You know, dear," she said, "that's the first robin I've heard this spring."

A similar story concerns the spinster who could not see too well. In order to hide her failing eyesight from her intended she stuck a pin in a tree. The next day, while walking in the forest with her affianced, she pointed to the tree, some hundred yards distant, and said, "Isn't that a pin sticking in that tree?" And as she ran to retrieve it—she tripped over a cow.

Sigmund Freud used this story to illustrate double meaning with sexual suggestiveness. An elderly gentleman, having devoted considerable time and extended lavish gifts upon a young actress, was sympathetically told by the lady that her heart was already given to another.

The elderly man politely said: "I never aspired as high as that."

Heinrich Heine was expert at proving that flattery need not be flattering. "This woman resembles the Venus de Milo in many

130

ways," he said. "Like her she is extraordinarily old, has no teeth, and has white spots on the yellow surface of her body."

Be good and you will be lonesome.

MARK TWAIN

A judge of the Victorian era came home from the assizes and, as usual, his wife asked if anything of interest took place.

"We tried a woman for wearing a one-piece bathing suit," the judge said solemnly.

"How shocking," his wife gasped. "What possible excuse could a woman have for exposing her person like that?"

Sighed the judge: "You should have seen her excuse."

An elderly lady, writing in her church newspaper, produced the following complimentary observation on the preaching talents of the new vicar: "We didn't know what sin was until he came to this parish."

"Who is that woman you spent hours talking to on the street?"

"That's our new neighbor, Mrs. Cross. She had to tell me something important and was too busy to come in."

A bachelor gentleman habitually spent his evenings with a widow who lived in his district. After a year or so a friend suggested that he marry the lady. "I have given it much thought," he said. "But where would I spend my evenings then?"

Declaration of a suffragette, after casting her first ballot:

"The conservative candidate was simply stunning. But the liberal was an excellent family man, and the socialist had the cutest brown hair. So I marked all three ballots, closed my eyes, shuffled them, put one in the box and tore up the others. It was the only fair thing to do."

Young lady to long line waiting to use telephone: "Don't worry, I won't be long. I just want to hang up on him."

Bachelors know more about women than married men—if they didn't they'd be married too.

H. L. MENCKEN

"That is the town house of the Duke of Westminster, one of our largest landed proprietors."
"Who landed him?" a female visitor asked.

Women do not believe everything they hear—but this doesn't prevent them from repeating it.

When a woman is in a train of thought someone is bound to get run down.

Following the separation of Poland from Russia, after World War I, a woman was notified that the new line of demarcation placed her home just inside the Polish border. "Good," she said. "I couldn't stand another of those Russian winters."

"Anything breakable in this package?" a postal clerk asked a woman who was mailing a Bible.
"No," she replied. "Nothing but the Ten Commandments."

Among the autobiographical blabbermouths George Moore stands out. Moore was an egotist who did not hesitate to use his invective talents promiscuously. He once called Thomas Hardy a miscarriage of George Eliot.
If his word can be accepted, he was an extraordinary ladies' man. At the time of publication of his memoirs those who knew him best were convinced that he lied, and had merely used sex as an extension of his ego. An anonymous critic, writing of this work, was responsible for a classic allusion to the male-female

relationship when he declared: "Some men kiss and tell. George Moore tells—but he does not kiss."

An apprentice seaman was standing his first watch alongside the captain. "Tell me, sir," he asked politely. "Do you believe women aboard a ship really bring bad luck?"

"Yes, son," the captain philosophized. "Same as they do ashore."

"How long should an engagement last?"
"Until the couple detests one another. Then they should marry."

A young New England housewife was the defendant in a proceeding which was merely a matter of formality. The district attorney politely asked: "In the course of your husband's absence we understand you shot a burglar. Is that correct?"

"Yes," the woman admitted.
"What became of the man?"
"The other burglar took him away," she said.
"There was another burglar?"
"Yes, sir," she stated. "The one I shot at."

In ancient times a woman was considered old at the age of forty. Today a woman of that age is only twenty-nine.

There is a mythological place where the population has remained constant some sixty years. Every time a baby is born somebody gets out of town.

She's descended of a long line her mother listened to.
GYPSY ROSE LEE, *tribute to a contemporary*

A justice of the peace, about to perform the ceremony of bondage, thought he recognized the blushing bride. "Did I not perform a marriage rite in which you took part some ten years ago?" he asked.

"Yes," she admitted. "My first husband has passed on."

"But at that time you said you were twenty-eight years of age, and now you again say you are twenty-eight years of age."

"Well," huffed the bride-to-be, "I'm not one of those women who say one thing one day and another thing the next."

"Sir," said the intrusive lady to a stranger seated next to her on the train, "smoking makes me sick."

"Well, then, madam," replied the stranger, "if I were you I'd give it up."

A prominent lady speaker was introduced to her staid audience, and, at precisely that moment she discovered her handkerchief missing. Remembering where she had placed another, she rose, and while the audience waited dug her hand into her bosom and probed in all directions. Then, realizing the audience's fascination, she muttered: "I know I had two when I came in."

On the beach at the French Riviera a tourist couple lay taking in the sun. Near them romped dozens of shapely females clad in barest bikini styles. The husband suddenly drew his wife's attention to one of the bathers. "Look at that girl there," he said. "The one in the full swimsuit. That's what I call decent beach attire, so modest and proper."

"Yes," his wife replied. "Some women will do anything to attract attention."

A young girl was telling one of her office companions of a recent experience. "I refused to marry Jim five months back, and he's been on a drinking binge ever since."

"That," said the other young lady, "is what I call carrying a celebration too far."

When Douglas Jerrold attended a ball and noticed a man dancing with a physically unendowed woman, he remarked: "That gentleman must be one of the Humane Society."

Men and Women; the Battle of the Sexes

"I wonder how many men I shall make unhappy when I marry?"

"How many men do you intend to marry?"

Overheard in a dark theater: "He not only lied to me about his yacht, but he made me row."

Men seldom elope with girls who take dope.

BEATICISM

A lady is one who never shows her underwear intentionally.

SCHOOL EXAM

Gentlemen who prefer blondes are usually married to brunettes.

There once was a man not unique
Who imagined himself quite a shique;
   But the girls didn't fall
   For the fellow at all.
He made only twenty a wique.

Epitaph in a British Abbey:
Here lies Ann Mann,
Lived an old maid,
Died an old Mann.

Temptation: something which when resisted brings happiness, and when yielded to brings greater happiness.

A mouse in her room woke Miss Dowd
She was frightened, it must be allowed.
   Soon a happy thought hit her,
   To scare off the critter,
She sat up in bed and meowed.

At a fancy ball in London a visiting clergyman, noting the low-cut dresses that were the vogue, was asked if he had ever beheld such a sight. "No," he replied. "Not since I was weaned."

Having spent a vacation in a nudist colony I was somewhat taken back when a lady shook my hand, and said: "Good-by, Mr. Nunn. I hope we see more of you."

GREGORY NUNN

She who hesitates—is extinct.

The spinster lady was taken aback when the roomer, in his cups, offered the first proposition she'd ever received. "Why, Mr. Blank," she protested. "Why would you make such a proposal to me?"

"I'll tell ya, honey," Blank whispered. "I gotta go to confession tomorrow and I'm a little short of material."

The minister performing the marriage rites was an uncle of the bride. To the groom he said: "Do you promise to treat her mother kindly? To love, honor and obey her entire family? To buy her a mink coat and spend your honeymoon in Florida? So help you God?"

"I do," the dazed groom replied.

"There," the reverend said to the bride. "*Now* are you satisfied?"

Doctors and the Medical Profession

If your time ain't come not even a doctor can kill you.

TWENTIETH-CENTURY PROVERB

There are three subjects on which the knowledge of the medical profession in general is woefully weak; they are manners, morals, and medicine. At this writing, due to certain doctrinaire policies of medical societies, the profession of Hippocrates is undergoing a critical re-evaluation in the eyes of many, most of whom are chagrined by the knowledge that so high a calling should recently fall so low in repute. They are, of course, wrong. The medical profession has always been in ill repute. Martialis told us: "Diaulus, lately a doctor, is now an undertaker; what he does as an undertaker he used also to do as a doctor." And from greater antiquity we get the following observations: "The doctor is to be more feared than the disease"; "Better a lucky physician than a learned one"; and the more contemporaneous: "Sickness soaks the purse."

Advancing chronologically we find: "Fond of lawsuits, little wealth; fond of doctors, little health"; "That patient's ear remorseless he assails; murders with jargon where his medicine fails"; "A young doctor makes a humpy churchyard." And the omnipresent monetary debate: "God heals, and the doctor takes the fee."

137

Nor was fee-splitting unknown, as witnessed by the old adage: "One doctor makes work for another."

Illustrious personages of the past on numerous occasions have laid the cause of their ill health to the presence of too many physicians.

It is said that Plutarch, in a fit of hypochondria, cried out for an undertaker. "But, master," a follower corrected, reminding the biographer he was not yet dead, "you mean a physician." "No," Plutarch answered, "I am eliminating the middleman."

Napoleon, who put more faith in the psychic than the physic, observed: "Medicine is a collection of uncertain prescriptions, the results of which, taken collectively, are more fatal than useful to mankind." Nor are medical societies especially fond of Bacon, for the philosopher wrote, in *Advancement of Learning*: "Medicine is a science which hath been, as we have said, more professed than laboured, and yet more laboured than advanced. The labour having been, in my judgement, rather in circle than in progression."

Records of eighteenth-century British assizes show that a case was decided on the basis of testimony given by a man said to be 140 years old. Some question was raised as to whether a man of 140 years could give proper testimony. To lend credence to his evidence a brace of youngsters offered corroboration; they were his sons, aged 119 and 123.

It casts a long shadow over the term "medical progress."

Medical practitioners are constantly in dispute with the legal profession. A physician was once summoned to a courtroom where an attorney had had a seizure. After examining his still form the doctor rose to go. "Is Lawyer Brown out of danger?" asked the judge.

"He's dead," said the medical man. "But I'm afraid he is far from being out of danger."

"I am sorry to drag you so far out into the suburbs on a dreadful night like this, doctor."

"That's okay. I have another patient in this vicinity, so I can kill two birds with one stone."

Lawyers have done their share of editorializing on the medical profession. Nineteenth-century records show this exchange. A physician presented his bill to the courts as a legal way of collecting fees due from a deceased person's estate. "Do you wish my bill sworn to?" the doctor asked.

"No," said the legalite. "Death of the deceased is sufficient evidence that you attended him professionally."

A man subject to blackout spasms collapsed on the street. An emergency ambulance rushed him to the nearest hospital where a physician made a cursory examination and ordered an immediate operation. As the operating room was being prepared a nurse, going through the man's clothing, found this note pinned to his wallet. "This is to let the house surgeon know that I am undergoing a plain case of fit. It is not appendicitis. My appendix has already been removed three times."

Hasty diagnosis and misplaced psychology often result in confusion. A man who had gone deaf underwent a thorough examination in an effort to find the root of his trouble. "It is quite evident," said the physician, obviously shooting in the dark, "that this is a case of excessive nervousness showing itself in psychosomatic form by deafness. Now I happen to know that gambling, alcohol, and sex stimulation are major causes of this type of disorder."

"What are you driving at, doc?"

"You'll have to give up poker, whisky, and sex."

"Are you crazy, doc?" bellowed the patient. "Just for a little hearing?"

A nineteenth-century journal is reported to have given wide play to death caused by extended use of tobacco. As an illustration it took a man in Cochonville, France, who dropped dead while smoking his pipe—at the age of 104.

In the slums of New York lived a physician named Hart, who was thoroughly dedicated to his patients. Most of them were poor first-generation immigrants, living in abject squalor. His bell rang one midnight, and when he wearily walked to the door in his nightshirt a woman stood there, shivering in the cold. After listening to her he dressed quickly and hurried to her flat, climbing six flights of wooden stairs. There he examined the woman's little girl. "You've a very sick little child there," he finally said. "You must keep constant watch over her. Get this prescription filled and follow the instructions carefully."

As he started to leave his eye took in the awful conditions under which the family lived. He made no mention of a fee and slipped a five-dollar bill beneath the prescription.

When he called the next afternoon the child was considerably improved. "I guess you found the money I left," he said modestly.

"Oh yes," the mother beamed. "Such a wonderful thing you did, it was enough for us to call in a better doctor."

The hospital supervisor sent for a young surgeon and lauded his efforts in the operating room the previous day. "Marvelous bit of work," the institution head complimented. "You operated just in time. One more day and the patient would have recovered without it."

Doctors are men who prescribe medicines of which they know little, to cure diseases of which they know less, in human beings of whom they know nothing.

VOLTAIRE

After the Civil War an army surgeon, who had distinguished himself in the field, was on a lecture tour. He always wound up his address with an impassioned oration on Antoine Laurent Lavoisier, the man who contributed to medical advancement through experiments with oxygen, combustion, and respiration; and who was executed on the guillotine during the French Revolution. After stressing that it took but a moment to sever his head and it will take centuries to replace it, the surgeon concluded by saying: "Lavoisier's last words were 'this probably saves me from the inconvenience of old age.' He distinguished himself in the fields of medicine and law, and as a tax collector. Now are there any questions."

"Yes," a voice called. "With a record like that why wasn't he executed a lot sooner?"

The age of specialization has given birth to some odd practices, particularly among medico faddists; the type of physician who caters to human vanity. To such a practitioner, specializing in diets, came a woman eager to lose weight. She was seated in the waiting room alone when she noticed a rate card on a table. It read: "Fees: First visit, $50. All subsequent visits, $10."

A moment later she was ushered into the physician's office, and shaking his hand, she said, "Well, doctor, here I am again."

The epitome of medical honesty was reached by a doctor who tired of the complaints of a certain hypochondriac. When the patient said, "Doctor, I feel the most excruciating pain every time I lift my arm," the doctor replied, "So don't lift it."

The oldest man alive today is reported to have celebrated his 120th birthday. His case is regarded as a triumph of nature over medical knowledge.

In the twenties there were persistent rumors of young doctors being tried in medical society star chamber proceedings, their crime being that of treating patients for indigestion when they could well have afforded appendicitis.

Samuel Bonom, one of the country's leading criminal lawyers, and currently a member of the New York State legislative body, tells of a friend with an unusual skin ailment who sought the services of a specialist. "Let me see your hands," the specialist ordered. The doctor became deeply engrossed in what he saw. "Hmm-mm," he mumbled, as he turned over first one hand then the other. "Hmm-mm. Ever had this before?"

"Yes," the man said.

"Well," diagnosed the specialist, "you've got it again."

A doctor once filed a report on the worst case of insomnia he had ever encountered. It was so bad that the patient couldn't fall asleep when it was time to get up.

A newspaper in suburbia has this opinion of local medical authority. "John Erickson, our distinguished fire chief, enters the hospital tomorrow for a routine checkup. He will leave a wife and four children."

Physicians are called upon for intimate advice no matter the occasion. One medical man tired of this and decided he would deny his occupation if the subject came up at a cocktail party. Upon being introduced to a woman he had never met, she started the conversation by saying: "I'm so very pleased to meet you, doctor. There's something I'd like to ask you. I have terrible rectal pains since my gallstone operation, and my kidneys are terrible too, to say nothing of my liver. Do you think there is a particular kind of exploratory that could find the cause?"

"I'm afraid I cannot help you, madam," he replied. "I'm not that kind of doctor. I happen to be a doctor of economics."

"Really," shrieked the woman delightedly. "So tell me, doctor, you think I should sell my Anaconda?"

Being human, doctors are reluctant to make house calls where receipt of payment is doubtful. Under these circumstances a physician diagnosed a patient's illness on the phone. "There is nothing wrong with your uncle. I have examined him thoroughly and I tell you he only thinks he's sick. He thinks he's sick."

A week later the doctor met the patient's nephew. "How's your uncle?" he asked.

"Worse," said the relative. "Now he thinks he's dead."

An internationally known surgeon felt he should attempt to establish some rapport with a man to whom he had given an estimate on a brain operation. "Your kids are no wilder than any of us when we were the same age," said the surgeon. "Why, when I was a boy I had a great ambition to be a pirate."

"You're very lucky, doctor," the patient replied. "It isn't every man who realizes the ambitions of his youth."

> "Is there no hope?" the sick man said.
> The silent doctor shook his head.
> And took his leave with signs of sorrow.
> Despairing of his fee tomorrow.
>
> JOHN GAY

During the middle years of Victoria's reign a smug professor at the medical college wrote on the blackboard, between classes, this legend: "Your esteemed professor informs his students that he has this day been appointed honorary physician to Her Majesty Queen Victoria."

When he returned he found these words printed below the announcement: "God save the Queen!!"

After undergoing extensive medical tests a man called to see if the results were available. "They're not," the doctor said curtly.

"Why not?" demanded the patient.

"Because," the doctor snapped. "I haven't figured out what kind of an operation you can afford."

"Doc, I have this awful insomnia. Can't you do something for me?"

"Certainly. Drink a pint of whisky every night before retiring."

"Will that cure it?"

"No. But it will make it a pleasure to stay awake."

On his sixth call following a dangerous operation, the doctor was surprised to hear the patient say: "Doctor, I am feeling so very much better. I want you to let me have your bill."

"Nonsense, my good man," opined the physician. "You are far from strong enough for that."

Many persons gauge a medical practitioner's skill by the quality of his office furniture and the amount of his consultation fees. A man once called on a doctor who had treated him for a malignant ailment. "Doctor," the patient said, "my daughters insisted that two other physicians come in for consultation, and their opinions are very different from yours."

"Do not feel badly about it," the doctor answered. "The autopsy will show who was right."

Naval medicine is unique, involving problems endemic to the nautical life. A petty officer assigned to a ship's hospital was being examined by a Navy department chief surgeon, prior to upgrading. "Now," said the surgeon. "Let us suppose you are called to the bridge because the captain has fainted. What is the first thing you would do?"

"I'd bring him to."

"Then what would you do?"

"I'd bring him two more."

An obstetrician, after examining a very pretty young lady said: "I've got good news for you, Mrs. Hayes——"

"It's *Miss* Hayes," the patient interrupted.

"Oh," said the doctor. "I've got bad news for you."

People who take cold baths never have rheumatism—but they have cold baths.

Doctors and the Medical Profession

In fleeing disease you fall into the hands of doctors.

LATIN PROVERB

A doctor who had been working on a theory concerning coffee and tea as the main cause of mankind's illnesses, was constantly trying to prove his point. He was expounding his belief to a patient of the upper class one day, and the man, having a mind of his own, was skeptical. "Let me prove the injurious nature of tea and coffee to you," insisted the doctor.

"You are welcome to try," the patient replied.

"Good. But once my point is made I want you to agree to abstain from these items."

"I'll agree."

"Tell me this: how often do you drink coffee and tea?"

"Constantly. From the time I get up to the time I go to sleep."

"Are you ever groggy when your head hits the pillow?"

"Quite often—in fact it is a perpetual symptom with me."

"Ah. . . . Now tell me, is this also accompanied by a dizziness?"

"Yes."

"And in the morning, when you rise, does your head throb? And is there a constant burning in your eyes?"

"Why, yes, there is."

"Well, sir," the doctor remarked with utter triumph and confidence. "That is the coffee and tea."

"Is it?" said the patient. "Well I'll be darned. And all the time I thought it was the whisky."

Glands may come and glands may go—but the monkey business will go on forever.

It was the patient's first day on a special diet and he was not particularly pleased. The nurse fed him one teaspoonful of instant pudding, a thimbleful of tea, and a protein cracker measuring a quarter-inch square. "Is that all I get?" he protested.

"That's all," the nurse replied. "Is there anything else I can do for you?"

145

"Yes," said the man. "Bring me a postage stamp, I'd like to read."

"Howdy, doc," said the operator of the country general store. "Where ya been?"

"Oh, I was up north for a week of hunting."

"Kill anything?"

"Not a darned thing."

"Heck, doc," said the old-timer. "You could-a done better'n that stayin' home and tendin' yer reg'lar trade."

Dr. Beaver rushed to the home of a stricken patient and found the poor man's wife waiting nervously. He rushed into the sickroom, but made the woman wait outside. Ten minutes later he rushed out. "Quick! Get me a chisel," he ordered.

The woman's face lost its color, but she hurriedly complied. Five minutes later the doctor flung open the door again. "This is very bad, very very bad. Get me a hammer, a saw, a Boy Scout knife, and an ax. It's worse than I thought."

She tore through the neighborhood until she had everything the doctor ordered. Then she ran back, rapped on the door, and when the doctor answered she handed him the tools. At the same time she pleaded. "Is there any hope, doctor?"

"How should I know?" the doctor answered. "I can't even get my satchel open."

A practical medical school in Switzerland gives each graduating student a batch of ten-year-old copies of *Life* magazine—so patients won't think they are new in the business.

"Don't look so glum," said the doctor cheerfully. "I've had the same ailment myself."

"Sure," moaned the patient. "But you didn't have the same doctor."

The ill woman had been to see hundreds of doctors all over the world and none of them could find the cause of her troubles. She paid exorbitant fees for tests and examinations that took a week to six months to complete. Though the doctors prescribed what were supposedly the proper drugs for her ailment, each came up with a different analysis—and nothing helped. One day the lady was visiting relatives in a very poor part of town when she passed a decrepit building on which hung a very old medical emblem. She entered a poor reception room and the doctor was seated there reading a dope sheet. Being one of those women who are prepared for anything, she happened to have all her X-rays along and showed them to him. As he examined them she told him every detail of her experiences. After an hour of listening he finally said: "Stick your tongue out."

She stuck her tongue out.

The doctor clucked a few times. "I'm afraid you have GOK," he said.

"GOK?" she shrieked. "Are you sure?"

"Positive. The clearest case of GOK I ever saw. Never been surer of anything in my whole life."

"Oh, dear. What sort of medicine will I have to take?"

"No medicine, ma'am. There just ain't no cure for GOK."

With that he told her his fee was two dollars and showed her to the door.

That night his phone rang and it was the woman's son. "Doctor," he said. "I understand mater was in to see you and you diagnosed her ailment as GOK."

"That's so."

"Might I ask how you arrived at your decision?"

The doctor said, "It's very simple. I examined them hundreds of X-rays, looked over them thousands of prescriptions, examined all that nice hemstitching where they operated. Then I looked at her tongue. There was no question about it. GOK all right."

"What is the nature of this illness?"

"It's an abbreviated illness."

"Abbreviated? I'm afraid I don't understand."

"GOK," the doctor replied, "stands for 'God only knows.'"

A notable case of wrong diagnosis concerns an officer on the staff of the Duke of Wellington. He was on his deathbed in a French hospital when word came that Napoleon had again thrown down the gauntlet by escaping from Elba. The officer called the senior doctor to him and demanded the truth regarding his condition. "I'm afraid, sir, you do not have long to live," the physician said. "A month, two months. With luck three months. Perhaps, if you take great care, four months."

"Then I may as soon die on the battlefield as here in a hospital bed," the brave man replied.

He rejoined his regiment, fought brilliantly, with the reckless abandon of a man who knows death is imminent, and at the Battle of Waterloo received a wound that took away parts of his lungs, his stomach, and his liver. But he would not stop; he insisted on being allowed to go on; helped defeat Napoleon, and died—forty years later.

Family and Friends

All peoples are your relatives, therefore expect only trouble from them.

ANCIENT CHINESE PROVERB

With pulpitry again serving as impetus for togetherness the curve has swung full, returning to the mores of very ancient days when mutual love between parents and children stood out 'mid the depravity of the times. The clergy, however, must share honors with the real estate lobby, whose high rent policies not only contribute to families staying together and praying together, but also in swearing together at real estate lobbies.

The opposite of togetherness occurred in the Dark Ages, when constant need of manpower for religious crusades created divine sanction for family abandonment. With celibacy before and after marriage widely encouraged, there was no reason for the men to stay home anyway. Thus, when the rallying cry to "serve God and escape Hell" was sounded, husbands knew exactly what it was they wished to escape.

Coal that wrought swords for the Crusaders also heated casts of a family defender, the chastity belt. The latter, in turn, inspired rank and file troubadours to originate an early erotica still in use.

149

Their tale began with a satire on the Knightly Oath of Primogeniture, somewhat in this fashion:

"I entrust by all oaths and obligations a key,
its nature known but to thee,
to fit a lock girdling the virtue of my lady. . . ."

Having foresworn his brother knight to no more than a bi-monthly castle visit, when he shall pass on to the wife a key "that she might properly exercise," the Crusader took his leave. Three days later, however, the trusted knight caught up with the band of Crusaders and sought out his brother, who greeted him jocularly, saying: "Why come you? Have you heard the call to Jerusalem?" And the other gasped breathlessly: "Nay. You delivered unto me the wrong key."

The question, to abstain or not to abstain, found champions of rank devoted to both propositions. Later critics of prudery found a spokesman in Erasmus of Rotterdam. His book, *Familiarium Colloquies*, was realistic, containing among other things this blessing to a pregnant woman: "Heaven grant that the burden you carry may have as easy an exit as it had an entrance."

Condemnation of *Colloquies* made it an immediate success, sales exceeding twenty-four thousand copies—remarkable for a time when only the elite and the pious could read.

As time went on, bad examples and situations of urgency lowered divorce requirements and imposed greater obstacles to family life. But whenever man, by nature a bigamist, threatened to sunder permanently the concept of marital unity, ministerial watchfulness was present to renew belief in honorable lineage.

So we come to the nineteenth century and find the battle engaged by a stern fundamentalist who refuses to brook anything that violates the old time religion. John Barleycorn has invaded his domain, community structure is threatened by drunken orgies. Something must be done and the Reverend Simeon K——, himself a bootlegger of no mean talent, decides to do it. Casting aside personal gain he throws down the gauntlet to conscienceless moonshiners, and issues the greatest proclamation for togetherness ever heard in his part of the country.

"If any man," his voice rings out, "at the seventh or eighth bottle, so forgets himself as to abuse and strike his wife and children, and spites his neighbor, and makes enemies of his friends, let him look to the preservation of his soul—*and stop after the sixth bottle.*"

A leading exponent of togetherness suggested the purchase of a house as a means of healing a family rift. "A house?" questioned the wife. "What would I do with a house? I was born in a hospital, schooled in a college, made love to in an automobile, and married in a church. I eat at restaurants, spend my mornings at the beach, my afternoons at canasta, and my evenings at a dance or a drive-in-theater. When I die I'll be laid out at an undertaker's and driven to the funeral in a hearse. All I need is a garage."

Home is where you go when the other places close.

JOE LAURIE, JR.

The only people I know who still believe in hell are the ones who had the proper kind of upbringing.

On his deathbed a Highlander was exhorted by his clergyman to repent all his crimes and recognize the necessity of forgiving his enemies. But the flame of centuries of feuding that burned in the clan MacGregor could not be easily extinguished and the clergyman was forced to hit hard on the dangers of hell that awaited if he refused. At last MacGregor agreed and the cleric called off the names of MacGregor's enemies.

"MacTavish," he pronounced solemnly.

"I forgive the clan MacTavish," the dying man muttered.

"McGonigle."

"I forgive the clan McGonigle."

"McSherry."

"McSherry? Aw, now, not the clan McSherry too."

"You must."

"Very will, thin I forgive the clan of McSherry, since there be no help fer it."

When the list had been gone through MacGregor called his son to him. "You heard my wurds," he said. "An' may it gang hard wi' you if you forgive 'em too."

A prodigal son returned from an extended trip abroad to learn his father had passed away.

"Why didn't you send me a letter telling me Father was ill?" he demanded of his sister.

"Why?" she questioned. "It wasn't my turn to write."

"What are diplomatic relations, Father?"

"There're no such people."

A true friend is one who likes you despite your achievements.

A group met in an attorney's office one day and listened attentively to the last wishes of their departed loved one.

After the usual formalities the lawyer came to the disposal section. "To my nephews and nieces, each of whose name is appended hereto, I leave the sum of five thousand dollars each," the lawyer read. "For each of my grandchildren, to be delivered to them upon attaining their majority, I leave a free and clear sum of twenty thousand dollars. And to my four children, each of whom I loved with equal devotion, I leave the amount of one hundred thousand dollars, to be paid free and clear to each individually. P.S.: Dear kids, this is the kind of will I would have liked to make if I had had the money."

Most of today's families are broke. It will just take a depression to make it official.

GREGORY NUNN

The apartheid policies of South Africa in 1960 caused a type of family separation akin to our own Civil War. When the young son of a prominent chieftain took a middle-of-the-road attitude on the thing, his father was greatly shaken.

"I'm afraid that boy of yours is not much credit to the family," a reporter said.

"Credit?" scoffed the old man. "Credit, indeed. The truth is, we regard him as the white sheep of the family."

A boy had been brought up with emphasis on the advantages of marrying into affluence. However, while away at college, he met a poor girl, fell in love, and married her. Knowing his parents, he asked a schoolmate to break the news to them. "What would be the best way?" asked his companion.

"Well," said the boy. "First tell them I died—then work up to the climax."

> Ten ancient commandments lousing up the fun.
> Along came prosperity—and then there were none.
>
> GERALD BARZAN

A burglar, unable to open the strong box in a plant he was robbing, took it home with him. "I've done everything I know to get the darned thing open," he told his wife. "I used the acetylene, and I've tried blasting it open. Nothing works."

"Don't give up yet, dear," she advised. "Let the baby play with it."

Sir William S. Gilbert characterized a friend this way. "No one can have a higher opinion of him than I have; and I think he's a dirty little beast."

Children are said to be delinquent when they reach the stage where they want to do what their parents are doing.

The son of an internationally recognized stock-market financier was brought into court for the third time, charged with using the mails for stock fraud. Respect for the family caused the judge to make a final appeal to the scion's father. "My good man," the magistrate said. "Your son has been brought here for the third time. In the past I have been lenient, out of regard for your good name, sir. But I confess now to a certain amount of pique at his constant wrongdoing."

"You are perfectly justified in your attitude, your honor," the financier replied. "I, too, have reached the point where I am thoroughly disgusted with him."

"Then why don't you show him the proper way of doing things?"

"That's just it, judge. I have. Time and again I've tried to drum the right way into his head," the magnate emphasized. "But the darned fool insists on signing his name to them circulars."

Sympathy is what you usually give to a relative when you don't want to lend him money.

A modern mother decided she had better talk to her teen-age daughter before the girl left for her second year at a fancy girl's college. The woman spared nothing, but hammered away at every facet of life she could think of, and in descriptive terms. When the lecture was over the mother said: "I hope you admire my frankness. It's the only way. No sense in hiding things, even if you might be somewhat immature to fully understand."

"Oh, mother," the girl said with awe. "You were magnificent. There're at least six things you told me that I never tried before."

"Can you recall your father's last words?"

"Father had no last words. Mother stayed with him to the end."

"Once upon a time——" a mother read, when her little girl interrupted.

"Mother dear," the child said. "Do all fairy tales start like that?"

154

"No, darling," advised mother. "Often they begin, 'Sorry, honey, I'm working late at the office tonight.'"

"If it wasn't for the wife and kids I'd give up this job," said the bearded lady.

Child psychology hints at possible disaster if a child isn't properly instructed in the values of absolute truth. A mother, who was a stickler for all phases of juvenile psychology, was appalled when her child entered the door and cried: "Mommy, there's a fire engine downstairs almost a block long."

"Now, Gregory Steven," the mother scolded. "For the fifty-millionth time I'm telling you, don't exaggerate."

"Father," asked an advanced coed, "let's be honest with one another. Were you ever in bed with another woman?"

"Yep," answered Father, folding his paper to the sports section.

"When?" gasped the girl.

"When I was born," said Father.

In France a farmer's sons found the breach between their personal ideologies so wide that neither could stand the presence of the other. In order to spare their parents the grief of having to choose between them both left home, and for a quarter century neither heard of the other. With the coming of World War I their aged parents sought, by a ruse, to bring them together. Their father sent both a telegram pleading urgent matters and asked that they meet him at the station.

One son, now a field marshal in the army of France, arrived on an easterly train wearing his finest uniform. The other son, now a cardinal in the church, arrived on a westerly train wearing the long frocked garment of his office. As the two came face to face for the first time in twenty-five years their parents stepped aside and listened hopefully for the signs of affection they felt must lie within. The churchman approached the field marshal and facetiously inquired: "I beg your pardon, stationmaster, but could you tell me when the next train leaves for Cannes?"

"I am really quite sorry," the other replied, "but I do not know, madam."

"Is there anything else I can do for you, darling," a father asked his daughter immediately after her wedding, "now that I've set your husband up in business?"

"Yes," said the girl, adjusting her bridal veil. "Robert wants you to buy him out."

Mealtime: When youngsters sit down to continue eating.

Children begin by loving their parents. After a time they judge them. Rarely if ever do they forgive them.

OSCAR WILDE

Adolescence is the period when the young discover their great responsibility to answer the phone.

The patriarch was on his deathbed. He had always subjected his sons to his will, particularly when it came to running the multi-million-dollar restaurant chain he had built. Knowing that his leave-taking was only a matter of moments he decided to disclose the secret of his success. He motioned them to him, and, as they gathered round his bedside, he said: "Boys, I'm taking off in a minute and I want you to know how I was able to build the chain. Remember and keep it to yourselves. Use only stale bread——" Here he was seized with a fit of coughing, and as he passed away he managed to choke out, "And slice the ham thin."

It is not necessary to have enemies if you go out of your way to make friends hate you.

FRANKLIN K. DANE

A friend is one who has the same enemies you have.

ABRAHAM LINCOLN

A Quaker girl regretted the passage of time which saw her without a husband. "It's a solemn thing to get married, I tell thee," her father soothed.

"I know that, Father," the girl agreed. "But I tell thee it is a great deal more solemn not to get married."

When some men discharge an obligation you can hear the report for miles around.

MARK . TWAIN

The acme of ingratitude is found in the all-time classic story dealing with friendship. A man called on a boyhood chum to ask for the loan of fifty dollars. "I'm sorry," said the friend, "but I will not loan it to you."

"But why? You're a millionaire now. What's fifty dollars to you? Besides, you'll get it back in a month."

"That's beside the point. I don't think I should loan you any money at all."

"I don't understand. We've known each other all our lives. We went to school together. Why, on the college exams it was me you copied from. And when we graduated in the depression, and you had no place to stay, I took you home with me, didn't I?"

"Yes."

"And when you needed money to start business, this same business that's now worth millions, didn't I hock my mother's ring, the last thing I had belonging to her, and give you the money?"

"Yes, you did."

"And during the war, when those Germans had us trapped and you were wounded, didn't I carry you out alive before you could die from loss of blood? And didn't I stay with you, giving you transfusion after transfusion, to keep you alive until I myself was anemic?"

"You don't hear me denying it."

157

"And when we got home, and your business was on the rocks, didn't I go to Washington and pull strings until you got a contract that put you back up there bigger than ever? And wasn't I the one who passed that Korean tip on to you when I could have cashed in myself, but didn't because I didn't want the market to go lopsided? And then, when we were——"

"That's right!!" the millionaire interrupted. "That was years ago. What have you done for me lately?"

"Pater was indefensibly cruel to me in his will," cried the disappointed heir. "Imagine, only one hundred million for me."

"Stop complaining," said his mother. "He might have cut you off altogether."

"Lady," said the bus driver to a woman who boarded the bus with fifteen children. "Are they all yours, or is it a picnic?"

"They're all mine," she replied. "And, believe me, it's no picnic."

If inflation continues the two car garage will be replaced by the two family garage.

SAMUEL BONOM

God could not be everywhere, so therefore he made mothers.

HEBREW PROVERB

A low flying bomber skimmed over occupied France, in 1942, and in the black of night dropped a specially trained group to rendezvous with the underground. It was super secret, and in order to avoid suspicions all of the participants had gone about their normal duties, unaware of the exact time of departure. The youngest in the group, the radio operator, had been home on leave when the call came and had left after saying he might be at the pub awhile.

In the blackness of the French countryside they hurried to a shelter prepared for them by the underground, and once inside set up signal apparatus for a fast contact. As the radioman unfurled his knapsack a collapsible umbrella fell out and rolled to the floor, landing amid guns, grenades, and powder charges. The leader stared in disbelief at this incongruity, and no one said a word for several moments, until the radioman asked: "Sir, did you ever have a mother?"

A certain millionaire who had achieved fame for his ability to resist charity, was asked to cash a check by a member of his club. "No, sir. No indeed. I wouldn't cash a check for my own mother," snapped the eccentric.

"I see," said the chastened man. "I suppose you know your family better than I."

A New York City schoolteacher was annoyed at a fifth-grade boy's obsession with the game of baseball. When asked to write a composition he always selected a phase of the national pastime. On the covers of his books he carried inning by inning accounts of the previous day's games, with gummed stickers of his heroes. In his pockets, where they always bulged till he appeared lopsided, were packs of chewing-gum baseball cards. But when he came to school with a glove and ball and placed them atop his desk, explaining that he had to pitch a game during the half-hour lunch period, it was too much. "You're overdoing this baseball business," she scolded gently. "Supposing there were two people drowning. You stood on the shore with just one life preserver. One of them was the leading hitter on the New York Yankees and the other was your father. Who would you throw it to?"

"That's easy," the boy said. "My father never hit .300 in his life."

The young couple was terribly put out by the unexpected arrival of her grandmother. Her announced intention of staying two weeks stretched into a month with no sign of relief. So they concocted a plan which supposedly would offend her the least and at the same time force her to go. At the dinner table that night the couple would deliberately get into a quarrel, forcing the old lady to take sides. If she sided with her granddaughter, the following day the girl would tell her regretfully that she must leave, out of respect to her husband. And if she sided with the husband, he would politely and sadly reverse the process.

At the dinner table that evening the wife clumsily spilled a pitcher of water into her husband's lap. "You clumsy moron!" he bellowed.

"How dare you speak to me that way?" she faked.

"How dare I speak to *you* that way. Why you're the clumsiest, the sloppiest, the most helpless idiotic wreck around the kitchen that I ever heard of in my life."

"And *you*," the wife shot back. "*You* say *I'm* sloppy. Did you ever hang up a shirt, or a tie, or a pair of pants? Did you ever offer to help with the dishes? I slave all day, and you come home like a king. 'Where's my dinner? Where's my newspaper? Where're my cigars?' I never heard of such a thing. What do you say, Grandma?"

"I'm not saying anything," Grandma replied. "I'm staying two more months."

When the Moors were at the height of their cultural development this story was told about them. A Moorish farmer called at the home of his neighbor and asked if he might borrow a rope. "Oh, good and faithful neighbor, I must regretfully refuse you this simple favor," spoke the man. "The rope you request cannot be given, for I use it to tie up my milk."

"But surely," replied the would-be borrower, "milk cannot be tied up with a rope?"

"By Allah," the refuser said. "When one does not want to do a thing one reason is as good as another."

A child, when newly born.
But grown up, a thorn.

MALAY PROVERB

At the art museum a little girl appeared fascinated by a series of religious paintings. "Mother," she asked, "do men ever go to heaven?"

"Certainly, dear," her mother replied. "Why do you ask?"

"Then why don't the angels ever have whiskers?"

"Oh, that," the woman nodded. "That's because they get there by a close shave."

A fool and his father's money can go places.

A salesman called at the home of an industrial tycoon. When a little girl answered the door, he asked, "Is your mommy home?"

"No," said the child. "Mommy is in Reno getting a divorce. And Daddy isn't home either."

"Are your brothers or sisters home?"

"No," answered the child politely. "Susan is at Barnard studying abnormal psychology, Peter is at Yale studying criminal pathology, Ellsworth is also at Yale studying all kinds of psychoses, and Cynthia is at Johns Hopkins studying dementia praecox. And when they all get through they're going to study Daddy."

A father in suburbia resisted the return-to-religion movement that had invaded the hinterlands. He had managed to study all religions and found none of them acceptable to his own philosophies. He explained this to the zealous clergyman who had called to lecture him on his absence from weekly services. "Then you have no belief in God?" asked the shocked cleric.

"I didn't say that," corrected the searcher. "I do believe in God. It is other things I question."

The clergyman grew stern. "What will you tell Him on that inevitable day when He asks what denominational faction you adhered to?" he asked. "And what will you tell him of your family? Where did they belong?"

"I suppose," the man shrugged, "that I'll tell Him we were Seventh Day Absentists."

Automobiles

What a lucky thing the wheel was invented before the automobile; otherwise, can you imagine the awful screeching?

SAMUEL HOFFENSTEIN

Economists classify the automobile as the key to an affluent society. Like many other professional positives, this too is naturally wrong. When one considers the primary method of purchase, the automobile is actually a symbol of serfdom. It was William Shakespeare who peered into the future to forecast the objective of those thirty-six easy car payments when he wrote: ". . . . to grace in captive bonds his chariot wheels."

Sixty years ago magazines and newspapers carried scathing articles dealing with the dangers of recklessness, hand-holding, curb-jumping, impetuous contest racing between automobiles on city streets, and warnings on the future as planned by designers of high-octane gasoline and super-speed engines. However, there was one marked difference. It was not danger to pedestrians that caused them concern, but the terrible injuries automobilists were sustaining when physically attacking each other over the right of way.

Parents complained of scandalous danger to their children, fearing not for their bodies but for their minds. They said automobilists, in their topless cars, were resorting to questionable practices —such as sitting closely huddled with their female passengers. They yearned for automobiles with tops, so that children might not be defiled by the indecorous language of drivers—especially when they collided.

The use of the automobile to encourage the immoral practice of "Elopement à la Gasoline" was decried. Cartoonists prophetically anticipated traffic jams on Fifth Avenue, and one publication ran a cartoon showing a gentleman interviewing an applicant for the position of chauffeur. The question put to the driver: "Got a good aim?"

But the most poignant plea came from the social historians. They despaired for the hapless American Indian. In the event of another uprising, they said, the poor Indian would not have a chance against mechanized cavalry on wheels. They needn't have worried. The same humanitarian instincts that moved industry to supply the Indians with guns would have bestirred the manufacturers' sense of fair play and the redskins would have gotten their cars. It was the sporting thing to do. . . .

A careful driver is one who honks his horn when he goes through a red light.

HENRY MORGAN

A great deal has been said and written concerning the New York City taxicab driver, with much verbal editorializing being unprintable. A magazine editor, however, once witnessed this incident. While driving through New York City's poverty-ridden waterfront section, an Irish hack driver was signaled by a poorly dressed, tiny woman of obviously wretched circumstances. When he pulled to the curb she hobbled toward him, one wrinkled hand clutching a torn head shawl tightly and the other extended tremblingly until it gave her support against the cab's door. "I understand you charge fifteen cents for the first quarter mile," she said softly.

"Yer right," the cabbie replied.

"I have to go to Dudley Hospital, my grandchild is there, I just found out. It's three long blocks to the subway, and it's very hard for me to walk up and down the steps. I was thinking, I have fifteen cents, but I was wondering if it isn't more than that from here."

"I should say not," the driver lied. The distance was five miles. "Fer fifteen cents ye kin go there'n back."

"Good, good," the tiny wizened woman said gratefully. "Would you please help me in? I'm very old, you know."

"Begorrah, lady," the cabbie said as he stepped out to assist her, "no matter what age ye are, ye don't look it." She leaned back proudly in her seat—and away they went.

A 1901 periodical contains a precursor of things to come: A reckless automobilist, garbed in the habit of goggles, white coat, and cap, tore down the street at a thoughtless and dangerous speed of twenty-five miles per hour. He knocked a man down, drove all four wheels over his prostrate form, and after going fifteen yards further, shouted: "Look out!!"

The man sat up and called: "Why? You coming back?"

The Russians will never invade us. There's no place to park.

An old-timer is one who remembers when it cost more to run a car than to park it. (1931)

Sign in a modern car-washing establishment:
"Automobiles washed, $1. Volkswagens dunked, 50¢."

A club of foreign car enthusiasts has asked the public's co-operation in not throwing chewing gum on the street. Their cars get stuck on it.

Problems connected with drunken driving appear insoluble. The drunkometer was looked upon as a deterrent for its psychological impact. It was felt that motorists would refrain from imbibing, as their denials could easily be refuted when they took a drunkometer test. But the plan passed into limbo when it was found that the majority of drivers were too drunk to take it.

A woman showed noble judgment when she recently returned her driver's license to a motor vehicle bureau. She said she was doing it because all the fun had gone out of driving. There were too many inexperienced pedestrians.

A diminutive schoolteacher, asked by a judge which part of her anatomy was damaged by contact with a foreign car, modestly replied: "If I wore a license plate, your honor, it would have been badly damaged."

An Episcopalian clergyman found that he was late for a testimonial dinner at which he was to be the guest of honor. He rushed out the door, hailed a passing taxicab, and told the driver: "I must get to the Waldorf-Astoria in five minutes. Drive as fast as you can. Don't stop for lights. Overlook the 'No Turn' signs. Drive on the left if you have to. I don't care what chances you take. I'll be responsible."

The cab shot away. On one street they leaped the sidewalk to avoid a traffic jam. On another they drove two blocks against the arrows. The driver went through five traffic lights and six safety zones, turning left into Broadway from a street where turns were not allowed. A pursuing patrol car finally caught up and forced the cab to one side. But the driver stepped on the gas and leaped away, until, after another quarter-mile chase, the patrol car came abreast and the patrolman, in a fine Irish brogue, yelled: "Stop! Stop, I say, or I'll plug the beegeezis out of every tire ya got!" The driver pulled to the side, and the patrolman stormed over. "Git outta yer seat, yer lunkheaded weasel," he roared, "and let's have yer license and ownership."

The minister stepped out instead, and the policeman gulped as he saw the liturgical garment, with choker and vest. "Beggin' yer pahdon, father," the officer said, removing his hat. "I hailed ye down so's I could warn the laddie to be careful when he gits three blocks further down. There's a very mean Protestant cop's got the duty, and ye might git pinched."

Many small companies have attempted to penetrate the automotive monopoly, with most having to give up the fight. On New York's clogged Canal Street a man driving one of these ill-fated products, chose to ignore the cacophony of horns behind him. An angry cop stalked over and barked: "Can't you move any faster?"

"I can," admitted the man. "But who'll be responsible for the car?"

A lady of means was piloting a Rolls Royce down Fifth Avenue when she halted near a traffic cop and started to give a confusing series of turn signals. First the arm shot skyward, then down, then it slithered around the mirror with pinkie in one direction and thumb in another. Next followed a series of pumping gestures in a north, south, east, west, and heavenly direction.

"Lady," the cop finally said, disgustedly. "I don't know whether yer pickin' cherries, pumpin' water, milkin' cows or heiling Hitlers —but this can't be the place fer it."

The woman's lips puckered as she fought to hold back a tear, and in a hurt tone she replied: "The same kind of confusion overcame me in France, and I must say you New York patrolmen could take a lesson from them."

"And what did the gendarme do, lady?" the cop asked facetiously.

"Well," she pouted, "if you *must* know. He kissed my hand."

It is difficult to say whether the driver confuses the pedestrian or the pedestrian confuses the driver. A woman knocked down a man, then looked out the window and said: "Don't you dare say what you're thinking. I've been driving nine years."

"You got nothing on me, lady," the man replied. "I been walking for sixty."

Qualms of conscience often overtake a hit-run driver, but sometimes, when he panics, the steadying influence of a compassionate rider will alter the situation. Such was the case when a teen-ager left the scene. A block from the point of contact his girl friend looked back and coaxed: "Ellery, I just saw the leg move. You can't let the poor man suffer. Turn around and hit him again."

A car manufacturer may have his new models designed by Dali —to confuse the witnesses.

The first thing that strikes a visitor in Paris is a taxi.

People will try anything if the price is right. A charity bazaar in New York raffled off a traffic ticket.

"Every city car that passes through here breaks the law by beating the speed limit. Now you've got to do something and do it fast," shouted an angry group at the small town mayor.

"Don't you worry now," the mayor said confidently. 'I'll raise the speed limit to 150. Let's see 'em beat that."

A green stamp fanatic in suburbia made her husband drive six miles out of his way that she might buy a pound of tomatoes at a store featuring a particular color stamp she needed to complete her fiftieth book. When they got back to the car, having completed the purchase, a traffic summons for a parking violation was stuck on the windshield. The husband, already questioning his own sanity, angrily removed it, and was about to tear it to bits when his wife stopped him. "Save the ticket, honey," she soothed. "That number might win a prize."

A standard intelligence quotient exam for six year olds asks this question: "What would you do if you owned a real automobile?" Twenty per cent of the kids answer: "I'd drive it."

"No, Henry, absolutely not," protested the co-ed in the drive-in-theater. "I won't allow you to do that in the car."
"Why?"
"Because you only have a learner's permit."

Remember the good old days when a woman's job was only to sit in the back and smile at cops?

"What would you do if the driver in the car ahead signaled a left turn?"
"Man or woman?"

"I'm losing my eyesight," said the high school boy. "An old woman, a middle-aged woman, four children, and a cop walked in front of my car today—and I didn't hit one of 'em."

Epitaph in an old English cemetery:
   Here lies Reverend Zekiel Bone
   Met his death in a safety zone.

Air travel will be much safer when they eliminate the automobile ride between the city and the airport.

"Tell me, reverend," said a sarcastic non-believer. "Do you honestly feel you've found the chain to eternal life."
"Not the whole chain, my boy," replied the cleric. "But I'm certain of one of the links."
"What's that?"
"Always look both ways on a one-way street."

"Did you have to pay anything to that man you ran over last week?"
"No, he happened to be a relative of my husband's, fortunately."

The eternal feuding between the legal and medical professions carries over into the field of mechanics. "What lawyers don't know about driving cars would fill what their profession cynically calls a brief," chided a doctor.

To which a lawyer replied: "And what doctors don't know about driving a car would fill what their profession laughingly calls a hospital."

As part of an examination on political office, an elementary schoolgirl was asked: "What was Lincoln?"
She answered: "A Ford with whiskers."

A turn of the century cartoon shows an automobile disappearing down the road in a cloud of dust, and a farmer scratching his head as he looks after it. The caption reads: "Them horses must 'a' bin goin' mighty fast when they broke loose from that carriage."

Two soldiers were indignant when a police officer stopped their jeep. "What'd we do?" one asked.
"Nothing," said the cop. "I just thought there was something wrong. You were only going ninety."

"I never knew profanity was so prevalent until I bought a car," said the country doctor.
"Do you hear much of it?"
"Yes," the doctor replied. "From everyone I hit."

"We'll have to skip the drive-in movie," a high school boy told his date. "Father won't let me have the car any more. He found out about the accident."
"How?"
"Remember the man we hit?"
"Yes."
"That was Father."

The Greatest Laughs of All Time

In America the automobile has become a big hit—and they aim it pretty good in Europe too.

Rules of the road call for a gentleman to allow a lady driver half of the road. It will be a lot easier once we find out which half they want. (1909)

Science, Transportation, and Progress

What we call progress is the exchange of one nuisance for another.

HAVELOCK ELLIS

Of all unsung heroes, those for whom the fewest melodies have been composed are the men of science. Having battled the small minds of the centuries they are content to carry on their experiments behind a shield of anonymity. Once their latest calculations have proven accurate they rarely seek their just financial deserts, but are satisfied to give patent privileges to those adept at marketing, while they return to the plodding rigors of research. That is why they are called mad scientists.

It should be noted, however, that the pioneers of progress were not entirely without tribute. In a cemetery outside of Paris the memory of a nineteenth-century wizard was kept alive by the symbol of his inventive genius: a lamp, which burned perpetually over his grave. On the headstone was this inscription:

"Here lies Pierre Fournier, inventor of the everlast lamp, which consumes only one centime's worth of oil an hour. He was a good father, a devoted son, and a cherished husband. His eternally mourning widow continues his business on the Rue Aux Trois. Goods sent to all parts of the city. Do not mistake the opposite shop for this."

171

For accuracy in the science of weather predicting the name of Clough is unsurpassed. Born in the mid sixteen hundreds, he made his reputation not only by foreseeing atmospheric conditions but by predicting popular reactions to climate. His infallibility can be traced to the use of a theory currently employed in our missile program—the margin for error. An excerpt from Clough's *Almanack* for the year 1702 illustrates his amazing talent:

"Perhaps from the 15th to the 23rd of January it will be very cold weather if it frese by the fire-side or on the sunny side of a fense at noon."

"For April, perhaps wet weather, if it Rains; now fair weather if the sun-shines; and windy or calm."

Clough capped his oracle by alerting the mercantile trade this way: "If now the weather do prove fair, People to Cambridge do repair."

There are no records extant of his ability with hurricanes, but it is a certainty that perhaps he was good at it, if he could guess them accurately, provided they came out as he said.

A man in Kentucky had four wives go off and leave him. The fifth he swapped for an old shotgun; now he has something that won't go off.

NINETEENTH-CENTURY REPORT

When the first American space ship landed on the moon a spaceman volunteered to reconnoiter the surrounding terrain. After some moments he reported by intercom that a strange creature, with a head shaped like a corkscrew, was heading towards him. "I'm going to blast him with my atomizer-gun," the spaceman shouted.

"No, don't do that," his commanding officer ordered. "Anything with a head like a corkscrew can't be bringing bad news."

First message sent to a deep-sea diver;
"Come up quick. The ship is sinking."

A Mississippi riverboat pilot was trying to calm a frightened woman making her first excursion. "Worry not, madam," he soothed. "I know every rock from here to the end of the line." Just then the boat struck a sharp object. "And that's one of 'em," he concluded.

A student-scientist has come up with a remarkable theory on the evolution of the mushroom. He submits that since the mushroom grows in damp places it is only natural that its shape be that of an umbrella.

If my theory of relativity is proven successful, Germany will claim me as a German and France will declare that I am a citizen of the world. Should my theory prove untrue, France will say that I am a German and Germany will declare that I am a Jew.

ALBERT EINSTEIN

With the world acutely aware that time may be running out, a story several hundred years old, and dealing with another instance of time dissipating itself, may be in order.

In a German village was installed a giant clock, to chime the hour and attract attention. The mayor was proud of this innovation and after some years the sound of the clock striking became imbedded into the subconscious.

One night the clock broke while striking midnight. The chimes continued to peel forth, and the mayor, in his sleep, counted each stroke until it reached thirteen; then he sprang up in bed, shook his wife, and shouted: "Greta, wake up! It's later than I ever knew it to be."

In the 1920s a flyer touring Europe reported he heard a rattling sound that indicated the plane's nuts and bolts were loose. Then he flew over Scotland and everything tightened up.

A gentleman drove his wife to the airport, where she boarded a jet plane to California. He then got stuck in New York City traffic, reaching home in time to accept a telegram that read: "Arrived safely. Love, Lulu."

There were twenty million fewer passengers riding the New York subways last year—and nobody noticed the difference.

The modern version of the "sick" style of humor appears to have originated in a railroad investigation. A man had been found dead on the tracks of a line by a trackwalker. The railroad employee, in the course of an ensuing investigation, was asked if the victim was a total stranger. "No, sir," the trackwalker said. "His legs were entirely gone, so I would say he was a partial stranger."

A British scientist spent years on a project, supported by a handsome grant. All of his labors, and all of his expenses, culminated in a report that man would eventually be born without teeth. As his society prepared to release this startling theory the plan was scuttled by a less erudite colleague, who pointed out that men were already born that way.

Edison did not invent the first talking machine. He invented the first one that could be turned off.

The Orson Welles radio drama about a Martian invasion was not the first incident wherein that medium caused a furore. The first time bagpipe music was broadcast in America two hundred people returned their sets to the mnaufacturer as being faulty, scores of people phoned the police department to report a terrible murder—and ten music lovers committed suicide.

It is said that two Indians were communicating with one another via smoke signal when the first experimental atomic explosion was ignited successfully at Los Alamos. As the mushroom cloud rose higher and higher, one of them remarked: "Gee, I wish I'd said that."

This is the machine age. The only thing people do by hand is scratch themselves.

JOE LAURIE, JR.

The modern home is going to be equipped with the latest in domestic kitchen appliances. You press a button and it lights the gas by rubbing two sticks together.

Science has discovered it is the lower part of the face that gives away one's thoughts, not the eyes. This is especially true when one opens the lower part of the face.

Television is turning out to be the most educational invention. Everytime a set is turned on folks rush for a book.

A professor at a technical college was surprised when his best pupil, having a choice of working with a railroad company or working with an atomic laboratory, chose the railroad company. He asked the young man to explain his choice.

"It's this way, sir," the student replied. "In a collision, there you are. But in an explosion, where are you?"

Polar exploration held the imagination of the public during the hectic twenties and early thirties. A shoe manufacturer, having besieged an explorer for a testimonial, received this citation: "They were the best boots I ever ate on a polar expedition."

The Society for Pharmaceutical Scientific Research is planning a special award to commemorate the memory of the man who invented the club sandwich.

GREGORY NUNN

The good state of Georgia contributed to Americana with this early story. A traveler was waiting for a train in a small town. Three hours passed, but no train appeared. He was about to negotiate for a horse to continue his travels when the station agent advised him not to trouble, the train would be along soon.

"How can you tell?" the traveler asked.

"I'm pretty certain of it," the station agent said. "Here comes the conductor's dog now."

When the streets of New York were electrified a prominent banker, who opposed the scheme as improbable, confessed to a society matron, "I am ashamed of my backwardness when it comes to modern science. Take this electric light, for instance. I haven't the slightest idea of how it works."

"It's very simple," the woman replied patronizingly. "You just press a button and the light comes on. Really, that's all there is to it."

In the twenties, when the railroads were besieged with numerous lawsuits as the result of passengers claiming injuries, they ordered all employees to file elaborate reports. Following a minor accident a porter submitted this detail: "There wuz no bones broken in the wreck and only one gentleman appeared to be hurt. I think it wuz his heart. He sat down by a leaking suitcase and shed tears."

A commuter complained to a conductor of the rail line's service. "If you don't like it, why don't you get out and walk?" the conductor said.

"I would," the commuter replied. "But I'm not expected home till the train arrives."

An Irish immigrant obtained a job as porter at the Palomar Observatory. His first night on the job he was fascinated by a scientist peering through the huge telescope. As the astronomer adjusted the lever a star fell. "Man aloive," the astounded Irishman exclaimed. "Yer a foine shot."

The Wright brothers hold another distinctive record. Following a forced landing in an apple orchard a report of fifty years ago credits them with being the first to climb down a tree without first having to climb up.

The plight of the Arab was illustrated some years ago during a severe drought. As part of America's aid to underprivileged nations this country dispatched a crew of top scientists to probe the desert wastelands of Transjordan in an effort to find untapped water supplies. After weeks of extensive digging their mission failed and they sent this report to the king:

"We regret, Abdullah, to report failure of our mission. We have dug the far reaches of your kingdom and were unable to locate a drop of water. Only oil."

A visitor to suburbia rushed to a station that rendered a hypothetical service. It was deserted. The man looked about, and finally a native wandered by. "Hey, when's the next train out of here?" the visitor called.

The native strolled over, scrutinized the rails, and said: "Looks like you just missed it."

"How can you tell?" the visitor asked.

"'Cause," said the native, "them tall weeds between the tracks is all flattened out."

All progress is based upon a universal innate desire on the part of every organism to live beyond its income.

SAMUEL BUTLER

As the result of his ride on a southern railway, Artemus Ward had this suggestion to make regarding the cow-catcher.

"It occurred to me it would be well to detach the cow-catcher from the front of the engine and hitch it to the rear of the train. For, you see, we are not liable to overtake a cow—but what's to prevent a cow strolling into a car and biting a passenger?"

"Is this a fast train?" an 1890 commuter asked the conductor.
"Yes, it is," he was told.

177

"I thought so," he replied. "Would you mind getting out and seeing what it is fast to."

The most popular form of humor on transportation systems is the slow train joke. Recently exhumed and applied to the commuter situation is the story of a woman who felt her labor pains while riding a suburban service. A great deal of fuss ensued, and when it was over the trainman said to her, "Young woman, you had no right getting on this train knowing you were in that condition."

"My good man," she replied. "I'll have you know that when I got on this train I was not in that condition."

A Scotsman paid his penny for a ferryboat ride, early in the nineteenth century. As the boat docked a diver, experimenting with August Siebe's new diving suit, came up. The Scotsman stared open-mouthed, and said: "If I'd known that I'd' a' walked over m'self."

In the late nineteenth century scientists in America were debating the relative merits of the senses. During one debate, in which effective arguments were heard favoring the sense of smell as superior to the sense of taste, all technological studies seemed to bear out the notion.

But scientists can be practical men, even in the face of science. One such expert, realizing his bookish arguments were futile, cast them aside and called for a hot whisky punch. He carried the decision for the negative when he drank it down, then turned to the opposition and said: "Now, gentlemen, smell it."

I never think of the future, it comes soon enough.

ALBERT EINSTEIN

An archaeologist was lecturing at a university when a student, apparently alarmed by one of his conclusions, rose and asked:

"Would you repeat that figure you gave when you predicted the end of the world?"

"I said in about fifty million years."

"Thank God," the student replied. "I thought you said fifteen million."

"The lie detector is a marvelous invention of science. Have you ever seen one?"

"Seen one? I married one."

Not all mass media experts feared organized pressure groups. In the early days of public relations the railroads were among the first to realize the value of the idea. A protest was forwarded to the p.r. executive at one of the railroads. It was written by a woman and centered around a poster hung in one of the railroad cars, in which a man was portrayed smoking a cigar. Not only was he smoking it, but he appeared to be getting pleasure from it, the woman declared.

The p.r. man sent the following reply:

"Be assured, madam, that the gentlemen in the poster was not contributing to the foul and vile habit of smoking tobacco. What he holds in his hand is merely marijuana."

The early days of the steamship supposedly saw this happen. One of the automatic ocean-going monsters was in trouble. Her decks were awash and she was coming apart in a severe storm. The passengers were alerted to abandon ship, and in a desperate attempt to signal help the captain sent up a host of distress rockets. He was about to order a second barrage when an old woman appeared on the flying deck and said: "Now see here, captain, this is not quite the time to be shooting off fireworks."

One of Bismarck's sternest critics was the scientist Rudolf Virchow. He was a member of the Prussian lower house, and later the Reichstag. A story is told of the time he so angered Bismarck, by outspoken criticisms of the latter's leadership, that the "iron chancellor" challenged him to a duel.

When Bismarck's representatives called on Virchow they found him hard at work on his anti-trichinosis experiments; the disease, at that time, was ravaging Germany.

Virchow accepted the challenge, but as the challenged party demanded the choice of weapons. When this was agreed to he held up two sausages. "One of these sausages is filled with trichinae; it is deadly," he said. "The other is perfectly wholesome. They cannot be told apart. Let His Excellency choose whichever of these he wishes, and eat it. I will eat the other."

The duel did not take place, nor was Virchow ever accused of cowardice.

Two learned professors were debating the debatable science of psychic phonomena. "This business of ectoplasmic ghosts is poppycock," said one. "I don't believe in such nonsense."

"Don't you?" said the other—and disappeared.

Science does not deny God, she goes one better. She makes him unnecessary.

FREETHINKERS OF LIEGE, 1865

Science is always wrong—it never solves a problem without creating ten more.

GEORGE BERNARD SHAW

At Moscow University the great legendary scientist, professor Vladik Krumski, performs his feats of wizardry. It is said that much of the Soviet success with their rocket launchings stems from his infallible weather predictions. He is never wrong.

Just before the Russians launched their most spectacular space probe they checked weather conditions as carefully as possible. The great Krumski was home with a virus but his assistants were certain of their calculations. The mighty rocket ship stood on the launching pad ready to go. The count-down had already started and everybody was tense, when the phong rang. "Stop the launching," Krumski's voice barked from the other end of the line. "It's going to rain."

"How can you be so positive, comrade?" a general asked. "No question about it," Krumski retorted. "My corns hurt."

On a farm road a henpecked husband was walking ahead of his wife when the great bomb fell, demolishing the world and leaving only this one couple alive. The man woke in a ditch and saw his wife standing over him. "Look, Elsie," he said, "next time you hit me like that I'm really gonna get angry."

Will Rogers, when asked to introduce a daring aviator who was continually planning a daring flight, and just as regularly postponing it, obliged in this manner: "Ladies and gentlemen, I would like to introduce that intrepid aviator, here today and here tomorrow——"

In the early days of the railroad the companies made it a policy to reimburse farmers for cattle killed on the line. As a consequence it appeared that only the best heads were attracted to the steel, if the financial claims of certain Kentucky farmers were the rule. After studying reports covering this situation, one railroad executive said: "I have reached the conclusion that nothing in Kentucky so improves livestock as crossing it with a locomotive."

When the giant railroads were absorbing the smaller lines throughout the country, one board chairman was amazed to find he had acquired a line with a perfect safety record. He called the president of the line to him and asked how it happened.

"Sir," said the president. "A collision on my line is impossible."

"Impossible is a big word," the chairman warned.

"In our case it is the truth," the president said proudly. "We only have one train."

The Greatest Laughs of All Time

Since I moved to the suburbs I found out the purpose of those railroad timetables. Without them there would be no way of knowing how late your train is.

GREGORY NUNN

Order of the Bath: First it's too cold, then it's too hot. Then you forgot the towel, next you slip on the soap—and finally the telephone rings.

An exploration team, penetrating the darkest area of Africa, reported finding a tribe of people that did not possess a single instrument of warfare. It is the first indication that there is still a part of the world that uncivilized.

A southern senator, voting against a bill to aid education, argued that the whole thing is a waste. "Science makes it impractical," he said. "Why, I once spent two years learnin' how to read; then they invented talkin' pictures and made the whole thing unnecessary."

One man's telephone is another man's wrong number.

Automation has deprived the telephone subscriber of the pleasure of speaking to the operator when he wants a number. Back in the days when this mechanical barrier did not exist, it was quite common to be misunderstood by the operator, and consequently a number of wrong connections would ensue. One subscriber, after undergoing the experience several times, shouted into his phone, "Am I crazy or are you?"
"Sorry, sir," the operator replied. "We do not supply that information."

Unquestionably, there is progress. The average American now pays twice as much in taxes as he formerly got in wages.

H. L. MENCKEN

Science, Transportation, and Progress

In the year 2100 space travel had become less bothersome than commuting. A visitor to Venus was strolling along the avenue when he saw a Venusian place a coin in what appeared to be a cigarette machine, and out popped a baby. The Venusian inserted another coin and out came another baby.

"Hey," called the visitor, "what kind of a gadget is that?"

"This is our baby machine," the native replied. "Don't you make babies the same way on Earth?"

"Are you insane?" challenged the Earthling. He then gave a graphic description of how babies were conceived on Earth.

"Oh," said the Venusian. "That's how we make trucks up here."

Food and Restaurants

Whenever cannibals are on the brink of starvation, Heaven, in its infinite mercy, sends them a nice plump missionary.

OSCAR WILDE

The fall and rise of a certain food product is as exciting as any conquest-over-tribulation story handed us by history. "Abstain from beans!" When Plutarch set aside his work on the great biographies to issue that warning the bean reached the nadir of its existence. Plutarch was not antibean without cause, for the seed of the pod had become involved with politicians and politics. It had become the instrument of the ballot, and instead of voting by straw the Greeks were voting by bean. The poll-takers of that day would carry two boxes with them and into one the citizenry would cast a bean to indicate their choice. The kind of bean used would depend upon the issue; for example, in expressing their opinions on a health bill they used kidney beans. It was this practice which led to the expression "You're full of beans," meaning a politican with a lot of popularity.

And when the masses stormed the palaces of old to demand their rights it was common practice for emperors to say "I'll give 'em beans." Which meant he would give them the right to vote.

In centuries that followed the bean became an article of scorn.

Thus we find Milton saying: "Convey each man his bean, or ballot, into the box." And Turner: "Beanes are harde of digestion and make troblesum dreams." In describing the lot of 1562 Britain one philosopher wrote: "Alwaie the bygger eateth the beane." From the standpoint of collective summation these would indicate that the people, instead of using the ballot, were eating it, and getting indigestion.

But now fate lent a hand. The ruling class, having done away with the right to vote, found itself with stacks of beans and no elections. Being frugal people they decided to give it to sailors as food. Immediately came an Admiralty report indicating a bean diet made the men "full of high spirits and energy." Therein lies an unsung clue to the defeat of the Spanish Armada.

Eventually the bean worked its way to this country, across the deltas of the Mississippi and the mountain ranges of the frontier, pausing momentarily in the Windy City before turning eastward. The rest we know. It was able to reach the heights of critical acceptance through its close identification with New England culture, and particularly that of the city of Boston. From then on everything was honey and roses, for the bean. . . .

British fondness for tea precludes a knowledge of other beverages. An American visiting London entered a tea shoppe and ordered coffee. It was served in a pot holding four measured cups. After downing the contents of one pot he ordered another, then another, and finally when he had called for his fourth the waiter said: "My word, sir, you most assuredly are fond of that brew."

"You bet I am," the American replied. "Or else I wouldn't be drinking so much water in order to get a little coffee."

"You're a beast," the bride wept. "I have never heard of anyone being so cruel. The way you treat me anybody visiting us would think I was the cook."

"Not if they stayed for dinner," the groom said.

Accidents will happen; that's why there are so many different kinds of croquettes.

God sends meat—the devil sends cooks.

CHARLES VI

A gentleman entered an exclusive restaurant on Thanksgiving Day and ordered a turkey sandwich. "Sorry, sir," the waiter said. "We are all out of turkey."

The man scowled and said: "Out of turkey on Thanksgiving? Well, then, bring me a chicken sandwich."

"Your request is redundant," the waiter frowned back. "If we had chicken, wouldn't I have brought you a turkey sandwich?"

> He may live without books—what is knowledge but grieving?
> He may live without hope—what is hope but deceiving?
> He may live without love—what is passion but pining?
> But where is the man that can live without dining?

OWEN MEREDITH

A Broadway playwright developed a Lincoln phobia. At a Fifty-first Street restaurant he pointed disdainfully to his cup and saucer, gestured at the waiter, and repeated the great emancipator's line: "Waiter, if this stuff is tea bring me coffee, and if it is coffee bring me tea."

"Okay," the waiter replied. "But, just for your own information, you're drinking cocoa."

George Bernard Shaw was at a loss for words but once in his lifetime. This took place when a publisher's messenger called at dinnertime, stared dumbfoundedly at the great man's vegetable plate, and asked: "Sir: Have you just finished or are you just starting?"

Food and Restaurants

A vacationer in New York bragged of an exceptionally good restaurant to other members of his excursion and organized a party the following evening to prove his point. When the members of the party ordered, the main course was microscopic, and the angry organizer sent for the manager. "My good man," he told the manager. "Yesterday I ate here and the chops were twice as thick, the garnishing twice as large, and the service four times as good."

"True," the manager agreed. "But yesterday you were seated near the window."

An eighteenth-century anecdote tells of the man who came to dinner, late. "You are always late to my dinners," complained the host.

"Ah, yes," the guest replied. "But I make up for it by leaving early."

John Barrymore never succeeded in his search for a stew that would give him heartburn immediately, instead of at three o'clock in the morning.

A Washington congressman was coarse in berating a waiter in one of the capital's good restaurants. The waiter listened patiently and when the tirade was over, he replied: "Excellency, my position of servitude forbids me to repudiate your remarks. But if it ever came to a choice of weapons, I would pick grammar."

The nineteenth-century English essayist, William Morris, always took his meals at the Eiffel Tower restaurant when in Paris. A friend once commented to him: "You must like the Tower very much to dine here so often."

"Like it?" Morris jeered. "It's the only place in Paris where I can avoid seeing the damned thing."

An English missionary, placed in a boiling pot by his captors, thought one of them looked familiar. "I say, old chap," he remarked as the water started to boil. "Haven't we met somewhere?"

"Yes," the cannibal replied. "We were in the same class at Oxford."

"What?" the missionary shouted with disbelief. "An Oxonian. And you still eat your fellow man?"

"Yes," the savage acknowledged. "But now I use a knife and fork."

A family of first generation Americans was taking its evening meal when a neighbor appeared, disregarded the dinner protocol, and launched into meaningless chatter. The grandfather of the group, unable to restrain himself, said: "Please, I am trying to eat in peace. And you come in every night and talk, talk, talk, talk. Can't you please, one night maybe, not talk?"

One of the younger members, a staunch defender of democratic tenets, reminded the old man: "The Constitution of the United States of America guarantees her the right to talk all she wants."

"I know, my child," Grandfather replied. "But the United States of America has a constitution that can stand it. Mine can't."

Although Frémont lost the 1856 presidential election to James Buchanan, out of the Republican wreckage emerged one of the greatest speakers of American history. Chauncey Depew took the stump for Frémont, and went on to gain possession of the after dinner rostrum. On one occasion Depew received the following introduction from a toastmaster: "The guest of honor is a man who needs no introduction. All you have to do is open his mouth, put a dinner inside, and out comes a speech."

Depew responded thus: "My good friend the toastmaster has told you what a wonderful man I am, that all you have to do is open my mouth, put in a dinner, and out comes a speech. I would like to tell you what a wonderful man *he* is. All you have to do is open *anybody's* mouth, put in *his* speech, and out comes *everybody's* dinner."

Depew stories were legion. A minister told how he responded to a feeble knock on his door one night and upon opening it beheld a half frozen tramp. The man pleaded for a meal, and the clergyman carefully prepared a platter, set it in front of the beggar, then bowed his head to pray. When the clergyman looked up he saw that the man had proceeded to devour the food without ceremony. "My dear fellow," interjected the minister, "don't you say something before dining?"

"I'm just like Chauncey Depew," the tramp replied. "We both does our best talkin' after we've et."

Abraham Lincoln, when served his first dish of ice cream, is reported to have said: "Waiter, it is not my intention to slander this hotel, but this here pudding is froze."

The modern cookbook has a blank space in the back—where you list the phone number of the nearest delicatessen.

The tomato herring is an odd species of fish, lurking in cans, and emerging only when unexpected company arrives.

An ancient tablet, *c.* 4000 B.C., tells of a mystic who vowed to learn the secret of life-without-food. Just as he was learning to live without eating—he died.

Life of woman is like milk, butter, and cheese. A girl is like milk, a woman like butter, and an old woman like cheese. All three may be excellent in their kind.

ANCIENT TEUTONIC PROVERB

Epitaph for a rich doctor:
> Here lies a physic, wan and pallid
> Made his chinks from potato salad. . . .

An item dealing with a jail break of the thirties relates that the ring leader confessed. He recalled that his wife sent him a cake with a file concealed, but he was not sure whether he had eaten the cake and sawed his way out with the file, or eaten the file and sawed his way out with the cake.

George Bernard Shaw, a stanch vegetarian, refused to attend a gala testimonial because the bill of fare was a vegetarian menu. He said: "The thought of two thousand people crunching celery at the same time horrified me."

"Waiter," said the surprised customer as he examined his check. "What's this eight dollars for?"

"For the chopped liver sandwich, sir."

"Yeah?" the customer nodded. "Who's liver was it? Rockefeller's?"

"Darling, how did you like the health salad?"

"It was great. Did you buy it yourself?"

It is inevitable that there must always be overzealous faddists to disturb the peace of the tired businessman who is minding his own business and getting a little paunchy around the waist.

"Never been sick a day in my life," said one health addict, throwing his chest out and slapping his flat waist. "Proper diet, fellas, right food, none of that rich, greasy stuff, no, sir." He jabbed the stomach of a relaxing neighbor and the man doubled over. "Putting it on, boy, watch it now." The picture of too damned much health went on. "Brothers, lemme tell you, from the time I was out of school to the time I entered the high flying forties, twenty years, I been leading the simple life. No sissfied delicacies, turning in early, no extravagances. Every day, summer and winter, in the sack at nine and up at five. Work from eight to one and then I grabbed me a quick lunch—plain, nothing fancy mind you—and then a hour's exercise. Then——"

"Excuse me, sir," interrupted the bartender. "What were you in for?"

"Was yours ham and eggs or ham and beans, sir?"
"Why?"
"'Cause we're all out of ham."

Lunchtime for sum folks, but jes' twelve a'clock for me.
SHARECROPPERS'S DIRGE

Society is composed of two great classes—those who have more dinners than appetite, and those who have more appetite than dinners.
NICHOLAS CHAMFORT

The artistic atmosphere is everywhere. Even my cook cannot escape it. She came into the studio today and said: "About the potatoes for lunch, sir; will you have them in the jockets or in the nood?"
JAMES MONTGOMERY FLAGG

When a noted Arctic explorer of the 1880s was proposed for a meritorious award, one of his contemporaries remarked, "He never commanded more than ten men, and he ate three of them."

"Waiter, one of this chicken's legs is shorter than the other."
"You gonna eat the chicken or rumba with it?"

"I won't eat such food. You'd better fetch the manager."
"That's no good, sir. He won't eat it either."

I often wondered why the English were tea drinkers—until I tasted their coffee.

If you want to eat well in England, eat three breakfasts.
SOMERSET MAUGHAM

The soup is never hot enough if the waiter can keep his thumb in it.

WILLIAM COLLIER

A husband, doing the shopping for his wife, paid eighty cents for a pound of apples, handed the clerk two singles, and started out the door. "You forgot your change, sir," the clerk called.

"Keep it," the man replied. "I stepped on a grape when I came in."

"Waiter!!" shouted an irate customer. "I can't tell whether this is coffee or tea. It tastes like benzine."

"If it tastes like benzine then it positively is coffee," the waiter said. "Our tea tastes like turpentine."

European reaction to American tourists, during the fifties and sixties, is no different than it was after World War I. A British report of forty years ago handles the usual problem with the usual exaggeration. "Hey, gasoong," a man shouted as a party entered the Claridge. "We want the swellest feed in the joint, toot sweet. And listen, gasoong, bring a couple of the most expensive quarts of champagne you got along with the eats—and the tooter the sweeter. We're Americans, see."

"Yes, sir." The waiter bowed politely. "I'll warn the other guests."

Marriage

As to marriage or celibacy, let a man take which course he will, he is sure to repent.

SOCRATES

"Life contains but two tragedies. One is not to get your heart's desire; the other is to get it." In choosing mates the greatest minds of the ages have bungled and had to live their days in quarrel. Xantippe, the wife of Socrates, became proverbial for her peevishness and ill humor. One day, when her invective got no reaction, she emptied a vessel of dirty water on the great teacher's head. Socrates' only response was philosophical: "After so much thunder I thought we should be apt to have some rain."

Milton, too, blessed himself with a shrew. When a member of the royal family called her a rose, he replied: "I am no judge of colors, and it may be so, for I feel the thorns daily."

The wife of a prominent Englishman constantly declared that upon his death she would dance on his grave; and she repeated the jibe regularly throughout recurring attacks the poor man suffered, including his last. But in expiration he foiled her plan, for contained in his will was an irrevocably legal codicil directing that his body be buried at sea. It is not by chance that the *Talmud* contains the following warning: "When a scholar goes out in search of a bride he should take an ignoramus along with him as an expert. . . ."

History has recorded many violent reactions in the game of love, but from the standpoint of objectivity, considering the personalities involved, and excluding bloodshed, the corrosive Alexander Pope captures the laurels. What might have stimulated his rancor in his ill-fated pursuit of Lady Montagu was the nature of the man who won, for there was some question as to Hervey's gender. When the contest was ended Pope labeled Hervey "Lord Fanny," then called him Sporus, after the youth Nero formally took as his wife. To perpetuate the cognomen, he wrote:

> Let Sporus tremble; what, that thing of silk,
> Sporus, that mere white curd of ass's milk?

As for Lady Montagu, she too acknowledged matters when she said: "This world consists of men, women, and Herveys."

But Pope, that classic blabbermouth, wrapped up the matter with this tribute to her ladyship:

> Avidien or his wife, no matter which,
> For him you'd call a dog and her a bitch.

Genius or not, it stands as the only time man had the last word. . . .

Marriage is the process whereby love ripens into vengeance.

> One Queen Artemisa, as old stories tell,
> When depriv'd of her husband she loved so well,
> In respect for the love and affection he'd show'd her,
> She reduc'd him to dust and she drank the powd'r.
> But Queen Netherplace, of a different complexion,
> When call'd on to ord'r the fun'ral direction,
> Would have eat h'r dead lor, on a slend'r pretense,
> Not to show h'r respect, but to save the expense.

ROBERT BURNS

Marriage

An Irish farmer called on his clergyman to seek advice. "It's about my poor friend James," said the man. "His lot does not look well for the future. His wife has been sentenced to five years, but she can get two off for good behavior."

"Tell James not to be worrying aforehand," the cleric advised. "She may not behave herself."

"What did your wife say about your coming in drunk last night?"

"If you have all day, I'll give you a condensed version."

The bride met her best girl friend at a luncheon one week after the wedding. "Weren't you taking an awful chance telling your husband all about your past mistakes on the day you were married?" the friend asked.

"I'll say I was," admitted the bride. "Some of them almost sobered him up."

Bride: My little peach.
Groom: My little plum.
Preacher: I now pronounce you fruit salad.

Mark Twain once debated the question of polygamy with a Mormon acquaintance. The discussion became heated, and finally the Mormon resorted to the Bible for his affirmative clincher. "Can you tell me of a single passage of Scripture wherein polygamy is forbidden?"

"Certainly," Twain replied. "No man can serve two masters."

"But, my dear," protested the henpecked husband. "I've done nothing. You've been talking for an hour and a half and I haven't said a word."

"I know," the wife replied. "But you listen like a wise guy."

Lips, however rosy, must be fed.

OLD SCOTCH PROVERB

195

In days of old a man who was a gentleman by instinct but a tailor by trade managed to amass a fortune. He sold his shop and moved to the country in anticipation of a life of dignified leisure. His wife was something of a shrew, and, like most wives, knew her husband's sensibilities. One of these was a feeling of shame regarding his previous occupation, and she harped on this string until she drove the man insane. Her needle was the word "scissors," and whenever the man seemed to be enjoying a light moment she would whisper it into his ear. Whereupon he would wheedle and storm. She kept his shears hidden; and often, when he was some distance away in the company of other men, she would stand on the balcony and hold up the instrument. One day, while they were strolling through the grounds of the manor, he drew his wife's attention to a forklike delta formed by a passing river. "It's very beautiful," she said. "It reminds me of an open scissors."

With an anguished cry he pushed her into the river. "I will pull you out if you promise never to say that word again," he shrieked at her.

"Scissors!!" she screamed, going beneath the surface. "Scissors!!" she shrieked again as she rose.

The third time she came to the surface thoroughly exhausted and too far gone to speak, but as the waters closed over her she threw up both arms, crossed her fingers—and disappeared.

An immigrant who worked his way up to the biggest fleet of pushcarts in the world knew he was dying and decided to face up to things. He therefore called an attorney to his bedside, and, after ordering his wife not to cry, started to dispose of his worldly possessions.

"My Cadillac with the push-button motorcycle-cop detector I leave to my son Cuthbert."

"Better you should leave it to Sol," Bertha interrupted. "He's a better driver."

"So let it be Sol," he whispered. "My Rolls Royce with the specially constructed Ford hot-rod engine I bequeath to my daughter Shirleen."

"You better give it to your nephew Borack," Bertha again interrupted. "He's a very conservative driver."

"All right, give it to Borack. My twelve-cylinder Volvo I give to my niece Charmagne."

"Personally, I think Celia should get it."

Unable to take more, he raised his head from the pillow and shouted: "Bertha, please, who's dying? You or me?"

Brigham Young forbade the showing of an English play in Salt Lake City, giving as reason: "I won't stand for such a fuss being made about one woman."

A European skeptic called on a rabbi to challenge him on a point the doubter considered an inconsistency in the Bible. "It puzzles me," he said. "When God tested Job, He took everything from him but left him his wife. Why?"

"The answer is simple," said the rabbi. "After God finished testing Job, He returned unto him twice what He had taken away. If Job's wife had also been removed, He would have had to give him two wives. And such a penalty not even God dared to inflict on him."

Judge: How dare you take fourteen wives?
Man: I was trying to find a good one.

"Darling," she called from her room. "Tomorrow is our twenty-fifth wedding anniversary. How about going out and killing a turkey."

"Ah," said the farmer. "Why kill a turkey for a mistake we made twenty-five years ago?"

Of all the calamities that befall mortal man, nothing is worse, or ever will be worse, than woman.

SOPHOCLES

197

A couple went walking in the country. It was a beautiful day, and as they approached a strange village chimes burst forth. "Aren't those lovely chimes?" she remarked.

"I'm sorry, dear," he replied. "What did you say?"

"I said the chimes, they're the most beautiful things I ever heard."

"I'm sorry, I can't hear you."

"The chimes, dear. Those beautiful, exquisite sounds coming from the next village. I have never heard such a gorgeous sound."

"I can't hear you," shouted the husband. "It's those damned chimes."

The two men entered the sumptuous house, and when they were alone one of them asked: "Was that your wife who opened the door?"

"Of course it was," said the other. "You think I would hire a maid that ugly?"

Following the funeral the widow, still in her mourning dress, called at the den of a medium and begged her to raise her departed husband. "Why do you want him so urgently?" asked the mystic.

"Because," she answered. "He died before I finished telling him exactly what I thought of him."

The marriage broker was hastily called aside by the "groom" after being introduced to the prospective bride. "This is ridiculous," he whispered angrily. "She is homely, she is old, her eyes are watery, her teeth are bad, and her skin is wretched."

"You may talk louder," the broker replied. "She's deaf too."

A woman never opens her mouth unless she has nothing to say.

A Hollywood actress appeared at her lawyer's office and instructed him to start divorce proceedings. Aware of the fact that they had been married less than a month, the lawyer said, "Come, now, you don't mean to say you wish to arrange for a divorce while you're still on your honeymoon? When did you quarrel?"

"At the church," the actress said. "He signed the register in letters twice as big as mine."

A woman applying for a legal separation was advised to give her husband a divorce. "What??" she protested. "After living with that bum for fifteen years, *now* I should make him happy?"

A Scottish gravedigger was asked if he ever had difficulty collecting his fee. He said it happened only once, and related the following: "It was when Swann buried his wife. Ye mind her, the un with the guid tongue. I had raised my kep and the mourners had gang, and when Swann stayed ahint. He says, says he, 'What will I be aw'n ye?' 'Siven and six,' says I. 'Tis o'er much', says he. 'Tis not,' says I. 'Tis o'er much in licht sandy soil like that,' says he. 'Sandy soil or hard clay, 'tis siven and six,' says I.

"He hands me a croon. Says I, 'Doon with anouther half-croon or up she comes.'

"And I niver seen a half-croon come sao smart oot o' a farmer's pooch."

Music played at weddings always reminds me of the music played for soldiers before they go off to battle.

HEINRICH HEINE

"You brute, you forgot the anniversary."
"What anniversary?"
"It's one year today that my driver's license was revoked."

Insanity: Grounds for divorce in some states; grounds for marriage in all.

There've been a lot of great war songs. Songs like "Over There" and "Keep the Homes Fires Burning." Then, during World War II, there was "Praise the Lord and Pass the Ammunition" and "Hot Time in the Town of Berlin." But the greatest battle tune ever written is still "The Wedding March."

The mother of the dead man looked accusingly at his wife and said, "I hope you realize he was driven to his grave."

"Certainly," said the widow. "What'd you expect him to do, walk?"

In the solemnity of pronouncing a death sentence the judge was moved to ask the prisoner, "Before your appointment with the electric chair, might there be a last request you wish to make?"

"Yes, your honor," replied the man. "I would like my wife to cook my last meal. Then I'll feel more like dying."

A grocer, while delivering orders in his station wagon, ran down and seriously injured an old lady. The lady sued and was awarded an amount large enough to drive the man out of business. After difficult times he managed to accumulate enough to try again. But a few months after opening his doors he struck an old gentleman with his delivery truck. The gentleman sued and collected big damages, enough to ruin him.

On a peaceful Sunday the grocer was sitting in his living room when his little boy entered and called out, "Father, Father, Mother's been run over by a great big bus."

The grocer's eyes filled with tears, and in a voice trembling with emotion he cried, "Thank the Lord, the luck's changed at last."

He who marries for money—earns it.

HEBREW PROVERB OF ANTIQUITY

Woman's word is never done.

TWENTIETH-CENTURY PROVERB

An early nineteenth-century bit of Americana concerns a farmer on the western frontier whose wife, a kindly woman, suddenly fell ill and died. Despite his advanced age, the man took to carousing and less than a month after the good woman was in her grave took himself another wife; a young flighty saloon girl, with excellent form, face, and questionable reputation.

His neighbors were quite indignant, for the deceased woman was much admired. So the night of the wedding a crowd—men, women, and children—gathered from many parts of the region. They stood underneath the nuptial window and beat on tin cans, pots, tubs, barrels, and blew loud blasts on raucous horns. Some even beat their fists on the side of the house. The farmer took all he could, and finally he threw open the window and shouted down: "For shame that folks come 'round here makin' a racket so soon after a funeral."

A college exam paper stated that "Socrates died from an overdose of wedlock."

"You say you can tell immediately if your husband is lying?" asked a neighbor. "How?"
"If his lips are moving he's lying."

Acrimony: What a divorced man gives his wife.

It is not bad luck to postpone a wedding—if you keep postponing it.

A man's lawyer called to congratulate him on his twenty-fifth wedding anniversary. "Why, you no good louse," the man cursed. "You stinkin' lousy bum."
"B-but I don't understand," muttered the attorney.
"So you don't understand, eh?" The man shook his finger menacingly under the barrister's nose. "Remember, right after I was married? I called you and said I was going to murder my wife. And you talked me out of it. You said I'd get twenty-five years!"
"Yes?"
"Well, tonight I would have been a free man!!"

Hollywood has started a wife-of-the-month club.

There are three kinds of women. Those one cannot live without, those one cannot live with—and those one lives with.

An Atlanta man was granted a divorce when he proved that his wife wasted lots of money trying to open eggs with a can opener.

Nothing annoys a woman more than to have friends drop in unexpectedly and find the house looking as it usually does.

Be kind to your mother-in-law; but pay for her board at some good hotel.

JOSH BILLINGS

At a séance a woman prevailed upon the medium to summon the spirit of her departed husband. After much cajoling, the spirit appeared. "How are you getting along, dear," the widow asked.

"Quite well, quite well," said the ghost. "Far better than ever I did during my thirty married years on earth."

"I'm grateful for that. And remember, darling, I shall soon join you in heaven."

The ghost replied, "I'm not in heaven."

Having missed his train to the suburbs a meek gentleman decided to fortify himself with a drink or two. Finding the liquor a great consolation he started back to the station, but lost his way. While groping about he happened to pass a zoo, and feeling sleepy, he opened the lion's cage and fell asleep with his head comfortably resting on the king of beasts' stomach.

The next day his wife set out to search for him and found him snoring blissfully in the middle of the lion's den. "Come out of there," she shrieked. "Come out, you little coward!"

The grief-stricken man threw himself across the grave and cried bitterly. "My life, how senseless it is! How worthless is everything about me because you are gone. If only you hadn't died, if only fate had not been so cruel as to take you from this world, how different everything would have been."

A clergyman happened by and to sooth the man offered a special prayer for the beloved departed, no charge. "I assume the person lying beneath this pitiable mound of earth was someone of importance to you," said the minister.

"Importance? I'll say it's someone of importance," moaned the man. "It's my wife's first husband."

"Sweetheart," his wife cooed. "Am I as dear to you today, on our tenth anniversary, as I was before we got married?"

"I don't know," he replied. "I didn't keep track of expenses before we got married."

After the wedding the groom took his father aside and asked if there was any advice he could offer. "Yes," said the old man. "Always keep a rabbit's foot in your pocket."

"Why?" asked the astonished groom.

"Because," said the man, "every time your wife sticks her hand in she'll think it's a mouse."

At a séance the curtains suddenly parted, the french doors flew open, and a forceful gust blew into the room. "Mr. Irvington, Mr. Irvington," the medium breathed. "I hear your wife knocking."

"No kidding?" said Irvington. "Who's she knocking now?"

Marriage is grounds for divorce.

Oriental folklore tells of the day following a quarrel over the proper upbringing of children when a husband greeted his wife by saying: "Good morning, mother of asses."

She replied: "Good morning, father of none."

In the early dawn a Scotsman sat by the bedside of his dying wife, her gentle face barely illumined by a flickering candle. "I dinna ken think I ken make it till mornin'," she sighed.

"Aye," heaved the Scotsman. "I dinna think ya ken. But donna worry. Ya ben a gud wife, th' best en all Punfermline. But there be wurk t' be dun and would na ya mind if I made f'r th' barn to get th' night's layin' and tak it ta toon for th' mark't?"

"Aye," she whispered. "Ye may go. Just lav me be here wi' the glowin' wax."

Sadly the man started for the door, then he turned, gazed at his wife, alive for the last time, and quietly said, "If ye feel y'sel' slippin' wud ya blow out th' candle?"

"My husband is a deceitful skunk," the woman cried to her mother. "Last night he pretended to believe me when he knew I was lying."

Monotony: The system that allows a man only one wife.

A citizen of ancient Rome sought to divorce his wife, and as a result was severely chastened by his friends, who asked: "Was she not chaste? Was she not fair?"

The Roman held out one of his shoes. "Is it not well made?" he said. "Is it not also new?" And when they had agreed that the shoe was both well made and new, the Roman replied: "Yet none of you can tell where it pinches me."

PLUTARCH

A gentleman named Brewer and his wife went to visit their son at an exclusive college. Since the boy was on the football team, and the squad was playing an important game the next day, he prevailed upon his parents to stay overnight and take in the event. Arrangements were made for them to stay at one of the fraternity houses.

During the night, however, the entire campus was disturbed by the senior Brewer's voice raised loudly in song. Young Brewer was furious, and the next day he took his father aside. "I hope you come again," he said. "But please, next time you do, do not sing so loudly."

"Sorry, son, it couldn't be helped," Brewer replied. "I had to sing loud, or they'd have heard your mother."

EPITAPH ON A HENPECKED SQUIRE
As father Adam first was fool'd
  A case that's still too common,
Here lies a man a woman rul'd,
  The Devil rul'd the woman.

ROBERT BURNS

"Now that you're married," said a lawyer to his best male client, "I suppose you're going to take out plenty of insurance."

"Nah," scoffed the man. "I don't think she's going to be dangerous."

A man once testified that the murder of his wife by his own hand had been a mercy killing. "How do you figure that?" asked the district attorney.

"Well," said the widower. "I'd rather kill a woman once than a different man every week."

Society-page item: "The bride wore a corsage of orchids, a flowered dress, and two cauliflower ears from a previous marriage."

Children

"No matter how bad a child is, he is still good for a tax exemption."

There is a legend said to emanate from the land of Akkad, which lay immediately north of Sumer, in the third millennium B.C. A pious man, married many years, was without offspring. In the course of one of the many wars that characterized the era he came upon a temple in a strange land. There he met a priest who told him the problem could be solved with the chanting of mystic psalms. The man returned home after establishing a communications system, using sacred messenger hawks between the holy man and himself.

Some months later a hawk delivered a message to the priest saying all was well, the man's wife was indeed with child. The priest's reply expressed joy and gave assurances that the psalms would continue.

The next message said the woman had been in labor for days, but nothing had happened. The priest repeated his assurances. Shortly thereafter came this message: "O holy purveyor of deeds and incantations, you are worthy to be blessed. I have a son." Before the priest could reply another hawk appeared bearing this news: "Blessed art thou, O purveyor of holy deeds. No sooner had I dispatched the news than I became the father of still another son."

As the priest changed his message of congratulation the hawks brought further news: "Mighty one, there is now also a daughter." Followed immediately by: "And still another daughter."

As the priest labored to prepare a reply suitable to the event another hawk appeared with a message reading: "FOR GOD'S SAKE, STOP THOSE DAMNED PSALMS."

So the legends of the East tell how children were the objects of man's first cuss word.

And children have been responsible for the creation of many cuss words since . . .

After much tribulation an American citizen succeeded in bringing his father from war-ravaged Europe to the golden shores of his adopted land. But the elder's experience had been such that he shook at the sight of friendly uniformed policemen, and the sound of approaching footsteps sent beads of perspiration cascading down his face. One afternoon the old man was in the park accompanied by the newly acquired joy of his life, his three-year-old granddaughter. Suddenly the sky became overcast, and a flash illuminated the area, followed by a resounding crash. The little girl placed an affectionate arm around the trembling old man, and in a reassuring tone said: "Don't be afraid, Grandpa. It's our thunder."

Questions, Answers, and Excuses

"Progress changes things rapidly, so the mind cannot possibly conceive of the future with genuine accuracy. Eleven years ago, in 1945, something came into existence that has since been the cause of great controversy. James, would you know what it was?"

"Me!"

History defined: "The Czar's wife was called the Czarina and the Czar's children were called the Czardines."

"Billy, how did you know that alcohol is good for a sprained leg?"
"My father always uses it when he sprains his throat."

Asked why he had come to school ten minutes late, a little boy replied: "I overwashed."

"John Smith is sick and can't attend classes today. He asked me to telephone you."
"All right. Who's this speaking?"
"This is my brother."

"What was the great difficulty George Washington had to contend with?"
"He couldn't tell a lie."

"If you have seven apples and I ask you for two, how many would you have left?"
"Seven."

"What distinguished foreigner assisted the colonies in the American Revolution?"
"God."

"If your father can do a certain job in one hour and your mother can do the same job in one hour, how long would it take them to do the job together?"
"With or without the time they spend arguing?"

"Which month has twenty-eight days?"
"They all have."

Children

"What happened when it rained forty days and forty nights, Billy?"

"The people said it was very unusual."

"What is the first and most important sacrament?"

"Marriage."

"You are wrong. First and foremost of the sacraments is baptism!"

"Not in our family. We're respectable."

"Who made you?"

"I don't know."

"You don't know? Why little Johnny knows and he's only four."

"He ought to. He hasn't been made as long as I have."

"According to Greek mythology Atlas supported the world. Now, how was Atlas supported?"

"He married a rich woman."

"What is the difference between a dog and a tree?"

"A tree is covered with bark and a dog is lined with it."

"Name six animals that inhabit the Arctic region."

"Three seals and three polar bears."

"How do you tell the difference between a Jersey cow and the other kind?"

"By the license plate."

"Arthur, can you tell me the shape of the earth?"

"It's round."

"What makes you so sure it's round?"

"Okay, then, it's square. Let's not have an argument about it."

"If you were preparing dinner for twenty people and only had sixteen potatoes, how would you divide each portion equally?"

"I'd mash 'em."

"What is one half of one tenth?"

"I don't know, but it can't be very much."

"My father and me, we know everything in the world."

"Where's Kalamazoo?"

"That's one my father knows."

"Mommie, do people who tell lies go to heaven?"

"Certainly not."

"Gosh, it must be awful lonesome up there with only God and George Washington."

"Young man, there were two cookies in the pantry this morning. May I ask how it happens that there is only one now?"

"Must have been so dark I didn't see the other one."

"See here, I wish I were your mother for twenty-four hours."

"I'll speak to my father. Maybe it can be arranged."

"What did Franklin get when he flew the kite in a thunderstorm?"

"Pneumonia."

"Mother, when Howdy Doody dies, and Rootie Kazootie too, will they go to heaven?"

"Of course, dear."

"Pretty nice for God, isn't it?"

"What do you call a man who doesn't believe in birth control?"

"Daddy."

To the ghetto dwellers of Eastern Europe it was a day of great consequence when a child reached the age of school attendance; tomorrow would be better, and the children must be prepared. In the home of Feyvel the brickmaker that day had come and gone. To mark the occasion the parents sat their son down to a repast of honeycake and watered wine. Feyvel said: "Tell me, my young son, tell me what you learned today. Did the rabbi show you the key to wisdom? Were you ushered into the sunshine of knowledge, the way to cure disease? Was your responsibility to mankind made clear? Tell me, my son, tell me what you learned today."

"I was taught the prayer for the dead," the boy said.

Feyvel's face reddened. "The prayer for the dead?" he shouted disbelievingly. "What is this? Summon the rabbi, bring him here. I demand an explanation."

In due course the rabbi arrived, and Feyvel said: "What's the idea of teaching my son, my hope, the prayer for the dead? Am I dying? Is my wife at death's door?"

"Don't get excited," the rabbi answered calmly. "The two of you should live so long as it will take him to learn it."

From the Mouths of Babes

A progressive school is a place where they teach children the same things they teach us right here—only the teacher is naked.

A cow is an animal that lays milk.

I would rather be a general than a private. Generals don't have to fight for their medals.

We buy Christmas seals every year to help a lot of poor people get tuberculosis.

My father was one of nine children. All the others are in jail. But my father isn't. He's a cop. If you can't beat 'em join 'em.

I would like to be a doctor, because I don't want to be a mother.

I have six brothers and sisters. Their ages are nine, eight, seven, five, four, three. The one missing is me.

Children who use bad language when they play marbles grow up to play golf.

There is no such thing as a devil. The devil is the same as Santa Claus. He's your father.

The doctor put me on a special diet. I wish chickens would lay something besides eggs.

A hypocrite is a boy who comes to school with a smile on his face.

During my vacation I never attended services. There was only one church, and I belonged to a different abomination.

One of the causes of feeble-mindedness is old age. Some people are born that way.

Gross exaggeration is 144 times as exaggerated as ordinary exaggeration.

Married men are only boys with their brains knocked out.

My father was a sergeant in the war. Personally, as a sergeant I can't see him.

Mark Antony was lucky. By the time he met Cleopatra Julius Caesar had already been there and she was able to teach Mark all the tricks Julius taught her.

Columbus discovered America in 1492, because it was so big how could he miss it.

The Chinese Communists ought to be very careful how they annoy the Indians. Look what they did to General Custer.

Children

The British are very superstitious people. They don't like February the 13th because it's George Washington's birthday.

George Washington was a very bad boy. He chopped down the cherry tree, and his father spanked his behind until it was red. That's why he stood up in the boat.

I don't mind that my father and mother got divorced, because they got married again. All my fathers and mothers have fathers and mothers. That makes eight people who spoil me.

I would like to be a disc jockey. It's a very good job, and you don't have to know anything about music.

The instrument the French used to cut off people's heads was called the Gillette.

Letters from Camp

Dear Folks:
Last Monday the counsellors took us on a hike. We picked huckleberries. Unless huckleberries have legs I swallowed a caterpillar. . . .

Dear Mother and Father:
You'll never guess who I met in camp. Remember that girl whose hair I stuck in the inkwell four years ago? Well she's here. Her hair is still blue. . . .

Dear Dad:
I am writing this letter to you *only* because this is *man-to-man stuff*. Last night we raided a dormitory in one of the girls' camps and I got a twelve-year-old girl's bloomers. Please don't tell mother. They won't fit her anyway. . . .

Dear Mother:

Last evening some of the boys from the camp across the lake came over, and they gave us dance lessons. They were very old. Some of them were thirteen. But I only danced the minuet because I remember what you told me about babies. . . .

My Son, My Son

Two elderly women became acquainted on the visitors' bus going to the State Penitentiary. After their sixth meeting one said: "Mrs. Franklin, you must come to my house for the celebration next week."

"Celebration? What kind of celebration?"

"My four sons are coming home next Friday."

"Next Friday? I thought they got ten years each for that robbery."

"They did. But they got three years off for good behavior."

"Ah," sighed Mrs. Franklin. "You must be a fine woman for the Lord to bless you with four such well-behaved sons."

The average child's place in the home is halfway between an adult and the television screen.

The mother of a young boy was embarrassed when he reached across the table to grab a roll from a platter. "Why did you do that?" she reprimanded. "Haven't you got a tongue?"

"Yes, Mother," the boy replied. "But my tongue is not as long as my arm."

A stranger came on a young boy standing atop a hill, his face turned radiantly toward the distant glow in the sky. "Son," said the stranger. "It's good to see the young folks in these parts admiring nature. I can see by the expression on your face that you appreciate the beauty of the sun as it sets in the western sky."

"That's no sun setting in the sky," the boy happily corrected. "That's my school burning down."

Children

A believer in telepathic spiritualism took her eight-year-old son to a séance. The medium had great talent, and in a moment the assemblage entered a trancelike state; all but the boy. "I want to talk to my grandfather," he told the medium.

"Hush," warned the medium.

"I will not hush," the boy challenged. "I want to talk to my grandfather."

"Oh, very well." The medium made several mystic passes and an apparition appeared against a black backdrop. "Here's your grandfather."

"Hi ya, Grandpa," the boy called. "Whadda you doing up there? You ain't dead."

On his first visit to the zoo a little boy stared at the caged stork for a long while. Then he turned to his father and exclaimed: "Gee, Dad, he doesn't recognize me."

The child came home from school sobbing. "Mother," he cried. "All the kids say I look like a monkey."

"Shut up," Mother ordered. "And comb your face."

The assignment was to name the eleven most important living Americans. After a few minutes of scribbling one little boy leaned toward another and asked, "Who you putting down for fullback?"

Names given children are often a key to the atmosphere in which their parents lived at the time the child was born. A few years back a little boy named Franklin D. Roosevelt started his formal education at a southern school. "So you're Franklin D. Roosevelt?" a teacher asked good-naturedly.

"I is, ma'am."

"And I imagine it is only natural that you try to be like him in every way?"

"Like who, ma'am?"

"Why, like Franklin D. Roosevelt, of course."

"Ma'am," said the boy politely. "I can't help bein' like Franklin D. Roosevelt, because *I is* Franklin D. Roosevelt."

A boy had employed subtle means to make known his desire to own a dog. Finally his father put this question to him: "If I gave you two hundred dollars, would you buy two one-hundred-dollar dogs, one two-hundred-dollar dog, or one one-hundred-dollar dog and put one hundred dollars in the bank for a rainy day?"

"Well . . ." The boy thought a moment. "If you leave it up to me, I'd buy two hundred one-dollar dogs."

A three-year-old musical genius was disturbed when the piano top closed on his hand during a rehearsal. A woman rushed forward and cooed: "Oo, did oo hurtie your ittsy bittsy finger?"

"Madam," said the prodigy. "I assure you the pain has ameliorated."

An insurance agent once made the mistake of trying to sell a man life insurance in the presence of his child. He pointed to the tot and said: "Let's face it; if you died tomorrow, Mr. Brown, where would your child be?"

"I'd be right here," the boy interjected. "The question is, where would Dad be?"

Having attained a certain standing in the community, a businessman hired a couple to perform domestic chores. One day the hired couple's little boy was told by the mistress of the house: "Run into town and buy two pounds of plums. But pinch a few to see if they are ripe."

Twenty minutes later the boy returned with his arms laden. "I pinched a couple like you told me, ma'am," the boy said. "And then when nobody was looking I pinched the rest."

Animals

Somebody must take a chance. The monkeys did who became men, and the monkeys who didn't are still jumping around in trees making faces at the monkeys who did.

LINCOLN STEFFENS

From which animal is man descended?

Initial evidence of the concept of evolution appears in the writings of the early Greeks. The Church, however, fearing danger to the biblical concept of divine creation, outlawed any development of evolutionary theories; thus imposing fifteen centuries of status quo. In 1859 Charles Robert Darwin combined the tricklings of the ages with his research to set forth *The Origin of Species*. Before the attendant storm settled men of conservative speech and sound reasoning were to issue hysterical disclaimers, beseeching God and the apes to "say it isn't so."

"The question is this: Is man an ape or an angel? I am on the side of the angels."

Benjamin Disraeli probably never believed men were angels, but he was a politician, and expediency dictated that he tell the people what they wanted to hear. His statement became a rallying cry for the anti-evolutionaries, many of whom were willing to

217

invoke inquisitorial authority while staking their right to wear wings.

In the summer of 1925, at Dayton, Tennessee, the trial of John Thomas Scopes dramatized the enormity of the struggle. Hindered by questionable tactics on the part of judicial authority, attorneys for the high school teacher accused of teaching evolution decided to surrender the case and place their hopes for scientific evaluation in the form of an appeal to a higher court. The appeal failed, but the State Supreme Court freed Scopes on a technicality, thus shutting off further argument. The right of the people to decide what would be taught in public schools, even if what they decided was ridiculous, remained unimpaired.

Man, in his anxiety to refute evidence that he is a monkey, manages to further the belief that he is an ass. . . .

The best way to avoid getting bitten on a tiger hunt is not to go on a tiger hunt.

Prior to making his famous ride Paul Revere met a horse peddler who said: "I've got an animal that will get you to Boston by five o'clock in the morning."

"Nope," Revere said. "What can anybody do in Boston at five o'clock in the morning?"

The smartest horse in the world was owned by Buffalo Bill. The old hunter fell from his horse one day right in the path of a charging buffalo herd. The animal dragged his unconscious master to safety, spread a blanket, built a fire, and pushed a pack of provisions next to him. Then the horse took off to find a doctor. Bill used to say there was only one trouble: he came back with a horse doctor.

A prospector once reported temperatures so high in Death Valley that a coyote was chasing a rabbit—and they were both walking.

Animals

Man is the only animal that blushes—or needs to.

MARK TWAIN

Baby Rabbit harped on the same subject until Mama Rabbit thought she would go out of her mind. Finally Mama Rabbit shouted: "If you must know, you were pulled out of a magician's hat. Now stop asking questions."

During a game hunt in northern Canada, Sir Archibald Defiant, the great British marksman, sent a charge into the thicket, then said to his man: "Chauncey, check and see the name of the species I just shot."

"Well, sir," Chauncey said on his return. "I've investigated, and he says his name is Brown."

The mother cow appeared at the psychiatrist's office with her offspring in tow. "I don't know what to do with him," she told the doctor. "He keeps asking for malteds."

Music hath charm to soothe a savage beast—but I'd try a revolver first.

JOSH BILLINGS

When it was discovered that women were responsible for a considerable number of housebreaking burglaries in a far eastern country, a newspaper editorial advised home owners to keep mice instead of watchdogs.

Mankind differs from the animals only by a little—and most people throw that away.

CONFUCIUS

If you pick up a starving dog and make him prosperous, he will not bite you. This is the principal difference between a man and a dog.

MARK TWAIN

Zoo: A place of refuge where wild animals are protected from people.

The Almighty once completed a tour of the universe and when He arrived at His final point of inspection, Earth, He asked St. Peter: "Why have you let the animals out of their cages?"

"A holiday, Master," St. Peter replied. "Today is Darwin's birthday."

A nature lover is a person who, when treed by a bear, enjoys the view.

A visitor to Australia was startled to see a kangaroo enter a bar, lean one foot on the rail, and order a horse's neck. The animal downed the drink, paid the tab, and started toward the door, when the stranger stopped it. "Pardon my awkwardness," he apologized, "but this is the first time I've ever seen a kangaroo in such a place."

"Let me tell you it'll bloody well be the last time too," the kangaroo replied. "Imagine, eight and six for a horse's neck."

A country gentleman once forgot to properly pen his dog for the night. The following day it was discovered that the dog had gotten into the house and wrought considerable havoc in the larder—eating everything there, except the dog biscuits.

It is said that when Hitler and his gang got to hell the first thing they saw was a pack of long-toothed wolves slaughtering and devouring a troop of SS men. The Nazis were disgusted by the sight, and Hitler said to one of his lieutenants: "How can anything be so unspeakably brutal?"

On hearing the remark, the leader of the wolf pack approached the Führer and said: "We're supposed to be a bunch of vicious, flesh-eating monsters. What's your excuse?"

At an army post in the Middle West there is a grave distinguished by a marker reading: "Here lies Victoria, an army mule, who in the course of duty kicked one general, two colonels, one major, three lieutenants, fourteen sergeants, thirty-six privates—and one bomb."

A story older than antiquity, and revived through the ages whenever applicable, concerns a Greek scholar who was one day bitten by a dog. Instead of seeking out a physician the scholar continued to inscribe a series of markings on numerous tablets. One of his pupils, hearing the news, came to him and insisted he take steps to have the wound cauterized. "I have something of greater importance that I am doing," the scholar replied.

"I see," the pupil answered. "You are transcribing your reactions to the poisons."

"No," the scholar said. "I am listing the statesmen I intend to bite when I go mad."

A tiger cub was chasing a frightened preserve visitor across an African plain when the tigress called from a mountain top: "Junior, stop it this instant! How often must you be told not to play with your food?"

An intellectual type of shaggy dog walked into the New York Public Library, wandered toward a librarian, and asked: "Can you please direct me to the section that contains the works of Booth Tarkington."

The librarian was stunned and silent.

"Now look here," the dog said angrily. "Do you or do you not carry the works of Booth Tarkington?"

"Er——" the librarian mumbled, barely catching her breath. "This is rather unusual."

"I suppose it is," the dog said sadly. "I guess nobody asks for Tarkington any more."

> I wish I loved the human race,
> I wish I loved its silly face,
> I wish I liked the way it walks,
> I wish I liked the way it talks,

And when I'm introduced to one,
I wish I thought, What Jolly Fun!

SIR WALTER RALEIGH

One day a big whale was deposited in a tank at the aquarium. All the other whales were very friendly except one that acted very aloof. "What's eating her?" the new arrival asked.

"Status," another whale explained. "Her folks swam over under the Mayflower."

A carrier pigeon came to rest on a ledge near the Pentagon. Behind it came another pigeon and landed beside the first, to chat.

"Where you going, pal?" asked the second pigeon.

"Section X, Building Nine, top secret division, to deliver an order," answered the first pigeon.

"What's the number of your order?"

"8642YYZ823MM-Q498723-ZS/–T–449089077, as appended."

"Better get a move on," said the second. "I got an order rescinding it."

"Uh oh," one cow warned another as the farmer approached. "Here comes old icy fingers."

A socially prominent dowager entered a Park Avenue restaurant with a French poodle. After placing the animal on a chair beside her, she comforted the poodle with baby talk. "Mama's itsy bitsy baby, mansy won't hurt you."

The waiter asked: "Your first dog, madam?"

A sparrow was late in arriving home for dinner. When he finally appeared he was thoroughly disheveled, and in an agitated voice explained to Mrs. Sparrow: "I was making great time hedge-hopping a bit, when I got caught in this badminton game. . . ."

Animals

Animals are prominent in suburbia. A commuter arrived home to find his wife in tears. "What's wrong, darling?" he asked.

"The dog ate a pie I made for you," she sobbed.

"Don't worry, dear," he soothed. "I'll buy you another dog."

"Now that school is starting I'm worried about Junior," Mrs. Turtle said. "His neck sticks all the way out, and I just know he'll catch cold."

"Stop worrying," Papa Turtle advised. "We'll buy him one of those people-neck sweaters."

Then there was the snail that ran the hundred-yard dash in a year and a half.

"Howdy, Ezra," a farmer called to his passing neighbor. "Got me a mule with distemper. How'd you treat your'n when he had it?"

"I give'd him turpentine," the other farmer answered, then snapped the wagon reins and said: "Giddap, Bessie."

On the return trip he was hailed again. "Say, Ezra, I give'd my mule turpentine and it killed him."

Ezra nodded. "Killed mine too. Giddap, Bessie."

An Irishman disputed Darwin's theory with his barber, who was a firm believer in it. To prove his point the barber left the room and a pet monkey he'd been training grabbed a brush, stirred the lather, and applied it to the Irishman's face. The monkey then took a razor, honed it to a fine edge, and was about to apply it to the customer's face, when the Irishman stopped him. "Naw ya don't," he cautioned. "Ye can soap up me face and towel me chin, but, begorrah, yer father's gunna shave me."

On the Isle of Man, a spot made famous by its refusal to abandon the donkey as a means of transportation, a preacher was unable to control his own mule. During Sunday services it poked its head in the window and brayed a raucous hee-haw, and kicked against the side of the building.

His patience gone, the preacher announced: "Brothers and sisters, is there not one among you who knows the formula for keeping that mule quiet?"

"I do, parson," a member interjected. "In order to keep that mule quiet all you needs do is tie a stone to his tail."

"Brothers and sisters," the preacher declared, "let he who is without sin tie the first stone."

A couple from moonshine country visited the Bronx Zoo. Everything was going along well until the woman began to beat the man over the head with her pocketbook. "Here now," a policeman interfered. "What's going on?"

"He called me a rhinoceros," the woman said.

"A rhinoceros hey? When was this?"

"Twenty years ago," the woman answered, taking another swing at the man.

"Twenty years? Then why pick today to get even?"

"Well, officer," the woman said, "until today I ain't never seen a rhinoceros."

A woman had a parakeet that was very lonely. One day she put a mirror in the cage to brighten it, and the parakeet fell in love with its own image. It was a touching experience to watch the bird snuggle up to the reflection and coo devotedly. One summer afternoon the woman went shopping and a strong wind wafted through an open window, toppling the cage to the floor. When the woman returned she discovered the bird had died—of a broken mirror.

Little Tommy, who lived in New York City, developed an inordinate fondness for the family parrot. One day the parrot disappeared and little Tommy was brokenhearted.

For two weeks he mourned, and then suddenly he seemed to

get over it. Seeing that the boy had come out of his trance Tommy's father decided to tell him the truth.

"Tommy," his father began. "Now that your grief has subsided I think it my duty to be frank and tell you what happened to the parrot. As you know, it is not natural for a human being to be so devoted to a creature the way you were devoted to that bird. The only way I could free you of this obsession was to lose it somewhere. I tried giving it away, but it always came back. I drove to Philadelphia and turned it loose, but it came back. Then I drove to Boston and turned it loose, but it again came back. Two weeks ago I took it to Florida, clipped its wings, and turned it loose in Miami, so I guess you realize he won't be back."

"Oh," little Tommy corrected. "He came back yesterday."

"Yesterday? But how?"

"He won't say, Pop," Tommy answered. "But are *his* feet sore!"

The mother of a large horde was disappointed to see an empty cage at the zoo. She therefore asked the keeper: "Where are the monkeys?"

"They're in the back, making love."

"Would they come out for peanuts?"

"Would you?"

An American researcher into the sex habits of the human female was criticized by a blue nose who asked: "Can you also tell me the sex habits of the hippopotamus?"

"That, madam," the researcher said, "would only interest another hippopotamus."

A man called on his neighbor one evening and found a card game in progress. One of the participants was the neighbor's dog. The hound sat in a chair, shuffled the cards, rapidly dealt them out, made a fanlike flip with the remainder, and set them down in the middle of the table.

"Hey," the visitor said to his neighbor. "That's some intelligent dog you've got there."

"He's not so smart," the neighbor sneered. "Whenever he gets three of a kind he wags his tail."

A pair of hippopotamuses were lolling in the waters of the Nile, their noses just above water, watching the sun settle to end what had been a beautiful day. Slowly one leaned closer to the other and nuzzled its ear. "Don't start anything now," the other hippopotamus said. "Remember, tomorrow's Monday."

A bunch of chickens was in the yard when a football flew over the fence and landed in their midst. A rooster waddled over, studied it, then said: "I'm not complaining, girls, but look at the work they're turning out next door."

A farmer met a rancher while vacationing in Europe, and before long they were friendly enough to talk about homey things.

"I got me a place with two hundred cows and a bull," the rancher said.

"Golly," the farmer said, "you must be a mighty independent man."

"No, sir," replied the rancher. "Not nearly so independent as that bull."

A canny Scot, in America but one day, went to work on a farm. "You sure can milk a cow," the farmer said. "How'd you learn that finger technique."

The Scot said: "I used to play the bagpipes."

A farmer had a little too much to drink and woke up in a pasture holding a rope in his hand. "Heck, now," he said as he stared at it, "I don't remember if I lost a horse or found a rope."

The trees in Siberia are miles apart—that's why the dogs are so fast.

BOB HOPE

Animals

A tall story from the cornbelt tells about a jackass that wandered into a cornfield, upset a little twig fire that burned there at night, and touched off the whole crop. The corn began to pop, and the jackass, seeing the popped corn piling up all around, thought it was snow; and despite the heat the critter imagined a frost had set in—and froze to death.

A tramp asked for some food at a farmhouse one day and was told that he could have all the eats he wanted if he would milk the cow. The farmer handed him a stool and the tramp set off for the barn. Half an hour later he was back at the farmhouse, battered, bruised, and without any milk. "Ah did mah best, suh," he told the farmer. "But ah'll be damned if I can get that cow of your'n to set on this stool."

In the old days of the railroad when an engineer ran over an animal he would stop the engine and hustle on up to the farmhouse to apologize. One day a railroad man struck and killed a cow. He stopped the train and was about to head for the nearest farmhouse when another farmer stopped him. "Better break it easy, like," the farmer said. "He's mighty ornery when it comes to anyone damagin' his producin' stock. Just tell him it was one of his boys."

A little dog came running into town with a big bone in his mouth, determined to bury it. But the roads were all tar and asphalt, and he dug hard without making any impression in the pavement. He just kept wandering around, ducking up one alley, then down another, stopping here and there and scratching desperately at the hard coating, when he at last came to a sign. He looked up at it for a minute, then took a harder bite on the bone, shot up the street, and disappeared in the distance running as fast as he could. A stranger, seeing it all, went over and looked at that sign. It read: TEN MILES TO A DIRT ROAD.

227

I never thought much of the courage of a lion-tamer. Inside the cage he is at least safe from other men.

GEORGE BERNARD SHAW

"Are there any sharks in these waters?" a skin diver asked a Mexican fisherman, as he prepared to enter the water.

"No, *señor*," the fisherman said impassively, holding onto his fishing pole as the rowboat bobbed gently.

A moment later the skin diver came to the surface. "Are you sure there're no sharks in the area I'm exploring?" he again asked the fisherman.

"No, *señor*," the fisherman assured him. "They are afraid of the crocodiles."

A theatrical agent was proud of the way he detected a phony act. To a producer he related this tale of a narrow escape. "This morning in walks a real beat-looking guy, says he has the greatest animal act in the world. He opens this satchel, and out pops a cat and two mice. The cat sits himself at the piano, makes with an arpeggio, and the two mice go into an old soft shoe. Then they do a circus chorus of 'Harvest Moon' and lead into 'Swanee.' But when they started to do 'The Indian Love Call' I threw the whole damned batch out of the office."

"Why?" screamed the producer.

The agent smiled. "That's when I found out the cat was a ventriloquist."

A French dignitary, while being entertained by an American friend, found his way barred by a barking dog. "Do not be afraid, Jacques," his host called. "You know the proverb; barking dogs do not bite."

"Quite true, *monsieur*," the Frenchman replied. "I know ze proverbe, you know ze proverbe—but ze dog, does he know ze proverbe?"

At the circus a man approached the sideshow barker and said: "Mister, I was wundrin' if you couldn't let me and the family

228

in fer half price. I got sixteen kids, and we're all dyin' to see the monkey."

"Sixteen kids?" the barker said in amazement. "Stay right where you are. I'll bring the monkey out to see you."

The Puritan hated bear-baiting, not because it gave pain to the bear, but because it gave pleasure to the spectators.

MACAULAY

For some years a naturalist named Murphy was haunted by the sound of a yellow warbler that had serenaded him one night while he was encamped in Missouri. After searching through scores of bird sanctuaries he finally came to one owned by a man named Finnegan. Finnegan was very co-operative, and after listening to Murphy's story of a yellow warbler he said: "I may have the bird you want." Scores of singing canaries were carefully screened, but none had the proper quality.

Some weeks later Murphy received a call from Finnegan and rushed over. In a sound-proof room at the sanctuary was a yellow warbler emitting glorious tones. "That's it!" Murphy cried. "What a voice! What color! What warmth! What a range of tone! I'll take it with me."

But on arriving home Murphy examined the bird closely and found that it had a wooden leg. Unable to control his disappointment he rushed back to the sanctuary and got Finnegan out of bed. "Finnegan, Finnegan," Murphy cried. "There's something wrong with the bird. It has only one leg."

"Now look, Murphy," Finnegan said disgustedly, "make up your mind once and for all. Exactly what is it you want, a singer or a dancer?"

A newspaper reporter once called to interview Rocky Mountain Jack, a hunter who reputedly had slain more than two hundred bears. "The American public would be especially interested in any narrow escapes you've had," the reporter said.

"Son," Rocky Mountain Jack replied, "if thar's been any narrow escapes the barrs had 'em."

When the zoology department of the University of Vienna was conducting experiments to determine whether or not animals can be taught to use their dormant faculties, a horse knocked at the door of Professor Umglic and said: "Professor, I would like very much to take that series of examinations I read about in the newspapers."

Umglic immediately put the horse through a series of evaluation tests, and the animal drew a perfect score. The horse then breezed through advanced examinations on the antiquities, social sciences, biology, and post-graduate psychology. Excited, the professor then laid a mathematics exam in front of the animal, but it was shoved aside.

"B-but I don't understand," the professor said.

"Come on now, Umglic," the mare said. "Who ever heard of a horse that could count?"

Gaming and Gambling

*The gambling known as business looks with severe disfavor
upon the business known as gambling.*

About 2600 years ago a call was sounded throughout the
Hellinistic world. Inspired by the Oracle of Delphi, it said, in
effect: "Hail, citizens! We summon you unto Olympia. To worship in the Temple of Zeus and where the best among you may
compete in sport." The call to this ingathering will forever resound to quicken the hearts of strong men everywhere, for, dispatched by an ancient bookmaking syndicate, it drew a sporting
crowd that assembled from Sinope to Marseilles. And with these
pilgrims came the seed of the first floating crap game.

Greece made gaming and gambling one, and men in togas
made book everywhere at the Olympiad. Ancient historians showed
no aversion to truth. So we find reference to dishonest practices
during the games: a rigged discus, a blunted javelin, loin cloths
filled with itching powder, nails on the track to discomfort the
runners. We hear of wrestlers who made better actors, and we
are told that mighty Eupolis, the prize fighter, engineered the
first ring tank job.

The gamblers of Greece did not use shills, and a player lucky enough to break the bank took home all the drachmae, without some parasitic strong-arm deducting five per cent for the house. The bit of culture known as the house cut was strongest in ancient India, where it was dignified by a government title in keeping with the spiritual atmosphere given anything that enriched the treasury. In India the houseman was called Superintendent of Public Games, with side duties of Holy Cutter of the Pot.

The Greeks, who had a word for everything, had a game for everything. What they did not invent they perfected. Checkers, chess, individual and team activity, dice, cards, all the pageantry of track and field. Only one game eluded their social order: Strip poker.

Partisan sportsmanship has a history of the unusual and the miraculous. The sick have grown strong upon hearing that their favorite team was victorious, while the strong have taken to their beds, heartbroken by the failure of some athletic idol. Friendships that have withstood the pressures of time have been shattered by the effect of the wind upon a driven ball. Sport has sometimes been the difference between life and death. An example of this is rumored to have taken place after the crash of '29. A young broker, wiped out in the calamity, stood atop the highest building in the financial district, delicately balanced, with both feet on a narrow railing. The pleadings of his associates were futile, and the appearance of police officers seemed to hasten the inevitable. Finally a man of the cloth arrived and advanced closer than the others. "Have you given thought to those who love you?" he asked. "Your family, your wife, your children, your mother?"

The broker refused to answer.

"Then consider the meaning of your act in the eyes of God," the clergyman continued. "He who made you in his own image, that you might live and enjoy the good things of life."

Again no answer.

The good reverend thought things over awhile. Suddenly his face brightened and he said: "Come off that ledge, my boy, and we'll both run up to the ball park and see the Giants play."

The young man seemed to soften, and finally he said: "No. I don't like the Giants."

"What?" the cleric shouted angrily. "Then, by golly, jump, you dirty Dodger fan."

A man of generous habits patronized the same restaurant daily. The atmosphere was pleasant, the food good, the service excellent. He was therefore surprised to find another waiter taking his order one day.

"Your regular waiter is here, sir," the new man said. "But he can no longer wait upon you."

"And why not?" the man asked indignantly.

"Well, sir, it's this way," the waiter explained. "We played cards last night. After he lost all his money I had the pleasure of winning you."

Fox hunting; the unspeakable after the uneatable.

OSCAR WILDE

The remains of a great gambler reposed in the chapel, and the most important bookies in the country were gathered to pay homage. After the usual formalities the clergyman began his eulogy: "My friends, let us remember that Ace Docker isn't really dead, but that he only sleeps——"

"Oh yeah?" a voice challenged from the rear. "I got fifty grand says he's dead."

A businessman's wife berated him on account of his devotion to the links. "If you keep spending so much time playing golf," she nagged, "you won't have anything set aside for a rainy day."

"I won't, hey?" he replied. "My desk is loaded with work I've got put aside for a rainy day."

Golfer (at end of round): Notice any improvement since last year?
Caddie: Polished your clubs, didn't you?

Wyatt Earp was a gentleman, all the way. He was playing a game of whist in Tombstone once, with three other men, one of whom had lost an eye. He suspected cheating, but he was too refined to accuse anyone. So he put his gun on the table and said: "The first man I catch cheating I'll shoot out his other eye."

"Did you have luck hunting snakes in India?"
"Marvelous luck. I didn't encounter a single snake."

"Let me see your license," the police officer said to the vacationer.
"Which one?" the man returned. "Marriage, car, driver's, fishing, hunting, camping, fire-prevention, trailer? Open the license trunk, dear."

One of the best fishing stories has an appropriate locale in the deep sea. A sportsman was having bad luck all day. As he baited his hook with a live minnow, the fish slithered out of his hand and landed in a large glass of whisky set on the gunwale. Regarding this as a good omen, the sportsman fingered the bait hopefully and sent it whirling on the end of a mighty cast. Soon there was a forceful tug on his line. With straining muscles he managed to reel in his catch. At the end of the line was a ferocious tiger shark, fighting desperately for its life against the minnow, which had it firmly by the throat and was throttling it to death.

Two duck hunters were swizzling in their rowboat, hidden in a marsh, when a flock appeared at high altitude. Taking uncertain aim, one of them fired into the mass and a single duck fell into the water. "Whatsha waste a shot fer?" asked the other. "The fall would 'a' killed it."

Marriage is like a prize fight—the preliminaries are better than the main event.

"When the breaks go against you there's nothing you can do about it," the gambler complained. "Even with cheating I can't win."

When the immortal Joe Louis was proving his right to the championship by taking on all comers, an opponent remarked: "I'm going to get me a sun tan so when I get together with Joe Louis they won't be able to tell us apart."

"They'll tell you apart," a cynic declared. "The one standing will be Louis."

Samuel Foote, the eighteenth-century dramatist, encountered a member of the royal court who complained that he had been thrown out of a second-story window for cheating at cards. He asked Foote what ought to be done about it. Foote replied: "Do not play so high."

Magellan went around the world in 1521—which isn't too many strokes when you consider the distance.

JOE LAURIE, JR.

Notre Dame was engaged in a gridiron struggle against Southern Methodist, in Dallas. A group of Catholic clerics watched tensely as S.M.U. carried deep into Notre Dame territory. The Irish stands were silent when suddenly a priest unfurled an S.M.U. banner and began to urge the ball carrier on. A young man politely asked why a priest would be cheering against a Catholic institution. "Son," the priest replied, "Once a Texan always a Texan."

A tiger hunt was organized in honor of a distinguished visitor to India, the President of the United States. Eastern manners showed to good advantage when, at the conclusion, a gun carrier was asked: "How did the President do?"

"His Excellency shot magnificently," the guide answered. "But heaven was very merciful to the tigers."

When James J. Corbett was ribbed on his poor ability to judge fighters, he replied: "So you think I am a poor judge of fighters? Well, let me tell you this. When I fought Jeffries at Coney Island, along about the third round I picked Jeffries to win."

Golf: A game that begins with a golfball and ends with a highball.

When Madison Square Garden was at its height it gave birth to this classic.

A fighter barely managed to survive the third round. As he slumped down in his corner his manager whispered: "Good fight, kid, good fight. He ain't laid a glove on ya."

"Yeah?" the fighter questioned. "Then keep an eye on the referee, 'cause someone is beating the hell out of me."

A stranger wandered into Laramie and got himself into a card game, where he did not do well. When a new hand had been dealt a wrangler standing behind him remarked: "I see where they're goin' to bury Abe Lincoln in a——"

"Gentlemen," interrupted the stranger. "If you lead with a spade I'll kill all of you."

Killing a man for cheating was accepted protocol during the frontier days, but as the West became civilized the formality of judicial inquiry was observed. At such a hearing a gambler was ask to explain why he was positive his late opponent had resorted to devious methods.

"I knew damned well he was cheating," the gambler replied. "'Cause he wasn't playing the hand I dealt him."

Gaming and Gambling

Oscar Wilde, when asked why he, an Englishman, did not play cricket, replied: "It requires one to assume such indecent postures."

The native guide rushed into camp. "Master," he shouted, "I have just observed many leopard tracks one mile north of here."
"Good boy, Sattu," the master replied. "Which way is South?"

Sign in caddie quarters at golf club: ALWAYS KEEP MOVING, DON'T STAND AROUND LOOKING STUPID, LIKE YOU WAS A MEMBER OF THE CLUB.

The lady teed the ball, swung lustily, and watched with apparent joy as a small object leaped away at a forty-five-degree angle. "Thank goodness it's gone at last," she sighed.
"It's not the ball that's gone, miss," the caddie replied. "It's your wristwatch."

Telegram: "Wife died. Can't tee off with you fellows at noon. See you at two."

"I am the recording secretary of a chess club," the man advised the judge who asked his occupation.
"And what are the duties?"
"I read the hours of the last meeting," he replied.

An inebriated man walked into the Automat, requested ten dollars' worth of nickels, and proceeded to pour them into the various slots. When he had accumulated several dozen sandwiches an employee approached, "Don't you think you've had enough?" he asked.
"What?" protested the drunk. "You want me to quit in the middle of a winning streak?"

"That caddie kept laughing and laughing at me," the dejected man told his wife.

"You should have knocked his head off," the wife sympathized.

"I would have," the man admitted. "But I didn't know what club to use."

There is but one good throw to the dice, which is to throw them away.

CHATFIELD

An aggressive fellow once accosted Andrew Carnegie in a restaurant and refused to leave the multimillionaire's table until Carnegie had agreed to purchase a sweepstakes ticket.

After some hesitation the tycoon agreed to the purchase in order to be free of the nuisance.

Some months later the fellow showed up at Carnegie's home. "You again!" the industrialist moaned. "What is it this time?"

"I have great news," the man said. "You won a hundred thousand dollars."

"Well, now," Carnegie replied, "that *is* something. I must say I admire your pluck. If you hadn't shown initiative I never would have won that money. This entitles you to a reward. You may have your choice of thirty thousand dollars immediately, or two hundred dollars a week as long as I live."

"I'll take the thirty thousand," the man answered. "Because with your luck you'll be dead in a week."

I listened to a football coach who spoke straight from the shoulder—at least I could detect no higher origin in anything he said.

DIXON RYAN FOX

A man was hailed into night court for walking the streets clad only in a barrel. "Are you a poker player?" the judge asked.

"No," the man said. "But I just left a couple of fellows who are."

A renowned statesman, addicted to the links, was having an off day while playing on a strange course. While walking to the next

238

hole he remarked to his caddie: "I guess you've seen worse players than I am."

There was no reply, and, thinking the caddie might not have heard, the statesman loudly repeated his statement.

"I heard you, sir," the caddie replied. "I was just considerin'."

There are two times in a man's life when he should not speculate—when he can't afford it, and when he can.

MARK TWAIN

A Kentucky landowner posted this sign: NO FISHING AND NO HUNTING. SURVIVORS WILL BE PROSECUTED.

Trust everybody—but cut the cards.

Wild Bill Hickok checked out in a poker game that made famous the immortal "dead man's hand." But there's a rumor concerning what happened after the shot was fired.

Calamity Jane leaned over and whispered something to the dying Bill. "Pay it no heed, Calamity," Bill said.

"But, Bill," Calamity said. "I tell ya he dealed himself four aces."

"So what?" were Bill's last words. "Ain't it his deal?"

A distinguished clergyman was engaged in playing golf with a Washington politician, when he carefully teed his ball, addressed it with the approved grace, raised his driver, and unleashed a tremendous swing. But the ball merely toppled off the pin, rolled a few feet, and died. The clerical gentleman frowned, shook his head, bit his lip, but said nothing. His companion, standing near by, remarked: "Doctor, that is the most profane silence I ever witnessed."

"Your honor," the woman complained in court, "My husband is an inveterate gambler. That's all he talks about—dice and cards,

239

and cards and more dice. He doesn't even remember the date on which we were married."

"What a lie!" the husband challenged. "That was the day I crapped out in Nevada after seven straight passes."

A parishioner was badly beating his minister at a game of golf. "Cheer up, reverend," the man consoled. "Remember, in the end you'll win. I expect that some day you'll be burying me."

"Even so," the cleric replied, "It will be your hole."

One day in suburbia a baseball flew over a hedge, bounced on a concrete walk, and crashed through a window. A moment later a tiny batsman appeared to ask for it. The man of the house was incensed. "How do you have the gall to show yourself around here?" he shouted. "You dare ask for the ball when you nearly killed one of my children with it!"

"Ah, mister," the kid replied. "You got eight children, but I only got one ball."

A beginner stepped onto the links, teed up the ball, measured his swing recklessly, and sent a prodigious drive into the blue yonder on his first try. The ball arched perfectly and came to rest inches from the cup. "Wonderful," his friend shouted. "The idea is to get the ball in the cup."

The novice looked indignantly at him, then said, "Why didn't you tell me that in the first place?"

If you play bridge badly you make your partner suffer—but if you play poker badly you make everybody happy.

A horse-player was dining at the track restaurant when he noticed that the lobster he ordered had a claw missing. He called the manager and demanded an explanation.

"Well you see, sir," the manager began, "lobsters are great fighters. They fight very much, and sometimes one loses a claw."

"Is that so?" the surprised gambler said. "Then take this one away and bring me a winner."

A newcomer wandered into Tombstone, and got himself in a game with some of the James boys, the Younger brothers, and the worst killer of them all, Cactus Jack. After an hour he had all the money.

"Friend," Cactus said, "I been studyin' yer hands these last times. You had three royal flushes, aces full a couple of times, and four of a kind six times runnin'. Wonder how you account fer that?"

"Just lucky, I guess," the newcomer replied.

"Yer a lot luckier'n you think." Cactus drew his gun, pointed it at the man's eye, then put it back in his holster. "The boys are willin' fer you to go yer way in one piece, providin' you don't linger. Yer really big luck was the fact that you happened to give yer performance at this here table during 'Be Kind to Strangers Week.'"

The man tore angrily from the brush, ran up to the Englishman, and shouted: "You blundering idiot. You almost hit my wife just then."

"Oh, I say, I *am* sorry," replied the Englishman, "Have a shot at mine."

Looks are sometimes deceiving. A man with a vacant look may have a full house.

Item in a British newspaper thirty years ago:

"At the Lincoln County picnic the rolling-pin contest was won by Mrs. W. H. Upsall, who threw the rolling pin sixty-seven feet. Mr. Upsall won the hundred-yard dash for married men."

I took up golf for the exercise—and all I keep getting is holes-in-one.

GREGORY NUNN

Business and Industry

Men, with crooked fingers like Harpies, seek from every stone an unholy gain. The sanctity of oaths has perished.

CERCIDEA, *Third Century* B.C.

Of the four elements that constitute the structure of man, the one that has changed the least is the major subcategory of economics known as business. It appears that everyone, through the ages, has been aware of its shortcomings, and, like the weather, nobody has been able to do anything about it. "Where there is a sea there are pirates" reads the oldest axiom of Asia past. "Milk the cow, but do not pull off the udder," is another bit of advice. Anarcharsis defined the market as a place set apart where men may deceive each other. And Theophrastus, whose writings indicate remarkable awareness on all subjects, observed: "Unconscionableness, to define it, is a neglect of reputation for the pursuit of filthy lucre."

Business groups, along with other pressure lobbies, constantly fight for their rights, but seldom acknowledge their responsibilities. Often they try to justify their actions by pointing out the instability of their pursuit and the necessity for preparation against a rainy day. If climate is the key to their performance it would appear they are preparing for a rainy century. And if it is the future that concerns them they need only turn to that great champion of industry, Calvin Coolidge, who came up with the indisputable prediction that, "Business will be either better or worse."

When price controls were done away with, the theory advanced was a fantasy based on the premise of things finding their own level. Left to its own devices, business launched a round of price increases to which unions responded with demands for higher wages. When labor-management tactics became ludicrous, Congress appointed a special group to investigate. "Don't you sympathize with the people whose life savings have shrunk away as the result of constant price increases?" a politician asked a manufacturer.

"I do sympathize with them," the industrialist replied. "Never let it be said that I was lacking in sympathy. I sympathize with them a great deal; and if I had my way I'd fix things so that I could sympathize with them twice as much."

That business ethics are on the upswing, however, is illustrated by this recent event. A sales executive for a large corporation used devious tactics in an effort to secure a lucrative contract. To obtain his goal he bribed an official, acted as a procurer, seduced and blackmailed a secretary, conspired to inflict bodily harm on the representative of a competitor, and organized a bacchanalian orgy. When the directors of his company were made aware of the tactics used they fired the executive—and shipped the merchandise.

It's a beginning. . . .

A trade magazine carried this institutional advertisement: CONGRATULATIONS TO THE X MANUFACTURING COMPANY AND TO ITS PRESIDENT, HARRISON K——. Ten years ago I couldn't borrow five cents from Mr. K——. Today he has a multimillion-dollar business, and I still can't borrow five cents from him.

I am glad to see that success hasn't changed him any.

A man applied to the State Liquor Authority for an alcohol license, and at an open hearing was asked to produce evidence of good moral character. "You mean to say," he protested, "that a man has to be of good moral character to sell *whisky?*"

During the noontime recreational activities the president of the corporation mounted the platform, accompanied by an overall-clad man off the assembly line, and made this speech.

"Ladies and gentlemen, you are about to see how American industry rewards those who are conscientious and hard-working. This man standing beside me has been with the company less than a year, during which time his unusual qualities have earned him salary increases in excess of one hundred dollars a week. I have watched him closely, observed with great pleasure the manner in which he has pitched in and gotten things done. Therefore I am pleased to announce that starting this very afternoon he gets out of his work clothes, comes into the executive branch, and takes over an office with the title of Executive Vice President in Charge of Policy at an annual wage of eighty thousand dollars. Congratulations to you, sir."

The workman shook the extended hand and said: "Gee, thanks, Dad."

"Business is so bad," complained one manufacturer, "that even the accounts who don't intend to pay ain't buying."

Accounts Receivable remains the biggest problem of business and industry. To facilitate receipts without offending, a polite method of dunning has been incorporated into every bookkeeping system.

An old-line manufacturer decided to prepare his own style of due notice, in keeping with the trend. After laboring several days he presented the sample letter to his secretary for comment.

"This certainly is a wonderful letter," she said. "It is well prepared and your expressions are very polite. However, there are two minor corrections. Dirty is spelled with one 't' and there is no 'c' in skunk."

If you build a better mousetrap the world will beat you out of the patent.

A Hollywood producer had this to say during a radio interview: "This business of me being surrounded by yes men is a lie. I hate a man who always says 'yes' to me. When I say 'no' I like a man who also says 'no.'"

With the volume of credit purchases increasing, private detective agencies are finding finance companies a better source of business than divorce lawyers. The president of a loan company called in a top detective and told him: "There's a wise guy going around the city saying he's a collector of ours. He's made himself a fortune. Why in one month he's collected more than all our real collectors put together. I want you to find him and find him quick. Expense is no object."

"Good," the detective said. "I'll have him in jail in less than a week."

"Jail?" corrected the executive. "I don't want to arrest him, I want to employ him."

A commuter railroad posted this sign in its terminal: WE HAVE AGREED TO LIVE UP TO THE RULING OF THE RAILROAD COMMISSION GUARANTEEING FAST, PROMPT SERVICE THREE TIMES A DAY. BUT DON'T DEPEND ON IT.

Real estate lobbies have given property owners an ethical code. When a tenant complained that his bathroom faucet was inoperative, his landlord made this proposal; "For a 15-per-cent increase I'll have the tub moved under the hole in the roof."

A utilities company petitioned for its fourth rate increase. At a public hearing an executive of the company made a long speech in which he said his company was not receiving credit that was its proper due; and concluded by declaring; "The people should 'Honor the Light Brigade.' "

One newspaper replied: " 'Oh, what a charge they made!' "

Credit is the system whereby a person who can't pay gets another person who can't pay to guarantee that he can pay.

CHARLES DICKENS

During the recession of the early twenties Henry Ford issued this statement: "Business will get better, but we won't know it when it does."

"Who knows?" one critic replied. "Maybe it already has."

A certain type of predatory opportunist puts in an appearance whenever people are in a position to offer money in exchange for services.

A story of the mid-nineteenth century tells of the man who, upon meeting a friend, told him he was going into business.

"What sort of business?" the friend asked.

"A partnership," the other replied.

"Are you putting in much capital?"

"No. I put in no capital. I put in the experience."

"And he puts in the capital, is that it?"

"Yes. We go into business for three years. He puts in the capital and I put in the experience. At the end of three years I will have the capital; and he will have the experience."

While many businesses have flourished others have been forced to close their doors. In the latter category is the neighborhood secondhand bookstore, rapidly becoming a memory.

A woman engaged in that ill-fated pursuit was closing her doors one evening when a man appeared, asked several questions concerning a book, and appeared ready to make a cash purchase. "Would you please come back and buy the book tomorrow?" the woman said.

"Why tomorrow?" the customer asked.

"Tomorrow is my husband's birthday," she replied, "and I want him to have a big surprise."

The boss's son has become a dynamo willing to overlook tradition in order to facilitate growth. Name-changing is one of the newer fads in many industries.

Hymowitz and Gorowitz had been partners for years. When their sons came into the business the young men felt a modern name was needed. It was decided that a round of name changes was in order and the firm became Laughton & Laughton. Some weeks after the change a buyer phoned and asked to speak to Mr. Laughton.

"Which Laughton do you want?" asked the operator, "Hymowitz or Gorowitz?"

Business mergers have characterized the postwar era to an unusual degree, causing anguished protests of monopoly and restraint of trade. And the small businessman often finds himself the flattered recipient of a gentleman's agreement to avoid competition. In this atmosphere of interbusiness assistance a bank leased a property immediately adjoining its building for the purpose of establishing a pizza confectionery. In time the new business flourished and the proprietor was confronted by an old friend who wished him well, and, at the same time, sought to borrow five dollars. "I'm sorry," said the businessman, "but I have an agreement with the bank. I don't make loans and they don't sell pizzas."

Statistics can prove anything. An old man asked a large insurance company to insure his life. "How old are you?" he was asked.

"Ninety-nine."

"We can't insure you. Ninety-nine is much too old to issue a policy against."

"Well," said the applicant, "I figured it would be O.K. Statistics show that very few people die at ninety-nine or over."

Upon receiving an order from one of their customers a steel company wired: "Regret to say we cannot ship tonnage requested until last shipment is paid for."
The customer wired back: "Cannot wait that long. Cancel order."

A financial institution learned that advertising gets immediate results. The day they advertised for a night watchman was also the night their safe was robbed.

The president of a large corporation received this denunciatory note from the chairman of the board: "You are not supposed to initial documents before I see them. Kindly erase your initials and initial the erasure."

The boardroom of a large corporation is said to have this sign displayed above the chairman's spot. "Don't say 'yes' until I've finished talking."

When the advantages of mail advertising became clear every type of business sought to capitalize on it. One insurance company sent out the following circular:
"Mr. Arthur B. of Sioux City had the misfortune to fall in front of a subway train while visiting New York City. Were it not for his ten-thousand-dollar policy, which he purchased from us, his family would have become public wards. Phone us today—you may be the lucky one tomorrow."

In a rising town fifty miles from the city a lovely religious structure was being built. "Hey," remarked a highway patrolman, "that sure is a gorgeous house of worship you're putting up there. What faith is it for?"

"Can't say yet," the builder replied. "I'm putting it up on speculation."

A New York businessman was vacationing in the wild West when he noticed an Indian selling blankets. He approached the redskin and asked him how much he wanted for the lot. "Hundred dollar," the Indian said.

"Too much," the businessman replied.

"Ninety dollar," the redskin said.

"Still too much."

"Eighty dollar?" the Indian asked hopefully.

"No," said the businessman. "I'll give you twenty-four dollars for the whole batch."

"Listen, wise guy," the Indian replied. "Bargains like Manhattan Island you ain't gonna get."

In the deep South of a century ago it was the custom of businessmen to accommodate the clergy at no charge whenever possible. A minister, passing through the Carolinas, stopped at a wayside inn where he took supper without offering a prayer, retired without offering a prayer, and the following day took his breakfast without offering a prayer. He was about to resume his journey when the proprietor presented a bill.

"Ah, my good man," the cleric explained, "I am a clergyman."

"Mebbe so," the owner responded. "But you came here, ate like a sinner, drank like a sinner, smoked like a sinner, and slept like a sinner. And now, sir, you'll pay like a sinner."

Desk: A wastebasket with drawers.

When a point of ethics bothered one entrepreneur he sought the advice of a friend. "I am faced with a dilemma. The other day I made a cash sale in the amount of three dollars and handed the man change for a ten-dollar bill. After he had left I noticed that he had actually handed me a hundred-dollar bill. Now from the standpoint of ethics I would like to know; should I or shouldn't I tell my partner?"

The fine line of propriety was illustrated when a prominent society lady returned an expensive coat to a department store, saying the style was atrocious and she had never worn it. In one of the pockets was a Bible.

A congressman, assigned to a committee whose purpose it was to cut down government spending explained the cost-plus contract this way; "Industry has been charging the government too much for their services. The cost-plus contract will eliminate that evil. This is an arrangement whereby the government allows a contractor to submit his costs, including expenses, and we in turn add a plus factor. It's really very simple. For example, if a thing costs one dollar to manufacture we allow them to charge us the one dollar plus another dollar. Industry cannot be greedy, they must be content with a 1-per-cent profit."

A classic business story concerns the efficiency expert who passed away. As his coffin was being carried from the church by six pallbearers the lid flew open, the efficiency expert sat up, and, addressing the undertaker, said: "If you put this thing on wheels you could lay off four men."

Finding himself in a predicament an elderly businessman decided to tell his wife the truth; so at the dinner table he declared: "My secretary is suing me for breach of promise."

"Ridiculous," said the wife. "At eighty-two what could you promise her?"

The son-in-law of the boss felt compelled to enter the office of his wife's father and say: "Sir, I'd like my salary raised."

"Don't worry," his father-in-law replied. "I've managed to raise it every week so far, haven't I?"

Every fall a rash of family deaths slowed production. In order to be better prepared, management hung this sign in the plant: THOSE OF YOU WHO ARE DESIROUS OF ATTENDING THE FUNERAL OF A NEAR AND DEAR RELATIVE ARE REQUESTED TO PLEASE NOTIFY THE SUPERVISOR BEFORE 11 A.M. THE DAY OF THE GAME.

A candy store operator was bemoaning the sad fate that had overtaken him. "I was a hard working clerk, earning a mere ten dollars a week," he told his clergyman, "when, like so many ill-advised young men, I fell in with shady characters and felt compelled to gamble."

"Ah," sympathized the cleric, "and the temptation cost you all your hard-accumulated savings!"

"No," said the man. "I won—and like a damned fool bought this lousy candy store."

The practice of mergers has extended to poultry farmers. Four chicken raisers, specializing in freshly laid eggs, combined their one-man operations and put in a sign on the property reading: WE HAVE TEN THOUSAND EMPLOYEES.

During the depression years a storekeeper whose property was being altered hung this sign in his window: NO BUSINESS, AS USUAL.

Don't take the will for the deed. Get the deed.
CREDO OF THE KIND-HEARTED

After the crash of '29 a Pennsylvania cemetery posted this notice, PERSONS ARE PROHIBITED FROM PICKING FLOWERS FROM ANY BUT THEIR OWN GRAVES.

Construction companies have catered to a new kind of advisor known as the "Sidewalk Superintendent." These curious passers-by make it a practice to stop wherever there is construction

251

going on, leaning over the rail, and for various periods of time remaining transfixed by the bustling activity. A New York City excavation carried this notice: SPECTATORS ARE REQUESTED TO PLEASE REFRAIN FROM FALLING OVER THE RAIL AS THERE ARE WORK-MEN DOWN BELOW.

In 1958 the administration issued statistics to show that a reported decline in business activity was purely imaginary, and suggested that in order to overcome needless pessimism industry should adopt the slogan "Business is good." The idea was approved by the National Association of Manufacturers and that organization polled certain members on the matter. One businessman replied: "There is no recession in this field, but we are having the worst boom in years."

LAW OF DIMINISHING INVESTMENTS: To get 10 per cent out of some businessmen you've got to be at least a fifty-fifty partner.

A leader in the pyramiding frozen food business offered a bribe of one hundred thousand dollars to a government inspector.

"Why so much?" the astonished federal man asked.

"Because," said the tycoon, "if I have to put chicken in the chicken pot pie I'm ruined."

If all the economists in the world were laid end to end—it wouldn't be a bad idea.

"You must eat ice cream, lots of ice cream," a doctor told an anemic patient. "It will build up your system."

"Please, doctor, don't make me do that!" begged the man. "I'm in the business, and I know how it's made."

The epidemic of expensive hotels has caused most of them to replace the old signs which read, HAVE YOU LEFT ANYTHING? to new ones which ask, HAVE YOU ANYTHING LEFT?

When it was discovered that employee morale was low in one of the industrial plants a public relations consultant was employed to institute a program of rectification. After several management conferences a plan was agreed upon and the workers were assembled to hear the program explained by the company president.

"When you have worked here five years you will receive a green certificate which says you have given five valuable years of service to the company," he announced. "When you have worked here ten years you will receive a beautiful blue certificate which says we appreciate very much the valuable services rendered the firm during the past ten years. And when you have worked here fifteen years you get a badge."

"What does the badge say?" the foreman asked.

"The badge says, 'This man has a green and a blue certificate.'"

"Look," said the businessman to his accountant. "Let's stop all those tricks. I want to pay my income tax in one lump."

"But you are permitted by law to pay it quarterly," the accountant explained.

"I know that," the boss replied. "But my heart can't take it four times a year."

Money

If you would know the value of money try to borrow some.
BENJAMIN FRANKLIN

If, as the poets say, love has moved mountains and forests, and so deeply touched the hearts of men that all of the oceans, and the rivers, and the lakes, are made up of tears love has shed, if this poetic lyricism be true, then the love of which they sing is the love of money.

It is the cause and effect of everything we do, the scale on which accomplishment is weighed. Make your point with money and you make it well. In politics: "A conservative is a fellow who thinks a rich man should have a square deal."

In economics: "A recession is a period in which you tighten up your belt. In a depression you have no belt to tighten up. And when you have no pants to hold up, it's a panic."

As for morals, no civilized culture has ever existed without its version of the greatest warning ever tolled: "Marry for money, my little sonny, a rich man's joke is always funny."

In the Dark Ages both the Church and the *Koran* forbade the charging of interest on loans. Though the *Talmud* specifically prohibited even the "dust" of interest, state laws barring the Jews from any other occupation forced them to undertake money-

254

lending as the sole means of survival. Gradually banking became more universal, with Christian bankers surpassing the Jews in scope and interest rates, until in 1208, Pope Innocent III warned against the enforcement of canon law excluding all usurers from the Church, "lest all churches might as well be closed." ("When it is a question of money all men are of the same religion." —VOLTAIRE.)

In an effort to curb the evils of moneylending the Church created a plan known as the "hills of love" (*montes pietatis*), whereby the needy might obtain interest-free loans by leaving whatever they themselves judged to be valuable. It failed, and paradoxically led to the creation of the pawnshop.

How much money is enough? No one has ever been able to answer. The shining example of philanthropy is sometimes tarnished when thought is given to how the philanthropist got it in the first place.

Where the pursuit of gold is concerned reputation hasn't mattered. Even Brutus was willing to risk his place as one of history's honorable men by loaning money at blood-letting interest rates. Then, as now, the philosophy of the distinguished followed the old English parable: "So we get the chinks, we will bear the stinks."

When the free-thinker movement was at its height in Europe, an Irish priest was invited to the home of a politician, the object being to humiliate the clergyman in a debate with several advanced thinkers.

The talks turned on the "callous attitude of the Church" in demanding money for a seat in heaven. "What do you say to this, father?" one of the bold campaigners said. "On my last visit to Italy I saw on the door of the Church of St. Agnes a list of indulgences, and actually saw written there a remission of one thousand years of punishment on payment of one lira. What do you say to that?"

"What do I say?" the priest repeated. "Why, I say it was dirt cheap."

In medieval England a man was tried for the crime of helping himself to the contents of a charity box. Though he was convicted and sentenced, he offered an eloquent defense. "M'lords, I am guilty of no wrongdoing," he said. "As I passed the box I noticed a sign reading 'For the Poor,' and so I helped myself. Am I not poor?"

To a form letter that began: "Dear Sir or Madam: May we ask why you didn't pay your taxes this year?" the tax department received this reply: "Dear Sir or Madam: I have not got the money."

A generous soul objected strongly when accosted for the second time in one week by the same derelict. "See here, my man," the sport protested, "did you not receive ten cents from me three days ago?"

"Yes, sir, I most assuredly did," the petitioner admitted. "But statistical surveys to the contrary, I find it difficult to maintain the standards I've grown accustomed to on three and one third cents a day."

At the conclusion of a press conference a United States senator said: "Thanks a billion, fellas. Since I'm on the Foreign Appropriations Committee, I'd feel like a cheap skate if I said 'thanks a million.'"

Few of us can stand prosperity—another man's, I mean.

MARK TWAIN

It is an easy matter for a stingy man to get rich—but what's the use?

Money

In Germany of the Kaiser's day the following advertisement appeared in a newspaper: "The gentleman who found a purse containing many marks on the Konigstrasse is requested to return it to the owner, as he was recognized."

Two days later this reply ran: "The recognized gentleman who found a purse containing many marks on the Konigstrasse invites the owner to call for it at his home."

A tale is told of a Scotchman who so desperately needed money he withdrew some from the bank.

A priest was consoling a lame beggar in France. "You must not rue your lot or chastise God for your fate," the kindly cleric advised. "You must count your blessings, for think how much more cruel it would be were you blind."

"You are right, father," the beggar agreed. "When I was blind the people always gave me counterfeit money."

Poverty is no disgrace—and that's the only good thing you can say about poverty.

A woman, having prevailed upon her husband to allow her to draw on his account, asked the bank manager to instruct her on the proper way to sign a check. "The same as you do a letter," the bank manager told her.

The following month all the checks were endorsed: "Yours truly, Ethel Culbertson."

A worried teller broke the news of pending problems to his wife by saying: "If the market does not go up, I've robbed a bank."

A philanthropist is a man who gives away what he should be giving back.

In Scotland of old lived the greatest of beggars, MacDuncan the Fool. In his village he was known to be an idiot, thoroughly daft, with no commonsense. "I am the leading citizen of Loch Heeman," a pawky Scot visiting London boasted. "We are known for our crops, our lots—and we have MacDuncan the Fool."

A visitor from Dublin once told how he had held out his purse and told MacDuncan to take any coin he wished. MacDuncan's eyes lit as the man poured the contents on the ground. The village people gathered to watch, while the beggar's smile changed to one of indecision and finally utter puzzlement as he brushed dirt from each coin and studied it. He flung aside the gold and silver and settled for the shiniest copper he found. The villagers laughed as they speculated on MacDuncan's consistency in being an idiot. Shining copper had again deceived him into passing up gold.

MacDuncan smiled, pleased with himself for making the villagers happy. "He always takes the big coin of small value," a native told the Dubliner.

Before leaving, the Irishman found MacDuncan alone and asked: "People say they offer you sixpence or a penny, and you always choose the penny. Do you not know the difference in value that you always take the penny?"

"Aye," replied the fool. "The difference I ken. But if I took the sixpence, do ye think they would try me again?"

A prominent family was selective in the man who might win the hand of their beautiful daughter. At last the time came and she was married, but little was known of the bridegroom. This bothered the local clergyman and he called one day to ask the matriarch: "This young man to whom you've given your daughter, does he have character?"

"He earns fifty thousand dollars a year," replied the lady. "What need has he of character?"

During the depression a husband brought home his pay envelope, containing eleven dollars. He withdrew a single dollar and handed the rest to his wife. The following week he reversed the process, taking ten dollars for himself and leaving her a single.

"But, sweetheart," she protested. "How on earth do you think I can manage an entire week on one dollar?"

"I don't know," he replied. "I had a rotten time of it last week. Now it's your turn."

At a charity ball a society matron spent the entire evening imbibing champagne, eating the spectacular foods, and cavorting with the nation's dignitaries. When the evening ended she called for her limousine, and as she was about to step into it an ill-clad man approached: "Please ma'am," he said, "could you let me have a coin? I've eaten nothing for two days."

"How much do you expect of me?" she said angrily. "Don't you realize I've been dancing all night for you?"

The reason some people are stingy is also the reason they are rich.

At a benefit for the impoverished of London an unexpected bit of glamor was added when George Bernard Shaw appeared. Shaw studied the crowd. A moment later he approached one of the less attractive dowagers and asked her to waltz with him. As they glided along the woman was overwhelmed, and she gushed: "Oh, Mr. Shaw, whatever made you ask poor little me to dance?"

Shaw replied gallantly: "This is a charity ball, isn't it?"

A man who had been wiped out in the '29 crash spent his time borrowing from those he knew. It was a test of friendship, to which some responded while others didn't. It remained, however, for the wife of a former associate to negate his last vestige of dignity. "Why do you waste your time begging?" she coldly snapped. "You should be working."

"Have you ever begged?" he asked quietly.

"Of course not," she snapped.

"Then," he said, "you don't know what work is."

When a familiar face was missing from the regular get-togethers the wife of one of the clique called to inquire the reason.

"You might as well know the truth," the man's wife said. "I put so much pressure on Bob to keep up appearances that he went out and got two years for stealing a Cadillac."

When Bob was paroled a few months later the couple found themselves ostracized by their old crowd; the woman who had called explained the reason.

"We can't mingle with criminals," she said bluntly. "Why did you have to steal a Cadillac? Couldn't you buy one and not pay for it, like the rest of us?"

> Mere wealth can't bring us happiness
> Mere wealth can't make us glad;
> But we'll always take a chance, I guess,
> At being rich and sad.

A Scotch lassie approached one of her elderly countrymen to ask if he wouldn't donate a shilling to the Lord.

"How auld be ye, lassie?" he asked.

"Eighteen."

"Well, nah," the Scot said: "I'm in my eightieth year. I'll be seein' Him long afore ye, so I'll just hand it to Him m'self."

> Want to make dough?
> Here's a plan to try:
> Buy stocks when they are low,
> Sell them when they're high.

"Now if I take this policy of yours," a businessman of the early thirties said to an insurance vendor, "and if my place burned down tomorrow, what would I get?"

"Oh," the agent replied. "Not less than ten years."

It's best to try to save a little while your earnings are small. It's impossible to save after you begin making money.

Money

Two highwaymen pursued a hard-riding minister along miles of English countryside, until they caught up to him. They found he had no money. "Aye, gentlemen, I'm sorry to disappoint you," the minister said. "I might indeed have something to give if I had such energetic fellows as you to pass the plate now and then."

A farmer was detained for questioning about an elections scandal. "Did you sell your vote?" the U. S. Attorney asked.

"No sirree, not me," the farmer protested. "I voted for that there fella 'cause I liked him."

"C'mon, now," threatened the attorney. "I have good evidence that he gave you five dollars."

"Well, now," the farmer said, "it's plain commonsense that when a feller gives ya five dollars ya like him."

There's another advantage in being poor. The doctor will cure you faster.

ELBERT HUBBARD

Take care of your pennies, and the dollars will take care of your heirs and lawyers.

The love of evil is the root of all money.

If you want to know what God thinks of money, look at the people he gives it to.

A Burns detective was placed at the entrance to one of New York City's temples during the high holidays, with specific instructions to keep out anyone who had not bought a ticket. The services were about to begin when a little man approached excitedly. "I've got to get in," he shouted when the Burns man stopped him.

"Where's your ticket?" the detective asked.

"Please," the little man begged. "You don't understand. I belong to another congregation, but I must get in. It's a matter of life or death. My sister is gravely ill, and I must find my brother inside to tell him."

The detective pondered a bit, then said: "Okay, go ahead in and find yer brother. But I'm warning ya, don't let me catch ya prayin'."

Poverty is a wonderful thing. It sticks to a man after all his friends have forsaken him.

Two relatives met, by accident, in a bank. "I'm glad to see you, Arnold," one said. "I'm desperate. I haven't got a nickel."

"You think you're bad off," Arnold replied. "When I cash this check I'll be four hundred dollars overdrawn."

Horace Greeley was once approached for a donation, the purpose of which was to save millions of his fellowmen from going to hell.

"I'll not give a damned cent," Greeley fired back. "Not half enough of them go there now."

Will Rogers chose this way to acknowledge an introduction at a banker's convention: "Gentlemen, you are as fine a group of men as ever foreclosed a mortgage on a widow. I'm glad to be among you Shylocks."

In the Middle West a deacon remonstrated with a congregation that had enjoyed a fine harvest and, as customary, declined to be generous with it. The church building, he pointed out, was in a state of utter dilapidation, the roof leaked, the walls threatened to buckle, and the heating system was fouled.

When he received no response he singled out each member individually and demanded his pledge. "Brother Johnson," he called. And Johnson made his pledge. "Brother Talbert," he called. And Talbert made his pledge. But when he got to Brother Entworth, the richest man in town, Entworth pledged only five dollars.

"Five dollars?" the deacon roared. "By all that's holy I swear, Brother Entworth, that the Almighty knows of your penuriousness."

At that moment a chunk of plaster fell from the roof and landed squarely on Brother Entworth's head. The deacon raised his arms in supplication and said: "We thank you, O Lord, now hit him again."

In old Europe a hardhearted baron held sway over an impoverished area. The baron forbade any to come begging, and when they did he had the hounds turned on them. One evening a man slipped through the fortifications and presented himself to the blue blood. He told a woeful tale of misery and degradation. The baron listened sympathetically until the man had finished. Then, with a tear in his eye, he rang for the captain of the guard. "Throw this man out," the nobleman ordered. "But do it gently. His story has softened my heart."

The ancient code of beggars is to let fellow guildsmen know of an easy mark. In France, prior to the Revolution, word spread of the generosity of a nobleman, and many beggars flocked to him. One day, while seeking out the castle, a beggar was stopped on the road by one of his fellows who told him not to bother going up to the estate. "The count is in a bad mood today. He is only giving two centimes to a caller," the returning beggar warned.

"I shall go anyway," the other replied. "Who is he that I should make him a present of two centimes?"

Profiteering reaches its melancholy peak during the times of war. In Russia, during World War II, a peasant woman called at the government collective to purchase a case of candles. "A thousand rubles," the cheating clerk said.

"A thousand rubles?" the woman protested. "I used to buy this much for two rubles."

"Don't you know there's a war on?" the clerk snapped.

"So what?" the woman snapped back. "You mean to say, comrade, that we're fighting with candles?"

One of the oldest bits of Americana concerns a bribed juror who was given fifty dollars to hold for a manslaughter conviction in a murder trial.

The verdict having been so rendered, the juror called at the home of the convicted man to collect his fee. "Here is your money," the man's father said, paying the debt. "It must have been difficult."

"It sure was," the juror acknowledged. "All the rest went in for acquittal."

A beggar sprawled on the street with a cup in his hand, a dog at his side, and a sign across his chest that read: HAVE MERCY ON THE BLIND. A man passed, tossed a coin into the cup, then reached down and said: "I put a half dollar in your cup and I'm taking forty cents change."

"That's a lie," the beggar said. "You only put in a quarter."

"Aha," the donor challenged. "You're not really blind. You're a fraud."

"You're mistaken," the beggar answered. "It's the dog that's blind—not me."

A clergyman visited the head of a family in the outskirts of Edinburgh. "John," he said, "I hope you are keeping family worship constantly."

"Aye, sir, I am," John answered. "In the time o' year when we ought."

"In the time of the year when you ought? I'm afraid I don't understand."

"It's plain to ken, sir, we canna' see to read the prayer book in winter."

"But John," the clergyman said. "You should buy candles."

"Aye, sir," John admitted. "But in that case I'm afraid the cost wud owergang the profit."

Money

In the thirties America was swept by a fad known as "Screeno," a game played in moving picture houses.

A Screeno jackpot winner left the theater after collecting her prizes. When she came in the door her son, noting her melancholy, asked if anything had happened at the movie.

"Yes," she said. "I won the Screeno jackpot. A mink coat, a fancy wardrobe from Bonwit Teller, a new car, a lifetime pass to all the Loew's Theaters, and five thousand dollars in cash."

"That's wonderful!!" the boy shouted. "Why are you so gloomy?"

"I don't care," she stomped. "Barrymore died at the end of the picture."

A traveling Texas couple stopped in Paris to buy several paintings by Dégas, three Renoirs, two Modiglianis, a Rembrandt, and a Cézanne. He paid three quarters of a million dollars in cash for them, then turned to his wife and said: "All right, honey, that takes care of the cards. Let's get the presents."

A Sister of Charity called on a businessman to solicit funds for the cause. "I would like very much to help you, sister," he said, "but I'm having the hardest time paying the money I owe around here."

"But you know," she said, "that you owe something to the Lord too."

"That's right, sister, that's right," the man admitted. "But He's not pushing me like some of my other creditors."

"Unexampled Parsimony" is the title given to this story in an old English jest book.

A broker, obsessed with the making of money all his life, called on one of his poor relatives, only to hear the man bemoan his bleak outlook. "Come now, Edward," the broker interrupted. "I've come to tell you that I have made out my will, and you are remembered handsomely, my boy."

"May the Good Lord bless your honor," the grateful man cried. "You will be rewarded by the Almighty for your charitable action, for you could not have thought of a more distressed family."

"Are you indeed so very poor, Edward?"

Edward's eyes filled with tears as he said: "Poor? sir, my family is starving."

"Hark ye then, Edward," the broker said, slamming one determined fist into the other. "I will pay your legacy immediately, if you will allow me a fair rate of discount."

There is nothing more demoralizing than a small but adequate income.

EDMUND WILSON

"I have come many miles, excellency," a beggar told a Polish nobleman. "Across the ice and through the snow, in feet ragged and bleeding, because I heard you were a very charitable man who bestows his munificence upon the poor."

"Tell me," the nobleman requested. "Are you taking the same route back by which you came?"

"Yes, Excellency."

"Then you may be of service," the nobleman said. "Deny the rumor for me."

Nineteenth-century Philadelphia court records are said to contain details of a hearing requested by the family of a deceased millionaire in which they sought to have the courts set aside his will. In the covenant he had left three quarters of his estate to his young widow. The family's attorney sought to prove the deceased was insane at the time of his passing by forcing the young, handsomely endowed widow to repeat his dying words.

"I would rather not," she insisted, and blushed.

"But you must," the lawyer fired. "The law demands that you do."

She declined once more, and only an appeal to the bench persuaded her to offer the testimony: "He said, 'Kiss me, Florrie, and open the other bottle of champagne.'"

At this point the judge cried out enthusiastically: "Sensible to the last!"

Theater and the Arts

Television has proved that sight has a definite odor.

The first encore was given to a Roman actor named Livius Andronicus. Andronicus was called back to repeat his speeches so often that he hired a boy to declaim for him, while he supplied the gestures. He called it an act of self defense. He was also the first ham. . . .

The first hiss took place in 1680, a dark year for the theater. There is no prior record of an audience being sufficiently stirred by the effort of player or playwright to emit sound by vibrating the tongue between the lips. The author thus immortalized was Fontenelle, and the play was *Aspar*, suitably termed a tragedy. Prior to this happening, audiences were content merely to fall asleep—much as they do today. . . .

Personal conduct clauses were introduced by Edward III (1312–77) when he ordered a company of players banished from London because "they represented scandalous, foolish things in alehouses and other places, to crowds of people."

The players got around the order by doing a series of religious presentations, until their success proved too much competition for the professional theologians—who were engaged in the same business. . . .

Theater and the Arts

The first English comedy was *Gammer Gurton's Needle,* produced early in the sixteenth century. It deals with the tribulations of an old hag who loses her needle while darning the seat of the main character's pants. There are no other needles in the village and the catastrophe carries through five acts, during which time the needle is lodged on the person of the main character in a spot more tender than the heart. . . .

The first tragedy of the theater is unrecorded, but there is every possibility that television will be the last.

A museum once boasted that America's intellectual interests were mounting as witnessed by the countless people who came to see its wonders. However, when a comfort station was erected on an adjoining corner, museum attendance fell off by two hundred thousand.

One of the shortest literary critiques on record is Voltaire's review of Rousseau's ode *To Posterity.* Said Voltaire: "This poem will never reach its destination."

If you can't give me your word of honor, give me your promise.

SAM GOLDWYN

The great American novel has not only been already written, it has already been rejected.

FRANKLIN K. DANE

Among caustic humorists in the field of music Rossini rates high. Franz Liszt once called on the master and in the course of the evening played a piece of music Rossini had never before heard. "What is it?" he asked the flamboyant Hungarian.

"It is a march I have written on the death of Meyerbeer," Liszt replied. "How do you like it, maestro?"

"My dear Liszt," Rossini said. "Don't you think it would have been better had you died and Meyerbeer written the march?"

Mark Twain was once the guest of a prominent society hostess at the New York Metropolitan Opera. The lady was extremely talkative throughout the performance, and afterward asked Twain: "I do hope you'll be my guest again. What do you say to next Thursday? The opera will be *Tosca*."

"I'd love to," Twain replied. "I've never heard you in that."

The great artists of the world are never puritans, and seldom even ordinarily respectable.

H. L. MENCKEN

Albert Einstein attended a concert in Berlin. During a solo performance Mrs. Einstein nudged him and said: "Look at Esterhazy, he has fallen asleep."

Einstein replied: "For that you wake me up?"

Shelley Berman on André Gide: "He was a Frenchman—and that makes him a little dirty to begin with."

I know only two tunes. One of them is "Yankee Doodle." The other one isn't.

U. S. GRANT

The pun as an art form is debatable; but it is generally conceded that Thomas Hood, in the closing lines of Sally Brown, set a standard neither surpassed nor equalled.

> "His death, which happened in his berth,
> At forty-odd befell;
> They went and told the sexton,
> And the sexton tolled the bell."

Actors must be on their guard. Louis Calhern was playing Lear and had entered the climactic passages of a soliloquy when a woman seated up front decided to breast-feed her crying baby. But the baby wouldn't respond, and in a voice audible to the entire theater the woman scolded: "Take it. Take it, or I'll give it to the actor."

In picture-making the writer is the most important clog in the wheel.

SAM GOLDWYN

The will of a dead actor requested that his body be cremated and 10 per cent of his ashes thrown in his agent's face.

Victor Hugo was extremely critical of Goethe. To a group of literary connoisseurs he once declared: "Goethe never wrote anything worth reading except *The Robbers*."

Reminded by one of his listeners that *The Robbers* had been written by Schiller, Hugo continued: "And even that is Schiller's."

An eighteenth century author presented a copy of his latest book to a female admirer. "Sire," she exclaimed, "this is not a first printing."

Bowing low, he answered: "Madam, I assure you any second printing of my work is even more rare."

Oscar Wilde, when told the story of a Denver man who was shot through the head when he turned his back to examine lithographs on a wall, said: "This shows how dangerous it is to interest oneself in bad art."

"I am thoroughly exhausted," Oscar Wilde told a friend. "This morning I put a comma in one of my poems."

"Was the afternoon's work equally exhausting?" the friend asked.

"Yes," replied Wilde. "This afternoon I took it out again."

I wouldn't belong to any organization that would have me for a member.

GROUCHO MARX, *on being invited to join an actors' club*

After achieving box office popularity as a cinematic artist a dramatic actor did not seem to enjoy the success. "I don't understand," his agent protested. "You're in demand. You have plenty of money and everything else you want."

"Bah," sneered the actor. "What good is money to me? Here I am with everything I want, and my poor old mother has to starve in a garret."

In Hollywood blood is thicker than talent.

At the old Star Burlesque a man approached the box office and demanded his money back. "Why?" asked the cashier.

"You advertised a chorus of seventy," he replied. "And not one of them looks over sixty."

The actor's tour was a great success. He outran every audience.

"I once played a house where every seat was on the aisle."
"How is that possible?"
"It was a long narrow theater."

Americans don't spend millions for amusement. They spend it in search of amusement.

Had the telegraph not immortalized Samuel F. B. Morse, this story would. Having completed a painting in which was depicted a man in the death agony, the inventor called upon his doctor for comment. The physician studied the painting closely, then said: "Malaria."

There is no great genius without a mixture of madness.

ARISTOTLE

"You can't use this story for a picture," the Hollywood censor told a top producer. "The leading character is a lesbian."

"Okay, then," the producer countered. "We'll make him a Hungarian."

Free Thoughts on Several Eminent Composers:

> Some cry up Haydn, some Mozart
> Just as the whim bites. For my part
> I do not care a farthing candle
> For either of them, nor for Handel.

CHARLES LAMB

Heywood Broun was once the defendant in an action brought by a performer he had called the world's worst actor. Later, when reviewing a performance by the same actor, Broun wrote: "Mr. Such-and-Such was not up to his usual standard."

The actor who played King Lear played the king as though he expected someone to play the ace.

EUGENE FIELD

I look upon reviews as a kind of children's disease which more or less attacks newborn books. There are cases on record where the healthiest succumbed to them, and the puniest have often survived them.

G. C. LICHTENBERG

No matter how well you perform there's always somebody of intelligent opinion who thinks it's lousy.

SIR LAURENCE OLIVIER

What's the good of having talent if you can't use it as an excuse for being unemployed?

GERALD BARZAN, *when offered a steady job*

In ancient England a merchant hired an artist for the purpose of conveying his portrait-in-oils to posterity. Terms were arranged,

273

among them the artist's surmise that the job would take a fortnight.

But it was completed in ten days. "You are cheating me of four days' work," the merchant protested.

"It matters not," said the artist. "The work is done."

"That, sir, is not business," the merchant protested. "I agreed to a set amount for a fortnight's work. I stand quite ready to pay the price, but you ought not spend fewer than the hours agreed."

Argument being useless, the painter took up his brush and applied his talents to four more sittings—lengthening little by little the ears of his patron.

When a Paris theatrical producer got into a heated discussion with an American, the Frenchman drew his card, threw it on the table, and stalked out of the room. The American stared at the card, took out his pen, wrote "admit bearer" on the back—and went off to the theater.

The critics:

A vast improvement can be made in the third act. Instead of the hero dying on the scaffold he should be shot by a firing squad. It would not only wake up the audience, but it would also let them know the show is over.

FRANKLIN K. DANE

He isn't the kind of performer who stops a show; he is content merely to slow it up.

ANONYMOUS

They couldn't find the artist, so they hung the picture.

Original source unknown

The rattlings of the milk-cans of human kindness.

(Guedella on the writings of James M. Barrie)

Excellent, were it not for its length.

CHAMFORT, *on a couplet*

The covers of this book are too far apart.

AMBROSE BIERCE

274

It was one of those plays in which all of the actors unfortunately enunciated very clearly.

ROBERT BENCHLEY

The dogs were poorly supported by the rest of the cast.

DON HERALD, review of *Uncle Tom's Cabin*

In the film version of *Kiss the Boys Goodbye,* the producers have kept the boys and kissed the script goodbye.

N. Y. *Times*

You can stay away anytime, because it is continuous.

ANONYMOUS

March came in like a lion and went out like a ham.

(Frank Nugent of Fredric March in *The Buccaneer*)

The title of *Wake Up and Live* ought to be changed to *Wake Up and Leave.*

WALTER WINCHELL

The House Beautiful is the play lousy.

DOROTHY PARKER

A non-conformist young man from the Middle West left his home for a career in the theater. After years of silence his father received word that a show in which he was performing would be on view at a Wichita theater. On opening night the actor's family appeared in strength. The play began, but neither the first nor second acts saw evidence of the prodigal farm boy. Finally, towards the end of the third act, he appeared in a soldier's costume, carrying a rifle. He paraded backwards and forward but said nothing. The elder farmer could not stand the humiliation; as the play neared its conclusion he rose from his seat and shouted: "Do something, Ephraim—for God's sake! If they don't let you talk, at least shoot!"

Madam Ernestine Schumann-Heink, at a Detroit concert, had to make her entrance from the rear of the orchestra pit. Quarters were cramped, and as she propelled her ample frame forward she began knocking down the music racks. "Sideways, madame," Conductor Gabrilowitsch whispered. "Go sideways."

"Mein gott," the great Schumann-Heink called back. "I haff no sideways."

A theatrical mystery concerns Shakespeare's intentions regarding Romeo and Juliet; was there an actual affair between the two? A theatrical historian once put the question to John Barrymore. "Did Shakespeare mean to give the impression of an illicit relationship between Romeo and Juliet?"

"I don't know what Shakespeare intended," Barrymore replied. "But every time I played Romeo I took Juliet out after the show."

Following a Broadway opening George M. Cohan offered this opinion to the playwright. "I saw your play tonight, and there is a great deal in it which is new and a great deal that is true. But, unfortunately, it happens that those portions which are new are not true, and those which are true are not new."

Will Rogers was a personal friend of the Prince of Wales. When it was rumored that Wales would make a good will tour of Africa, to be climaxed by a hunt, Rogers was asked if the latter was true. "Sure," he replied. "The Prince is going to shoot wild animals as fast as they come out of their cages."

"Where did you get the plot for your second novel?"
"From the film version of my first."

The most embarrassing moment in the life of a performer took place on the stage of the Palace Theater. A magician, having called upon an impartial youngster in the audience to assist him, asked: "Now, my boy, have you ever seen me before?"
The boy replied: "No, Daddy."

The peak of critical disdain occurred when a gunman approached the box office of a theater and said: "The play stinks—give me everybody's money back."

Late fifteenth-century repartee tells the incident of a patron who accosted an artist with the remark: "It is incredible that you paint so beautifully, yet beget such ugly children."

"Yes, sire," agreed the artist. "But, you see, I make my children in the darkness and I do my painting in the light."

Bert Swor, as principal comedian with Fields' minstrels, shared the same dressing room with Al Fields. Swor was a fresh air lover while Fields feared the cold. Upon arriving at the theater and being assigned their dressing room, Swor would promptly open the window and Fields would close it just as quickly. During one engagement the routine was followed for ten minutes until Swor took a chair and broke the window. "There," he said. "Now we both have our way. It's open and it's closed."

Harry Houdini, the Handcuff King, told this story to Al Jolson. Houdini arranged to be handcuffed and leg-ironed on a bridge in Scotland; then he was to be tossed over the side. A stunt of this kind usually drew tremendous crowds, but when the great Houdini stood on the bridge ready to do the trick not a single viewer showed up to watch him. It was a toll bridge.

Sol Hess, creator of the Nebbs, attended the funeral of an actor friend. The deceased had the misfortune to be married to a shrew. After he detailed phases of the funeral to Joe Laurie, Jr., Laurie asked: "How did he look?"

Hess said: "Relieved."

A young actor visited Broadway for the first time. He approached the owner of one of the traditional theaters and asked in awe: "Did John Barrymore really play here?"

"Yes," boasted the owner. "But he won't again. He fell off the trapeze three times."

A stage-strutting hero once remarked to the great Garrick: "Shakespeare haunts me night and day."

"That you are so haunted is not to be wondered at," Garrick answered. "In every character of that author you attempted to present, have you not most cruelly murdered him?"

After his first performance of *Hamlet* in London, Barrymore was backstage thinking he had failed, when one of those old time fellows in Inverness cape, pop-up hat, and cane with ivory knob, came into the dressing room. He became very emotional, threw himself to his knees, groped for Barrymore's hand to kiss, and said throatily: "O Master! I enjoyed your performance so much!" Barrymore replied: "Not half so much as I am enjoying yours."

Fred Allen constantly fought sponsor interference. A pressure group once protested a remark he made on the air, threatening to cease using the sponsor's product. Allen was forced to retract. Since the product was a laxative he did it this way: "The prospect that they would go through life constipated so frightened the agency that they made me apologize."

I always wanted to be on the stage. I didn't want to do *Hamlet*, so I did the next best thing—omelette. I laid eggs.

MAXIE ROSENBLOOM

The practice of submitting any kind of book to Sam Goldwyn for possible movie consideration has led to unusual commentaries. After World War II someone placed a copy of *The Making of Yesterday, The diaries of Raoul de Roussy de Sales, 1938-1942* on his desk. Goldwyn stared at it, and his jaw slowly dropped. "How do you like that?" he said, amazed. "Four years old and the kid keeps a diary."

Hissing, now in disrepute, was an integral part of the stage a century ago. At a small theater in Vermont *The Forty Thieves* was being performed to an audience of seven. Displeased at the acting of a particular performer, the customers hissed him energetically. Whereupon the manager brought his full company of thieves on stage—and out-hissed the audience.

I was once so broke I forgot whether you cut steak with a knife or drink it with a spoon.

BOB HOPE

Television is called a medium because anything good on it is rare.

FRED ALLEN

When John Erskine was scheduled to lecture in Chattanooga, Dr. Alexander Guerry, president of the university, went to the station to greet him. Not having met Erskine before, the doctor approached two men in turn, mistaking each for his guest.

Guerry later told the educator of the experience. "I asked one gentleman if he were John Erskine and he said, with emphasis, 'I should say not.' I asked another, and he said, 'I wish I were.' Which shows at least one man read your books."

"It does," Erskine agreed. "But which one?"

The mistakes of radio announcers have become a part of show-business lore. Herbert Hoover, when President, was once introduced as "Hoobert Heever." A product named Hind's Hand Cream was characterized throughout a commercial as "Hand's Hind Cream." Ruppert's Beer entered the hall of fame as "Buppert's Rear." But none of these matched the announcer for a mattress company who advised the audience to "demand the breast in bed."

In the fields of art the art of rejection is, for the most part, artless. The performing arts has its "Don't call us, we'll call you"— an unimaginative cliché and a notch below the writing field's "The editors have read your manuscript and find it unsuitable to our present needs."

George M. Cohan once received a substandard play accompanied by a beautiful letter in the hand of the playwright. To soften the letdown, Cohan sent the following wire: "We have read your letter and your play and are giving serious consideration to producing your letter."

On one occasion Herbert Beerbohm Tree broke the news this way: "My dear Sir: I have read your play. Oh, my dear sir! Yours faithfully, Herbert Beerbohm Tree."

Oriental propriety, however, demands a warmer approach. And so, early in the century, the following standard rejection form was used by a Chinese editor:

"Illustrious brother of the sun and moon, look upon the slave who rolls at thy feet, who kisses the earth before thee, and demands of thy charity permission to speak and live. We have read the manuscript with delight. By the bones of our ancestors we swear that never before have we encountered such a masterpiece. Should we print it His Majesty the emperor would order us to take it as a criterion and never again print anything which was not equal to it. As that would not be possible before 10,000 years, all trembling we return this manuscript and beg thee 10,000 pardons. See my head at thy feet, and I am the slave of thy servant.

The Editor."

Occupations and Professions

*When more and more people are thrown out of work, un-
employment results.*

CALVIN COOLIDGE

A secretarial career, or that of a domestic, barber, civil servant,
truck driver, laborer, etc., may seem dull compared to the higher
callings. Still, each has its reasons for being and its gratifications.
In the words of Douglas Jerrold: "The ugliest of trades have
their moments. Were I a grave digger, or perhaps a hangman,
there are some people for whom I could work with a great deal
of pleasure."

Earning a livelihood outside the élite professions has its advantages. It is less confining. The upper professional usually has
his career planned for him before the age of self-determination.
Following a score of parental and academic brainwashing years he
is not apt to rebel against limited horizons. Instead he is
content to lean on the cushion of prestige that accompanies high
fees. In a little while the urge to bring in wildcat oil wells and
breathe the air of the lumberjack is pushed into a brain recess,
to appear momentarily when watching a travelogue, or an adagio
dancer.

The ordinary breadwinner is lucky. He can try as many fields as he likes, until, after mountains of unemployment checks, he at last finds his niche, or gets married, in which case he stays put.

Cumulative vocational experience pays off. I can recall a Horatio Alger kind of true-life tale. A man who tried many things failed as a stock-market speculator, failed as a supermarket operator, failed as an advertising executive, failed as a government employee, and failed in a score of other businesses and vocations. But perseverance conquered, and he made a fortune—writing books on why men fail. . . .

The dictation taker is not without honor in history. A report says: At Marengo, whilst Napoleon reconnoitered the enemy's movements, and gave his orders in writing, a cannon ball struck the officer to whom he was dictating, and threw him mutilated on the ground. Napoleon ordered another secretary; he came. At the moment when Napoleon resumed his dispatch, the wounded man raised himself. "General!" said he, in a dying voice, "General —we stopped there." He repeated the last words that Napoleon had dictated—and died.

If I had my way that story would be framed and hung over every water cooler in the country.

The lot of a burglar is a hard one. Having been found guilty, a second story man stood before the British magistrate awaiting his due. "Have you anything to say before I pass sentence?" the judge solemnly asked.

"Yes, m'lord," said the burglar. "It's a bit thick bein' identified by a bloke wot kept 'is 'ead under the bedclothes the 'ole time."

A young man applied for a job at the bank, giving two ministers as reference. "We don't work here on Sundays," said the interviewer. "Can't you get references from anyone who sees you on weekdays?"

"I was forced to break my engagement to that young schoolteacher," sighed the lad. "I was late one night, and she wanted me to bring a written excuse from my mother."

Occupations and Professions

A vice president is a person who finds a molehill on his desk in the morning and must make a mountain out of it by five P.M.

FRED ALLEN

The hazards of certain occupations couldn't possibly involve more risk than that taken by a professional forger. There is a case on record wherein such a craftsman worked diligently to do an expert job on a check drawn against a millionaire's account. He labored six months to attain perfection—only to have it come back marked "Insufficient Funds."

In England a manufacturer wished to encourage church attendance on the part of his factory help, particularly with regards to fast days. He said that if they went to church they would receive full wages for the day in the same manner as if they'd spent the time at the plant.

Shortly after the announcement the shop foreman came forward and told his employer the men had decided that if he would pay time and a half they would also attend evening services.

A certain labor union, notorious for employing ex-convicts, is reputed to keep jailed members alert to their opportunities, particularly around parole time, by sending notices to the effect that "There are Only Forty Shoplifting Days to Xmas."

When the elder Dumas lay dying a faithful servant, who worshiped his master, was moved to a point where his sobs filled the death room. Dumas turned towards him, and in a voice barely audible, said: "Do not weep, my friend. If I want anything up there—I'll ring for you."

Chauncey Depew would constantly remark upon the peculiarities of New Englanders. He told the story of a certain section in Vermont where the only pleasure the citizens had was attendance at funerals. He attended such an event, and, as the preacher finished his message, the undertaker announced: "Friends, there will be a slight delay in the festivities on account of the corpse has been mislaid."

When the Brooklyn *Daily Eagle* closed its doors an elderly gentleman, at work in the composing room some fifty years, was told he would be pensioned off. "Doggonit," he cussed. "When I started here they said it was gonna be a steady job."

During the course of a heated argument between a clergyman and a magistrate over the relative merits of their authority, the clergyman, a bishop, said, "This debate is senseless. You, as a judge, can only say 'you be hanged'; whereas I, have the power to say 'you be damned.'"

"True," admitted the jurist. "But when a judge says to a man 'You be hanged,' he's hanged."

Sign in a tonsorial college: THE OPINIONS EXPRESSED BY THE BARBERS ARE STRICTLY THEIR OWN.

A kindly old lady was watching a construction job. As the work grew heavier one of the men took off his hat, cast it aside, and continued to swing his pick bareheaded. The sun beat down on him, but he didn't seem to mind. However, the old lady began to fidget and finally she ran over to him, saying: "Mister, don't you know the sun will injure your brain if you expose it like that?"

"Lady," said the laborer, "do you think I'd be doin' this kinda work if I had a brain?"

Another addition to the list of dead occupations is the second story man. He went out of existence with the ranch-style home.

As the foreman was making the rounds at noontime he noticed one of his men eating a sandwich while blood dripped from a deep gash in his forehead. "Bill," shouted the foreman, "you've hurt yourself. Why don'tcha rush over to the dispensary?"

"Nothing doing," replied Bill. "Not on me lunch hour."

"Beulah, I see a spider web in the corner. To what do you attribute that?"

"I'd say to a spider, mu'm."

The telephone company received a complaint from one of their subscribers regarding the awful language used by several linemen working on the wires outside her window. One of the men was called to his supervisor's office and asked to explain. He denied all, giving this version of the incident. "Me and Jack Chalmers are on this job, see? Jack is away up on the pole, and I'm working about ten feet below, when he suddenly drops some hot lead and it goes right down me back. Now all I said was, 'You are getting rather careless, Jack, and I think it would be much wiser if you adhered to safety regulation number two.'"

The boss called two of the office help into his inner sanctum. "I hear you and Bob here almost had a fight," he said.

"Yes," said Bob. "It would-a been a terrible fracas, too, only there wasn't nobody around to hold us apart."

Right in the middle of a hot poker game at the fire house the phone rang. "Who is it?" asked the chief.

"Please, help, you've got to help me," a frantic voice shouted. "My house is on fire."

"Calm yerself, lady. Now tell me, did you try puttin' water on it?"

"Yes, yes I did."

"Well, then," said the chief, "there's no sense our rushin' over. That's all we do."

"Why did you fire my son as a caddy?" asked the angry woman. "Was he lazy?"

"No," said the pro. "He could do the work all right. But he couldn't learn not to laugh."

A southern congregation was considering the relative merits of several ministers, one of whom was to be given the post of resident preacher. It was a hard decision, and they finally settled on Zeb Dilten. "Why'd you pick Zeb?" the constable asked one of the elders.

"Wal, it's like this," said the elder. "It's true he ain't much on sermons, because he's gotta tend his own farm and orchard. But he's mighty movin' in prayer when it's caterpillar and cankerworm time."

An early nineteenth-century story tells of the call-house madam who, through a mixup, found herself in front of the Pearly Gates. She rang the bell, and St. Peter called out, "Who's that?"

"It's me. Flossie LaCouche."

"Flossie LaCouche? What are you doing in these precincts?"

"I wanna get in! Waddaya think I'm doin'?"

"Well, all right," St. Peter answered, as he swung the gates open. "You can come in—but I know you're not going to like it here."

A train was crossing the Canadian border on its way to New York, during that time when the country was dry. A redcap assisted a man who was getting off at the first American stop. "Careful with that luggage, boy," warned the passenger.

"Suh," the porter said proudly, "Ah toted thousands of dese yere kind of suitcases, and Ah'm proud to say that never once't did Ah let de bottles rattle."

A carnival worker called on a psychiatrist, but he refused to sit and discuss the case; rather, he preferred to do it from a standing position, unique in psychiatry. "It's on account of my work at the carnival," said the man.

"Just exactly what do you do there?" asked the doctor.

"I put my head through a canvas and people throw baseballs at me. I can't sit for weeks at a time," the man explained.

"What has throwing baseballs at your head got to do with sitting down?"

"Oh, I forgot to tell you about my side line," the man said. "I also rented out my behind for a dart game."

Honor the undertaker. He always carries out what he undertakes.
GERALD BARZAN

"My good man," said the dentist. "You don't have to pay me now."

"Pay you?" said the patient. "I'm counting my money before you gimme the gas."

A shop foreman was constantly agitating about the mass of unemployment in this country. "Look, Charlie," said the proprietor, "I don't see why you should fuss so much about unemployment. After all, you've got a pretty steady job here."

"That's what bothers me," said Charlie. "I feel bad to think of all those bums loafing while I gotta work."

A construction engineer was being tried for traffic violation in a Georgia court. "Mr. Buildem," the judge said. "We have taken into consideration your considered opinion regarding the badness of the roads hereabouts, as indicated in your sworn testimony. As a result the court has decided not to fine you a hundred dollars as the law permits."

"That's extremely kind of you, judge," said Buildem.

"We try to be fair," continued the magistrate, "and instead of the hundred-dollar fine we're going to sentence you to work on the road for two weeks, in the hope that your superior wisdom as a road expert will improve them considerably."

A story that most editors will tell a novice reporter concerns the young apprentice journalist whose first assignment was to interview a Catholic priest. When the journalism school graduate arrived at the church the Reverend Father was receiving confessions. The reporter went down the aisle until he reached the confessional box; there he put his face against the side and, sighting the priest, said: "I should like to see you, sir; I am a reporter for the Providence *Puritan*."

Softly the priest said: "In a moment."

After a while the priest emerged from the confessional box, walked to the reporter, and in a careful whisper said: "Young man, I have listened to confessions for more than forty years, but yours is the worst one I ever heard."

An industrialist finally had a good year, having obtained a federal contract to produce whatever it was that would be needed to sell through government surplus. He decided to become a gentleman farmer, and with that in mind visited some acreage that was up for sale. The owner showed him around the place, then asked him what he thought. "Well," said the businessman, "milkin' cows sure looks easy, and I'm certain I could do it myself. But, tell me, how do you shut it off?"

An efficiency expert is a man who knows less than you about your business and gets paid more for telling you how to run it than you could possibly make even if you ran it right instead of the way he told you to.

The master of the house was put out with the new Irish maid. "Why did you tell the mistress what time I came in this morning when I specifically asked you not to?"

"Sure, sir, Oi did not tell her," protested the maid. "She asked me what time you came in an' Oi tould her Oi was so busy getting breakfast Oi didn't look at the clock."

Outside one of the army recruiting camps there is a barber shop with a sign reading, "Military haircuts repaired here."

"Do you want a meal bad enough to work for it?"
"I'm just hungry, mum, not desperate."

"What does your father work at, Johnny?"
"At intervals."

There is now a friendly undertaker who signs his letters,
"Eventually yours."

"That's right, madam," the employment-agency director said,
"we have the best nursemaids in the city. Every one of them is
less than five feet tall."
"What has that got to do with it?"
"Why," said the agency man, "if they drop a baby it doesn't
have far to fall."

"They stopped my pay down at the foundry."
"Why was that?"
"I think firing me had something to do with it."

A passenger on a Chicago-bound train complained to the porter.
"Do you know I found one black shoe and one brown shoe
under my berth?"
"Dammit," said the porter. "It's the second time I done that
this morning."

"Is your mistress home?" a caller asked the maid.
"Can't tell till you raises your veil, mum," said the maid. "If
you've got a big wart in the middle of your nose she ain't."

"Doc," said the construction worker to the psychiatrist, "I don't
think I can stand my work any more."
"Why?" asked the doctor. "The riveting getting on your
nerves?"
"It ain't that," said the patient. "I don't mind the riveting.
It's the guy next to me. He hums all day."

"This storm is awful," the reporter screamed into the phone.
"Wind velocity is over one hundred miles. The sleet blinds you.

289

The flood waters are rising. Boss, I tell you it's no night for man or beast."

"Great!!" shouted the editor. "I'll send a couple of photographers to cover it."

"My husband is an efficiency expert."

"What does his work involve?"

"Well, it's hard to describe, but if we women did it they'd call it nagging."

A gentleman named O'Hara, back on the ould sod, was hired as an assistant stationmaster. His first day on the job, as a train arrived, he called out, "Change here for Limerickgalwayandmayo."

The stationmaster was critical. "Haven't I told you, Clarence, that you are to sing out the stations? Clearly and distinctly."

"I will, sir," said the chagrined O'Hara. When the next train arrived his fine Irish tenor came over the loudspeaker, singing:

"Sweet dreamland faces
    Passing to and fro
Change here for Limerick,
    Galway and Mayo."

A gentleman, having been admitted to Heaven, decided to spend his vacation in Purgatory and purchased a round trip ticket, with that objective in mind. He arrived at Purgatory early in the morning and was amazed to find everybody sitting about in relaxed positions.

"I don't get it," he remarked to one of the denizens. "I'm a citizen of Heaven. And what happens? I have to work steady from five in the morning to seven at night. And down here, where, let's face it, things are supposed to be so much tougher, why you're all sitting around with nothing to do at eight in the morning."

"It's not hard to figure out," said the Purgatory citizen. "You see, we have just as much work down here, but there's more of us to do it, so we get through sooner."

When the interviewer asked the applicant for the secretarial job if she had any outstanding capabilities, she said, "Yes. I've won over two thousand dollars in slogan contests."

"That's fine, but we need somebody who's bright during office hours."

"Well," said the girl, "this was during office hours."

The lady persisted in walking to the bus driver and asking, "Is this Grand Concourse?"

"No," said the driver.

Two stops later she asked again, "Is this Grand Concourse?"

"No, it's not, lady," said the driver.

And so it went until she had asked the same question eight times. "Will you tell me when we're there?" she finally asked.

"I won't have to," said the driver.

"Then how will I know?"

"By the smile on my face," said the driver.

A foreman on a railroad project sent an accident report to the safety engineer, with this note attached: "Enclosed find report on accident when the piano fell on Casey's foot. Where it says 'Remarks' do you want mine or Casey's?"

Virginia, the maid, notified Mrs. Bluchip that she was resigning her position to work for the Smiths. "Well, now," said Mrs. Bluchip, "I think I shall tell Mrs. Smith about your terrible temper."

"Oh, thank you, mum," said Virginia. "P'raps it'll make 'er mind 'er *p*s and *q*s."

"Madam," said the young maid, "I'm afraid I can no longer work here. I've a terrible problem."

"Let me hear it. Perhaps we can help you," said Madam.

"Well you see, ma'm—I—I'm in a child-bearing way, and as you know I am not married and it presents all sorts of problems."

"Now don't you worry about that," said the lady. "We'll just adopt the baby ourselves, pay all your expenses, and care for you so that you can stay on."

The maid thanked her. But the following year the story was repeated; then the year after that, and the year after that. Four years later, the maid came forward and again announced her resignation. "And it's not what you think, ma'm," she said. "It's just that I can't work in a place where there are so darned many children."

"Odd, Malcolm," said Sir Leslie, the British industrialist. "You are always ten to fifteen minutes late and you live only next door, while your brother Hamilton is always on time and he's many metres distant."

"That's easy explained, sir," replied Malcolm. "If 'e 'appens to be late a bit 'e can 'urry. But hif Hi'm late Hi'm 'ere."

Some years after the crash of '29 the ex-stockbroker found himself employed in an antique shop; but the first day on the job he smashed a Ming vase. The store manager was upset and told the ex-broker that he would have to pay for the vase by forfeiting half his weekly wage.

"How much was the thing worth?" asked the former Wall Streeter.

"Eight hundred dollars," said the manager.

"Hurrah!"

"And why the merriment?"

"Hurrah!" he shouted again. "A steady job at last."

A young lady newly transferred from the Chicago office of a large advertising agency to the New York division of the same company, was receiving instructions her first day on the job.

"Now, Miss Bilt," said the man in charge of the branch, "there is nothing difficult about working with me. Your duties here will be the same as they were in Chicago."

"Fine," she said. "Kiss me, and let's get started."

During the war, when domestic help was especially hard to come by, a group of Westchesterites formed a "Cook-of-the-Month-Club."

"I know I'm dictating too many letters these days," the executive told his wife. "Last night when I said my prayers I finished them with 'Yours truly.'"

A young lady volunteered for the first aid course given by her local Civil Defense group. She was walking down the avenue one day when she saw a man lying face down in the gutter. She leaned down to his prostrate form and began massaging his back and his sides, rubbing frantically with all her strength. She continued to work feverishly for ten minutes until the man looked up and said: "Lady, I don't know what you're doin', but I'm tryin' to get this electric cable down the manhole."

When the great railroads were being built across the United States two Irish laborers, friends from way back, met on the streets of a northern California town. "Wher've ye been?" Murphy asked Callahan.

"Workin' on the railroad, but it was too damned hot," complained Callahan. "Why whin Oi was working in Arizona they marked off the thermometer at a hundred twinty degrees in the shade."

"Well, now, they could'na been too bad," said Murphy. "Not if they let you work in the shade."

During the great depression an Ivy Leaguer dropped into his club on New York's upper east side. There, to his great delight, he met an old classmate. After much backslapping the arrival asked his old classmate how things were going. "Frankly, not so hot," he answered. "I lost my job at the exchange immediately following the crash and haven't been able to find work since. The rent is unpaid for some four months; we are to be evicted next week. Neither the wife nor I have had a decent meal in over a year. We save anything good for the children. Were it not for New York City relief I wouldn't have the clothes I'm wearing."

"Come, come," said the other. "No need to feel so bad. After all, what are friends for? Here's my card. Come to see me tomorrow, and I assure you there is a spot open that will more than make up for the lean years."

"I—I can't make it tomorrow?"

"Really?" Surprise showed on the benefactor's face. "Why not?"

"I've got to march in the parade of the unemployed," the man answered.

An apprentice electrician was standing by watching the journeyman mechanic work, but at no time was he asked to do anything. For an entire week this went on and finally the helper asked, "Say, do you charge for my time?"

"Of course."

"But I haven't done anything since I got here."

The electrician said nothing, but went on about his work. At the end of the day, as the two were leaving, he said to the apprentice: "Okay, if you gotta be so damned conscientious, go ahead and turn off the lights."

The honest courtesans of Athens were forerunners of the modern call girl though the disciples of Aphrodite achieved status denied twentieth century professionals. Their biographers were the great historians of the day and it was traditional for the noblest Greeks to compete openly for their favors. Among those to succumb, only to meet with rejection, was Myron, the foremost student of Ageladas and one of the great artists of antiquity. In his senility Myron called upon Lais of Corinth, the most beautiful woman who ever lived. His objective was purely professional in the artistic sense, but when she disrobed and he beheld her without restrictions, Myron felt rejuvenated. Possessed of considerable fortune, he offered his entire estate for a single night, only to meet with rejection and the loss of her modeling services as well.

Certain his appearance had been responsible for the rejection, Myron got himself up as did the dandies of his day, shaving his beard, trimming his hair, discarding the robe of the scholar for the red garb of flaming youth. The next morning, pleased with his appearance, he rouged his cheeks and presented himself to Lais to bid for her favors. "Poor boy," Lais replied, seeing through the subterfuge, "you ask today what I refused your father yesterday."

Salesmanship and Salesmen

I'll sell my soul before my swoon,
It's not for sale, my swoon's immune.

ODGEN NASH

The practice of recruiting army generals into the ranks of corporate sales leadership following a well-publicized war, is an old one. Today's militarist-turned-salesman is distinguished by a single characteristic. Having gone from logistics to sales statistics they seem to feel an austere personality is in order; they forget that a rich man's joke is always funny. In the vast history of army into business only one man stands out with sufficient brightness worthy of note. He was General Horace Porter, West Point graduate, diplomat, aide-de-camp to General U. S. Grant during the Civil War, and salesman-humorist extraordinary.

Following the great conflict Porter became a corporation executive, affiliated with the Pullman Company. As a representative of that firm he was called on to make speeches in various sections of the country. And he always responded by crumbling the shibboleths of the audience he was addressing. Asked by a Massachusetts crowd to comment on the reasons why Yankee soldiers, during the Civil War, were willing to re-enlist and keep fighting though facing death, Porter replied: "They'd do anything not to go back to New England." Commenting on the many Pilgrim families in that area who possessed articles belonging to the vessel that brought the founding fathers to this country, he said: "With the Pilgrims' addiction to kleptomania the captain of the Mayflower was fortunate to get out of the harbor with anything that wasn't nailed down."

Nor did Porter shy from tackling the strongest industrial cartel of the period, the railroad combine. In response to criticism from the railroads, Porter, in his executive capacity for the Pullman Company, answered: "Of course we cannot be expected to do as much for the traveling public as the railway companies. They at times put their passengers to death; we only put them to sleep."

Porter's high-water mark came in a speech on the origin of the word "deadheads." "It is well known that the term was derived from a practice upon a Missouri railroad, where, by decision of the courts the railroad company had been held liable in heavy damages in case of accident where a passenger lost an arm or a leg, but when he was killed outright his friends seldom sued, and he never did; and the company never lost any money in such cases. In fact a grateful mother-in-law would occasionally pay the company a bonus. The conductors on that railroad were all armed with hatchets, and in case of an accident they were instructed to go around and knock every wounded passenger in the head—thus saving the company large amounts of money. And these were reported to the general office as 'deadheads,' and in railway circles the term has since been applied to passengers where no money consideration is involved."

When a salesman is removed from one territory and assigned to another it is customary to help the new man with his itinerary. "I understand Bushtown is fairly new on the agenda," the novitiate remarked. "Company had you go there often?"

"Once in the last year," the veteran replied.

"What hotel would you recommend?"

"The Royal."

"You stopped there?"

"No," said the old-timer. "But I tried all the others."

To "dynamite" is a procedure where a salesman sells anything he can find that anybody wants.

The dynamiter, in this case, was a man named Boris. "What's a good place to go?" Boris asked.

"Try Madison Square Garden. There's always something going on there in the way of commercial exhibits," he was told. "And remember, whenever you see a buyer going to buy something take him aside and tell him you can get it cheaper."

Boris took off for the Garden, where a kennel show was in progress. As he reached the lobby he heard a woman negotiating with a kennel operator. "I'm afraid fourteen hundred dollars for a pomeranian is too much," she said.

The kennel man told her he could do no better, then suggested she think it over and let him know. When the man was gone Boris saw his chance to dynamite and lit the fuse. "Pardon me, madam," he called. "Excuse me for listening in, but let me tell you I have a very classy pomeranian and the price is extra good. I can let you have it for eleven hundred dollars."

The woman was overjoyed. She gave Boris her name and address and asked him to please make delivery before the end of the week.

When she was gone he rushed to the phone and called the office. "How's things going?" Mr. Inside asked.

"Marvelous, I made a terrific sale," Boris shouted jubilantly. "But tell me, Seymour; what's a pomeranian?"

Counter-irritant: A woman who tortures a salesclerk and then doesn't buy anything.

An insurance salesman was called on by the president of the company to report on the technique he used to sell a one million dollar policy.

"Men," the ace began, "I followed the rule book. When I got

to his office, knowing what sticklers doctors are, I made sure to arrive on the button for our appointment. But the place was jammed. I waited four hours to see him, and he appreciated it. He told me that it was a pleasure to meet a salesman who knows how to conduct himself in a professional man's office. I smiled, warmly let him know that it was quite all right, and used this cue to ask him about himself. I listened attentively to every word, going out of my way to agree with the wonderful opinion he had of himself. He talked three hours, then asked me to come back. I did the next week, went through the same procedures, made the sale, and when I left his office I knew I'd made a friend for life." Then, after a pause, he concluded: "But boy!! What an enemy *he* made."

A shoe store chain had a problem. Spot surveys showed their sales personnel always busy, yet merchandise was not moving off the shelves. A firm of business consultants told the president, "We found your problem. Get rid of the relatives. You have three hundred relatives working for you."

"I can't do that," the president protested. "They're all on the wife's side."

"Very well. Then instruct them to measure the feet of the lady customers without asking them the size they wear."

"What good'll that do?"

"Well," said the consultant. "It's a lot quicker to measure their feet than to argue with them."

A gentleman of the road was doing a less than satisfactory job for a whistle manufacturer and was called to the home office for a chat with the manager. The executive, an advocate of amateur analysis, told the man: "I think I know your trouble, Blakely. Somewhere in your childhood is a cataclysmic experience. Now I know something of psychology. I've given you a test, and it proves that you have a saturation dementia inferioriosa."

"What in hell is that?" asked the dynamiter.

"An overly large amount of inferiority complexes. Your attitude is inferior. Your approach is inferior. Your entire outlook is inferior. This test is infallible, and it detects conclusively the presence of inferiority."

The salesman nodded thoughtfully, then asked: "Did you test the whistle?"

I once worked as a salesman and was very independent. I took orders from no one.

GERALD BARZAN

Door-to-door salesmen often encounter the unexpected. A dynamiter pushing a combination lawnmower-vacuum cleaner reported to his regional manager, "I went up to this fancy house, rang the bell, and the butler came to the door absolutely nude."

"If the man was absolutely nude how did you know it was the butler?"

"Well," he said. "I could see it wasn't the maid."

A salesman applying for a job with a new company boasted that he wrote more business than any ten men the previous year—and had the cancellations to prove it.

"When a man falls way down as you have, Botchman, there must be a reason," the company president lectured a salesman. "A salesman has got to know his item thoroughly. Now what can you honestly say for your product?"

"For one thing," Botchman replied, "I honestly wish t'hell someone would buy it."

"I'd like to buy some shirts for my husband," a woman told a retail sales clerk. "But I don't know his collar size."

"Thirteen, madam."

"How can you be sure?"

"Men whose wives buy their shirts are always that size."

At a department store a female sales clerk was catering to an affluent customer, with orders to allow her any privilege requested. For three hours the woman tried on intimate feminine undergear until the counters were clogged with rejected items. "That lady," said the clerk, "completes the stock."

"Oh dear," said the woman, disappointed. "Is that all the panties you have?"

"All," confirmed the clerk, "except the pair I have on."

A specimen peculiar to the selling field is the 'sideline' carrier. This is a salesman who usually travels for one firm that provides the bulk of his income, while supplementing his tax burden with any number of items for other companies.

A sideline man called on a favorite account in Kansas City, only to find the proprietor in a despondent mood. Despite this, the vendor ran down his list. Perfume, lawnmowers, baseball gloves, children's wear, men's ties, ladies' brassieres, foreign cars, farm equipment, wallets, ball point pens, pens that write, pencil sharpeners, toys, encyclopedias, French pictures, Band aids. . . . He was going rapidly through another sample case when the store owner stopped him. "Look, it's no use. There's nothing I can use," he said nervously. "Business is so bad I'm going home and commit suicide."

"Suicide?" the drummer quickly dug into a sample case and called out: "Knives, ropes, razors, guns, carbolic acid, portable gas pipes——"

When a recession set in the sales manager of a large industrial firm called in his top salesman. "Jack," he said, "We're in an awful slump. I hate to interrupt your home time, but you've got to go out and hustle up some business."

"But the season is over," protested the salesman. "Why I practically had to cry to get any business when things were booming this year."

"You've got it," the sales manager said excitedly. "We'll send you to a dramatic school for a week. They'll teach you how to cry real tears. Then you'll get out there and cry for the company. Cry like you've never cried before."

After a week at school the salesman hit the road, and six weeks later returned to the home base. "Any orders, Jack?" the sales manager expectantly asked.

"Nope, not a single order."

"Not *one* order?" the sales exec. said disbelievingly. "Did you cry?"

"Cry? *Did* I cry?" repeated the salesman, "I cried to the President of General Motors. I cried to the chairman of Anaconda Copper. I cried on six floors of the General Electric Building, and they cleaned every floor of the Pentagon with my tears."

"And no orders?"

"No," the man said. "But I got eighty-six dollars for myself."

In the New England countryside of the twenties, this sign was posted: TRAVELING SALESMAN ARE NOT PERMITTED IN THIS VILLAGE.

Below, in phosphorescent green, a paint salesman appended: THAT'S WHY IT'S A VILLAGE.

When dealing with buyers and purchasing agents, salesmen have to cope with peculiarities of the individual. At one office the senior buyer was notorious for his anti-immigration feeling and would not order from anyone whose name sounded "otherside-ish." This eliminated the Irish, the Italians, the Poles, and the East European Hebrew; as well as anyone else whose name did not resound with pure Anglo-Saxon syllables. Four salesmen met in the reception room of this company one day, chatted as they waited to be called, and then one decided name introductions were in order. "My name is Gaines," he said. "And yours?"

"Gable," the second replied.

"And yours?"

"Guest," the third said.

"And yours?"

"Also Ginsburg," answered the fourth.

Salesmanship and Salesmen

A successful sales executive is a man who can keep both feet firmly implanted on the desk—and give the impression they belong there.

FRANKLIN K. DANE

The bane of the soft spoken super salesman, known as the closer, is the cautious prospect who insists on reading carefully every word of the sales contract. Nineteenth-century Americana tells of an insurance company that set up shop among the Pennsylvania Dutch. Its policy clauses contained an unusual amount of escape words, having scattered throughout much small print and a profusion of "provided," "only on condition that," "whereas the preceding would not apply" and so on.

A prudent Quaker, having taken a policy for several thousand dollars, carefully read the contract. So perplexed did he become that in the morning he called at the office and said to the insurance agent: "Friend, I have studied thy policy and do not see where in case of fire I am insured at all."

"Well, friend," the agent responded, "if thou art it is an inadvertence."

A real estate salesman stressed the points of a piece of land he was trying to unload on what looked to be a pigeon. "Mark what I tell you," the real estater pressured. "The death rate in this suburb is lower than any other part of the country."

"I believe you," answered the intended victim. "I wouldn't be found dead here myself."

His first day in suburbia a new resident decided to be friendly. He walked down the block and when he saw a neighbor carting out buckets from the bottom section of a split level, he called out, "Hi there!"

"Hi," the neighbor replied, as he emptied the two buckets in a recently dug well.

"How's the land lie out this way?" the newcomer called.

"It ain't the land that lies," the neighbor called back. "It's the real-estate salesman."

A widow, about to remarry, was visited by her insurance salesman. "Hello, Mrs. Brown," he said, removing his hat. "I thought you might want to arrange another policy. Your first husband had such good luck with his."

For the traveling man road accommodations remain a problem. Two salesmen became friendly at a roadside tavern. "Ever been to Fleatowne?" one asked.

"Yes," said the other.

"Good," the other said happily. "I'll be visiting there for the first time next week. Maybe you could tell me which is the best hotel to stay at?"

"I could—but I won't."

"Why not?"

"Because," said the veteran, "you'd never believe it."

A salesman merchandising a business service called on an executive with whom he had an appointment. But the man's secretary said: "Mr. Hampden is too busy to speak with you today."

"Look honey," he replied. "Tell Hampden he won't have to say a word."

A book legger found himself in an obscure town with nothing to do for several days. Under these conditions it is standard practice to consult the nearest taxi driver. "Any place a guy can wet his whistle around here?" the drummer asked.

"Nope," the hackman said. "State's been dry since 1890."

Leaning closer the drummer asked in a hushed voice, "Any girls around who'd like company?"

"Nope," said the hackie. "Nothing like that around here since Adah Menken had a group passing through in *Mazeppa*."

Having exhausted the priority choices the salesman inquired into the basic things; movies, billiard parlors, running crap game, general-store cracker-barrel sessions and the like. To each he received a negative. "Tell me," he finally said, "what form of amusement do you have here."

"Well," said the taxi driver, "come on down to the drugstore. There is a freshman home from the university."

At the end of the business day an executive agreed to see an office-equipment go-getter. When he had been admitted and sat facing the prospect, the executive said: "You should feel honored, young fellow, I refused to see twelve salesmen today."

"I know," said the equipment man. "I'm them."